Bauer

S0-BRD-970

The Customer Advocate
and the
Customer Saboteur

Also available from ASQ Quality Press:

Beyond the Ultimate Question: A Systematic Approach to Improve Customer Loyalty
Bob E. Hayes

Measuring Customer Satisfaction and Loyalty: Survey Design, Use, and Statistical Analysis Methods, Third Edition
Bob E. Hayes

Managing the Customer Experience: A Measurement-Based Approach
Morris Wilburn

Customer Satisfaction Research Management
Danica Allen

Competing for Customers and Winning with Value: Breakthrough Strategies for Market Dominance
R. Eric Reidenbach and Reginald W. Goeke

Analysis of Customer Satisfaction Data
Danica Allen and Tanniru R. Rao

Six Sigma Marketing: From Cutting Costs to Growing Market Share
R. Eric Reidenbach

ANSI/ISO/ASQ Q10002-2004: Quality management—Customer satisfaction—Guidelines for complaints handling in organizations
ANSI/ISO/ASQ

The Certified Manager of Quality/Organizational Excellence Handbook, Third Edition
Russell T. Westcott, editor

The Quality Toolbox, Second Edition
Nancy R. Tague

Making Change Work: Practical Tools for Overcoming Human Resistance to Change
Brien Palmer

Innovation Generation: Creating an Innovation Process and an Innovative Culture
Peter Merrill

To request a complimentary catalog of ASQ Quality Press publications, call 800-248-1946, or visit our website at http://www.asq.org/quality-press.

The Customer Advocate and the Customer Saboteur

Linking Social Word-of-Mouth, Brand Impression, and Stakeholder Behavior

Michael W. Lowenstein

ASQ Quality Press
Milwaukee, Wisconsin

American Society for Quality, Quality Press, Milwaukee 53203

© 2012 by ASQ

All rights reserved. Published 2011

Printed in the United States of America

16 15 14 13 12 11   5 4 3 2 1

Library of Congress Cataloging-in-Publication Data

Lowenstein, Michael W., 1942–.

   The customer advocate and the customer saboteur : linking social word-of-mouth, brand impression, and stakeholder behavior / Michael W. Lowenstein.

     p. cm.

   Includes bibliographical references and index.

   ISBN 978-0-87389-811-9 (alk. paper)

   1. Customer loyalty.   2. Customer services.   3. Customer relations.   I. Title.

HF5415.5.L685 2011

658.8'12—dc22

2011015231

Publisher: William A. Tony

Acquisitions Editor: Matt Meinholz

Project Editor: Paul O'Mara

Production Administrator: Randall Benson

ASQ Mission: The American Society for Quality advances individual, organizational, and community excellence worldwide through learning, quality improvement, and knowledge exchange.

Attention Bookstores, Wholesalers, Schools, and Corporations: ASQ Quality Press books, video, audio, and software are available at quantity discounts with bulk purchases for business, educational, or instructional use. For information, please contact ASQ Quality Press at 800-248-1946, or write to ASQ Quality Press, P.O. Box 3005, Milwaukee, WI 53201-3005.

To place orders or to request a free copy of the ASQ Quality Press Publications Catalog, visit our website at http://www.asq.org/quality-press.

∞ Printed on acid-free paper

Quality Press
600 N. Plankinton Ave.
Milwaukee, WI 53203-2914
E-mail: authors@asq.org

The Global Voice of Quality™

To Susan,
my truth woman

and

in loving memory of my mother,
Sylvia Yoffee Lowenstein

Contents

List of Figures and Tables

Preface

Why Customer Loyalty Matters (and It Absolutely Does!) but May Not Be Enough

Businesses, hoping to capitalize on the explosive potential power of word-of-mouth in their marketing programs, have come to something of an epiphany. The seemingly simple process of people talking to one another about a product or service, a behavior that has been around for as long as humans have lived in civilized communities, is not as easy to manage as they once believed, nor in most cases has it generated the lofty and consistent results they had expected.

Over the past decade, the concept, and effective execution, of off-line and online social (and business-related) word-of-mouth has become extremely important to marketers as, increasingly, business-to-consumer (B2C) and business-to-business (B2B) customers have shown distrust, disinterest, and disdain for most supplier messages conveyed through traditional media.

Several books have served to raise awareness of such new-age social word-of-mouth marketing components as influencer relations, buzz, viral communication, neural networks, online community, collaboration, consumer-generated media (blogs, boards, user forums, online reviews, and direct supplier feedback), and other peer-to-peer dialogue. However, given the availability of techniques such as text mining, analytics, electronic (consumer-generated) content monitoring and harvesting, and downstream behavior analysis, they have barely scratched the surface in defining how to use these techniques and assess their effectiveness to achieve and sustain success.

Today, we are witnessing customer-driven marketing through empowerment and self-management, and companies have often found themselves in the backseat of the new customer–supplier relationships. They are forced to modify existing communication techniques or create new ones so that they can be positioned to generate advocates (and avoid or minimize sabotage) among their customer bases. How they use, or misuse, these new-age relationships and techniques, and how they assess the return-on-customer effectiveness and level of monetization of their initiatives will change how social word-of-mouth is pursued by both small and large enterprises.

The false sense of simplicity surrounding the early application of social word-of-mouth techniques has given way to real challenges that businesses must address:

- What is true word-of-mouth versus artificial word-of-mouth, and why is it essential for marketers to distinguish between the real and engineered versions?

- How do marketers build plans around social word-of-mouth, run an effective word-of-mouth program, and track its success?

- Is social word-of-mouth the same in every market or geographic situation? If not, what are the key differences for marketers to understand?

- Why is customer advocacy the ultimate attainment of behavior in behalf of a brand or supplier? What is customer sabotage and how can it be avoided?

- What kinds of research and metrics are available to monitor the revenue impact of social word-of-mouth and advocacy among customers?

- How does word-of-mouth compare with recommendation as a downstream behavior lever? Why is the act of recommendation considerably more complex, and less prevalent as an action, than originally believed?

- What is necessary to get staff buy-in, and what are the roles and effects of employee advocacy and sabotage in word-of-mouth?

- What is the real, likely future of social word-of-mouth marketing?

The Customer Advocate and the Customer Saboteur offers a comprehensive overview of and actionable insight into the social word-of-mouth landscape:

- How we got here

- How true, original, credible, and authentic word-of-mouth campaigns can be generated and modeled

- How appropriate measures need to be applied to assess strategic and tactical campaign effectiveness

- Why customer advocacy is the ultimate goal of word-of-mouth

- How to minimize customer sabotage

- How technology tools are being integrated to facilitate learning from word-of-mouth campaigns

- How employee behavior links to customer advocacy behavior

- How social word-of-mouth is addressed differently around the world

- How the core concept is likely to morph going forward vis-à-vis marketing and leveraging customer behavior

For many years, marketing practitioners have focused on customer loyalty. How do you measure it, how do you protect it, and how do you reward customers for their loyal behavior? What we are now coming to understand is that creating a loyal customer may not be enough to prevent risk and even loss. Customers may say that they are loyal to the brand and that they will use the brand again, but given the opportunity, they will often switch with little or no hesitation. We have seen this in industries such as retail, wireless telecom, credit cards, and travel, each of which has spent more than almost any other industry on loyalty tools. However, the switching virus has spread to many other B2B and B2C sectors to the point where it is at pandemic levels.

At the same time, we are seeing brands such as Google, Red Bull, Zappos, Apple, Umpqua Bank, Wegmans Food Markets, IKEA, and Harley-Davidson, each having a dedicated and enthusiastic group of customers who are more than just loyal; they are customer *advocates*. Once these select companies built a critical mass of customer advocates, they began to enjoy benefits that most brands could only dream of. They get massive social word-of-mouth exposure, they have lower customer acquisition costs and marketing budgets, they have lower customer service costs (or none in the case of Google), they can enter new market areas, and so forth. The most remarkable example of customer advocacy may be Google, which not only doesn't do any marketing (in the traditional sense) but also doesn't have any customer service. And yet, Google still has a large cadre of users who are passionate about its value proposition.

Customer loyalty, in and of itself, principally focuses on retaining customers, cross-selling to customers, upselling customers, and creating "barriers to exit" in the macro sense. In today's interconnected world, with active vendor substitution, search-and-switch migration, and high churn rates an everyday reality, traditional approaches to customer behavior and experience management can often fall short. Advocacy, the highest expression of customer loyalty behavior, will be the standard for successful brand and corporate performance going forward.

Business and academic thought leaders have discovered the powerful leverage and impact of customer advocacy on marketplace behavior. Major consulting organizations have led the way regarding application and business outcome of advocacy. In a time requiring extreme marketing budget accountability, my colleagues at Market Probe and I have conducted groundbreaking research in multiple business sectors that absolutely makes the monetizing outcome case for customer advocacy. In the following chapters, all of this will be shared with you.

Acknowledgments

First and foremost, I would like to thank T. R. Rao, PhD, president and CEO of Market Probe, for his encouragement and support throughout the book development process. His leadership and deep understanding of the value of customer and brand advocacy to companies around the world are gratefully acknowledged. The concept and the outline for this work were born at previous employers, but apart from me, it had no other champion until I joined Market Probe as executive vice president, bringing passion for advocacy and its application with me. Again, my sincere gratitude to T. R.

Thanks also to senior colleagues at Market Probe: principally, Tom Fusso, PhD, John Morton, Judy Ricker, Lisa Wiland, John Gilbert, Jack Jefferson, Dominique Vanmarsenille, Marcus Hallam, Saji Kumar, and Viraag Agnihotri for their support and sharing of insights.

My appreciation also goes to professional and academic colleagues who provided content, insight, counsel, inspiration, or all of these: Leslie Gaines-Ross, PhD, chief reputation strategist at Weber Shandwick, who wrote the afterword; Jeanne Bliss; Jill Griffin; Colin Shaw; Bob Thompson; Stephan Sigaud; Pete Serron; Jodie Brinkerhoff; Carolyn Setlow; Stuart Roesel; Howard Lax, PhD; Ruth Breece; Joan Fredericks; David Smallen; Tim Wragg, PhD; Professor Philip Kotler, PhD;

Professor Jagdish Sheth, PhD; Professor Adrian Payne PhD; and Professor Bernd Stauss PhD.

Thanks to key staff at ASQ Quality Press: Matt Meinholz, acquisitions editor, and Paul O'Mara, CQIA, project editor. Thanks also to the staff at Kinetic Publishing Services, LLC.

Finally, thanks to my family, especially my wife Susan, to whom the book is dedicated. She put up with my frequent, preoccupied escapes to the third-floor man cave/office in our home, where I was surrounded by piles of files (our home is otherwise very neat and tidy), to research and write for close to a year.

Introduction

This book could have been introduced in many ways. From my perspective, the most effective and honest introduction is the way the concept for *The Customer Advocate and the Customer Saboteur* was initially presented to ASQ Quality Press.

NEED AND PURPOSE

Today, marketers must be aware that customers are so inundated and overwhelmed with messages, impressions, and the availability of product and service information that they've gone in large measure to alternative, informal, and less traditional methods of helping them decide what and where to buy. At the heart of seeking sources for decision input is *trust*, along with its cousins *credibility*, *relevance*, *objectivity*, and *authenticity*.

This is an era where spam, pop-up ads, telemarketing, and other types of targeted, "push" advertising and marketing communication—indeed, most long-standing forms of electronic and print messaging and promotion—receive low trust and believability scores in survey after survey of customers. Beyond permission e-mail, supplier and brand websites, and the like, customer trust is consistently highest for word-of-mouth. How high? While the aggregate value of print and electronic advertising as a decision-making influence has remained about the same since 1977, word-of-mouth has doubled in leveraging power to the point where it is the dominant communication device in our society. Through public studies, it has been learned that more than 90% of customers identify word-of-mouth as the best, most reliable, and most relevant source of ideas and information about products and services. This is about the same percentage that finds it the most trustworthy and objective source. More than a trend, this is marketing transformed.

As a result, no matter how well suppliers believe they understand their customers' needs and their online and off-line behaviors on an individual basis, they must have new insights and both a strategy and array of tactics that will help customers create influence and personal leverage, peer to peer and situation by situation. What this means as an end goal is creation of *active customer advocacy*, a state of elective, personal, often deep-rooted and emotional engagement between a purchaser and a supplier that goes beyond satisfaction, beyond delight, and even beyond loyalty.

Advocacy represents the highest level of customer involvement achievable; interaction with suppliers on an individual and emotional level well past the typical functional, passive relationship between supplier and customer; and having customers proactively and voluntarily convey their experiences to friends, relatives, and colleagues. Advocacy is not merely a different spin on gaining insight about customer purchase, referral, and communication behavior. It is also built on trust, through real, authentic experiences.

Arguably, because the name of the game is rational and emotional value optimization, learning about how customers perceive suppliers, brands, and products or services and then having them carry their experiences and consideration forward as active advocates is, or will become, the *only* way to think about them. Companies will need to make significant adjustments from traditional push marketing to an environment where customers expect personalized interest and collaborative, supportive communication and engagement.

WHY WOULD SOMEONE BUY AND READ THIS BOOK?

This book focuses on (1) advocacy and alienation (with the latter possibly resulting in sabotage)—two related but lightly covered elements of downstream social word-of-mouth outcomes, and areas where I have singular experience, (2) both the online and off-line impact of social word-of-mouth, with coverage of key online/off-line differences in leverage and use by industry and demographic group (age, education, ethnicity, gender, etc.), and (3) "inside-out" (customer support, blogging, company-sponsored online communities, and employees' attitudes and actions) as well as "outside-in" advocacy creation by customers themselves.

There is a great deal of information and interest surrounding the impact of online social media and neural networks on customer communication and decision making—indeed, their overall influence on marketing strategy and tactics. These will be covered in depth. However, numerous studies (including mine) have proved that off-line informal communication has greater influence on B2C consumers and significantly more impact on B2B customers. The book will identify online and off-line methods for creating customer advocacy and how to leverage them.

In addition, customer advocacy and customer sabotage are subjects that have incredible bottom-line importance, but companies are really just beginning to learn about the concepts (and there is confusion among those who know the terms, which this book will seek to eliminate through common definitions), and few have successfully applied outside-in or inside-out advocacy creation in their marketing and customer experience initiatives. The book will offer proof through data and case examples of how to create advocacy and minimize sabotage.

WHY WOULD A LEADING HOUSE PUBLISH THIS BOOK?

Social media influence on decision making and downstream customer behavior, along with the impact of customer experience (particularly around advocacy and sabotage), are already tremendously important to all companies. But the themes of this book are definitely "what's next" for companies. Advocacy is still a fairly embryonic concept for marketers, but there is already a strong groundswell of interest and investment in optimizing it. Companies are very actively looking for advocacy enhancement solutions and methods of minimizing or eliminating customer indifference and sabotage. This book features a lot of my original research in this space, as well as support findings from other studies and how-tos for successful application through case examples.

WHY AM I DEVELOPING THIS BOOK?

I've been passionate about what influences stakeholder behavior for over 30 years. I was a pioneer in understanding the effect of social media on customers (I wrote the afterword and several sections for *Customer.Community*, a 2002 book on this subject by consultants Drew Banks and Kim Daus). I've written, or co-written, 4 books and over 125 articles and columns on customer-related subjects and served as advisor to two customer loyalty portals. Specifically regarding customer advocacy, I've conducted many customer research studies since 2004 that show the consistency and superiority of advocacy—over loyalty, commitment, and recommendation—as a conceptual and evaluative framework for helping any company both understand and optimize customer behavior. Further, these studies have focused on what prioritized actions companies can take to enhance advocacy and minimize sabotage, and these will be presented in the book. Next, the linkage of internal processes and employee focus and action on customer behavior receives little attention, but my colleagues at Market Probe and I have also conducted original research in this area, and it will be featured in the book.

WHY DO PEOPLE/BUSINESSES NEED HELP ON THIS TOPIC AT THIS TIME?

Creating customer advocacy from the inside out (customer experience—people and processes) and the outside in (neural, peer-to-peer communication) can make a huge profit impact on any marketing initiative and the overall enterprise, irrespective of size or industry. There are books on the challenges and opportunities represented by word-of-mouth and social media, but they typically have little proof or guidance as to how these tools can be directly linked to desired customer behavior. Further, there is not much coverage, if any, in these books on inside-out influence of employees or the negative impact of customer sabotage on businesses.

WHY IS THIS TOPIC IMPORTANT *NOW*?

Many companies put pressure on marketing, sales, and customer service budgets, and they are being tasked and challenged to optimize customer loyalty behavior through whatever cost-effective means are available. There is increasing awareness, as well as belief, that social media and word-of-mouth can be leveraged to enhance relationships with customers (but can also threaten them), but most information and books are general how-tos or focus on the abstract theory behind the topics.

WHAT IS THE BOOK DESIGNED TO ACCOMPLISH?

I've developed both a "why" book—with a lot of exclusive research from Harris Interactive (on communication generators and receivers, and downstream action as a result of experience and received communication), plus studies by Keller Fay, Right-Now, OTX, Forrester, and others—and, having established the platform and proof of value, a how-to with success examples.

Also, customer sabotage—from both inside and outside the organization—is powerful but rarely discussed. This book examines sabotage in detail.

DISTINCTIVE VALUE

Just as no book had addressed the back end of the customer life cycle (or the full life cycle), as Jill Griffin and I did in our 2001 book written for Jossey-Bass, *Customer WinBack*, there has been no book that addresses how online and off-line social word-of-mouth can be leveraged, how to define and create customer advocacy (and minimize customer sabotage), and how to practice inside-out value-building, through employees and consistent top-end customer experience delivery, for advocacy creation.

Virtually all other books address components of what creates and sustains customer advocacy (and also customer sabotage). No other books cover these subjects both broadly and in depth.

What I've endeavored to provide all readers of *The Customer Advocate and the Customer Saboteur* is both overpromise in terms of content and insight and overdelivery in terms of perceived value. These are core elements in the creation of trust and advocacy.

Michael W. Lowenstein, PhD, CMC
March 31, 2011

1

What Are Customer Advocacy and Customer Sabotage (aka "Badvocacy")?

Chushin wa ni kun ni tzukaezu: *A truly loyal subject does not serve two masters.*

—JAPANESE PROVERB TAKEN FROM SSU-MA CH'IEN, HISTORIAN OF ANCIENT CHINA

Kevin O'Brien, chief marketing officer at RiverStar, a customer experience solution provider, posted the following blog entry on the CustomerThink marketing and customer relationship portal:

Best Buy Transcends the Retail Experience

I have never received a level of service where all touch points were in sync with each other, and where every step of the way was the epitome of how to create a most outstanding customer experience. Here is my story in a nutshell.

My Pre-Experience Best Buy Impression

Best Buy is a place to wander the aisles, explore new music and play new games. Best Buy is the place with young, blue shirted Geeks(quad) that talk in tech/gen Y speak about anything gaming or electronics related. Like any other retailer, pick what you like and proceed to the checkout counter. At this stage, I am vendor neutral, and price is the only competitive advantage.

Game Changing Experience

Nothing yet at this point. Just another retail experience.

I Shop Around for a Few Televisions

I am building a house and am considering a whole house audio/video solution. Best Buy has TV's on sale, including 3 years/no interest financing. My thoughts are to buy the TV's on a deal like this so I don't have to finance them through the bank loan. I run over to Best Buy and after numerous questions and demos of every available 40–55 inch television, I decided to purchase 4 new Samsung TV's. Martin, my sales associate, provides me one last demo of a 400 DVD changer per my request and uses a Control4 (whole house audio/video control system) panel to navigate the device. Ironically, I had been considering a Control4 system (not normally offered by big-box retailers) and I had no idea that Best Buy offered Control4.

Game Changing Experience

Martin told me to NOT buy the televisions today, but to hold off until they have a person come to our new house to assess our wiring configuration and planned layout. Steve, from Geek Squad, was out to review the home within 48 hours.

Best Buy Makes a Proposal

Best Buy gives me a proposal??? I thought I'd just pick up a few things and give them my credit card. Within 48 hours after the on-site review, a 10 page PDF lands in my email inbox detailing a complete installed system, including a parts list, with full installation with training.

Game Changing Experience

Steve ropes in Josh, who runs sales for the Magnolia department (ultimately the decision maker for the pricing), and a Control4 representative to meet me at the store to answer EVERY single question I have. The 4 of them (including Martin) take as much time as I need to understand my concerns and issues. I walk away with no stone unturned and am completely educated on the system, the benefits and the future of the Control4 product.

Best Buy Bends Over Backward

I assess the Best Buy proposal and review it against 2 others; mentally agreeing that Best Buy is the direction I would like to go for this solution. The experience to date has been great. The backing of a huge retailer, with the personalized service is something that gives me a sense of comfort with this type of investment. After a number of discussions, Best Buy wins my business.

Game Changing Experience

Best Buy reevaluated their proposal, added a number of significant upgrades and dropped the price to well under the competition in order to meet my budget.

Their price flexibility coupled with outstanding service commitment was impossible to pass up.

The Credit Card Application

In order to get the benefits of the financing terms, I needed to open a HSBC account for my Best Buy card.

Game Changing Experience

They override their standard credit card limit in order to finance the complete purchase. I relax in their family room setting after being offered a beverage of my choice and wait comfortably while they pull strings to arrange the financing that I need for this purchase. Other than a few security questions that I needed to answer, I sat back while the Best Buy financing representative did the rest.

Product Exchanges

There are hundreds of variables in these installations with the type of equipment varying based on the on-site configuration during the install. Additionally, Best Buy deals with various product vendors and will pull in other product to complete the solution (even if they don't directly resell the product).

Game Changing Experience

Best Buy was having difficulty getting a specific product (Atlona) through a reseller, so they told me to go direct to the manufacturer to get the best price for this component. Martin set up the connection with Atlona (the manufacturer) to give me a price that was 25% less than what Best Buy had already budgeted and charged for the item. They initiated this process! In addition to the Altona device, there have been 2 other scenarios where components weren't needed or were swapped out to provide me with a better option. The Geek Squad crew, who have been doing the installs, has been managing the product back and forth for me without my ever needing to return to the store for exchanges.

Installation Process

Now, keep in mind that the configuration, installation and training of this system takes 2–3 installers about 5 days or more to complete. So, these guys have been in and out of my house (now that we have moved in) on a weekly basis for the past 2 weeks (my only complaint). Because Best Buy is a newer dealer of Control4, their certified expertise is limited; ending up as a piece meal installation over a number of weeks in order to spread the techs across multiple projects.

Game Changing Experience

We've been waiting anxiously (TV's mounted with no ability to watch them!) for a few weeks and at one juncture, I complained to the top brass that this install is dragging out and intertwined between other jobs. I circled back with Steve and Martin and told them that I need a TV up by Friday night (Celtics vs. Bulls), no questions asked. They worked overtime to rearrange schedules to make certain that my viewing of the game was possible. In fact, the district manager was out that day working on my house with the installer to make certain that we would get to where we needed to be by game time. The project still wasn't complete, but they made it work.

COMMUNICATION and SERVICE is the overriding Game Changing Experience.

This experience for me has changed the way I not only view Best Buy as an organization, but how I shop with Best Buy. My communication with Martin ranges every channel available: cell phone/text/email. When I need something, regardless of the time of day, or whether or not he is working, I get a response and an answer. In fact, I had an interest in a smaller TV for our master bedroom and all I did was call up Martin, let him know what I was looking for, dropped by the store and loaded up the car. The personal service that they have provided me throughout the process has made me feel like I am their only customer. The whole team is always in sync with each other and the message they send to their premiere customers is consistent and precise.

As long as they continue to operate in this way, I will be a Best Buy customer for life. (O'Brien 2010)

Kevin, gentle reader, is an *advocate* for Best Buy. Not only has he communicated the details of his positive purchase experience and relationship with Best Buy in the blogosphere (to date, more than 1000 people have seen this posting), but he has sealed his endorsement by stating his willingness to be upsold and cross-sold over an extended period. Among several notes back to Kevin, his blog prompted this positive response:

Best Buy Experience

Hi Kevin

I have recently had a great Best Buy experience as well and plan to buy my TV from them when my renovations are completed and the carpet goes down and we unwrap the furniture.

The TV shopping experience was eye-popping, with scores of different screens on the floor that would do the job . . . the technology has certainly moved a long way in five years since I bought my last set.

I found the Best Buy staff in the Marina CA store to be interested and engaged in what my needs were and providing useful advice that changed a couple of my ideas on how to provision programming.

You might be able to buy the same set slightly cheaper at Walmart or Costco . . . frankly I don't care if I pay a bit more, the advice and service at Best Buy is worth the premium.

Thanks for sharing.

The response Kevin received is but one example of the viral and interactive nature of positive and negative expressions of brand impression through experience and the resulting informal, peer-to-peer word-of-mouth behavior that takes place both online and off-line.

Here's another public online expression of a positive retail experience, this one from a blog by marketing consultant Jim Joseph (2010):

I had an amazing shopping experience this past weekend—Eataly—a full blown retail celebration of Italy that just opened in Manhattan near the corner of 23rd and 5th.

Eataly is the latest project from Italian chefs and restaurateurs Mario Batali and Lidia Matticchio along with her son Joe Bastianich. It's a concept that comes from Italy where gourmet food retailers have executed it to perfection.

The space in Manhattan is amazing as it mixes retail selections with cafes with deli counters with education about the regions and foods of Italy. You can spend hours in the place having snacks, grabbing a drink, eating a meal, and of course shopping for food to bring home.

All authentically from Italy. There's even a beer garden on the roof, and a "school" where you can take cooking classes. Culinary heaven, straight from Italy.

The merchandising is perfection, much like its Italian origins. Plenty of food products and kitchen ware in every category to choose from along with posters that explain where the products come from and even how to use them.

It's so much fun to see something new in retail, I just couldn't get enough—even though 50,000 square feet in Manhattan is no small feat.

Note that in both Kevin O'Brien's and Jim Joseph's blogs there was no outright or even indirect recommendation that anyone reading their statements of positive experiences should go to Best Buy or to Eataly. As will be covered in the chapter addressing the differences between customer advocacy and customer referral or recommendation, only word-of-mouth and positive brand impression are needed for advocating behavior to occur. Also discussed in that chapter is that word-of-mouth is at least as powerful a force as recommendation—in fact, positive word-of-mouth is expressed with greater frequency than recommendation.

Advocacy occurs when customers select a single supplier from among all those they might consider, giving that supplier the highest share of spend possible and informally (without any form of compensation) telling others about how positive the relationship is and how much value and benefit they derive from it. Advocacy incorporates opinions formed from customers' transactional and other contact experiences with a brand or supplier, but it is built on a foundation of strategic, positive purchase and communication behavior. This level of behavior results when the customer is favorable toward a supplier and not only purchases consistently from that supplier over others but also actively tells peers about the personal value and benefit received from the relationship.

How is advocacy different from satisfaction or loyalty (or even recommendation or referral), which so many companies use as a key indicator of performance and effective customer management, even offering incentive payments and promotions based on it? Satisfaction, because it depends principally on attitudes and recent transactions as well as the tangible, functional elements of value, isn't dependable, because it doesn't correlate very well with long-term relationships and bonds with suppliers or with key monetary measures like share of spend.

Loyalty, though it recognizes a longer-term relationship and more active purchasing from fewer suppliers or a single supplier, often doesn't take into account the power and influence of peer-to-peer communication or the level of brand favorability. These important differences are neither semantics nor hair-splitting. Much of the dialogue and discussion of customer loyalty (including the creation of customer loyalty research models) does not include either the emotional and relationship elements of brand perception or the strong influence of word-of-mouth in decision making. These components cannot be found in typical coverage of customer loyalty behavior.

Customer recommendation and referral, which will be covered in a chapter of its own, is more a manifestation of loyalty behavior than the desired behavior itself. As noted earlier, multiple customer research studies have determined that informal word-of-mouth drives at least as much (positive and negative) downstream behavior as recommendation.

Advocacy is clearly a different concept and set of opinions and behaviors. Advocacy not only considers the likelihood to have an exclusive purchasing relationship but also incorporates both strong brand-based, emotional kinship and active, positive, and voluntary communication about, and in behalf of, the chosen supplier.

By focusing on advocacy (and mitigating or eliminating sabotage), companies are able to strategically and positively differentiate their value proposition while simultaneously creating optimum levels of desired customer behavior. This chapter will identify multiple examples of companies that do this well. Two are Harley-Davidson, which has been able to create a growing corps of enthusiastic owners (with very little advertising) through its million-member Harley Owners Group, and IKEA, which has differentiated itself within the home furnishings retail category by offering unique products, services, and purchase experiences to a highly devoted customer base.

THE RAPID EVOLUTION FROM TOTAL QUALITY, SATISFACTION, LOYALTY, AND RECOMMENDATION MEASUREMENT

The next chapter traces the history of customer advocacy. Here, we will briefly cover the history of *research* associated with customer attitude and behavior, leading to the manner in which customer studies have needed to morph over time with changing market conditions.

Formal research on customer opinions has been going on since the 1950s. Much of it had to do with perceptions of product/service quality and satisfaction, engagement, and eventually loyalty and recommendation. For decades, data on these attitudes and feelings were sufficient to provide companies with general insight and direction. By the early 1990s, control of brand and supplier selection had shifted away from companies and moved to consumers, a result of several pivotal, converging factors:

1. Growing internet penetration and cell phone usage as communications enablers

2. Oversaturation of "push" advertising and promotional messaging through traditional mass electronic and print media

3. Heightened public distrust in the honesty and authenticity of corporations

This was a major, seismic change in the way businesses regarded customers and the nature of information needed from them.

Beginning around 2000, major consulting organizations began to recognize that these critical changes were likely to have a profound impact on businesses. Instead of relying solely on such historical measures as satisfaction, loyalty, engagement, and recommendation, companies would need to identify and focus on something more contemporary, more actionable, and more predictive of key monetizing business outcomes, such as share of wallet. That "something" was ultimately defined as *customer advocacy*, that is, behavior driven by a strong bond with the preferred brand and active, voluntary online and off-line word-of-mouth in behalf of that brand.

Consulting companies conducted many insightful advocacy studies, issuing statements such as the following:

> Advocacy is a deeply-rooted, emotional connection which relies on trusted, effective non-traditional communication and engagement channels. (Hollins and Setlow 2007)

> Word-of-mouth is the primary factor behind 20 to 50% of all purchasing decisions. And its influence will probably grow . . . (Bughin, Doogan, and Vetvik 2010, 2)

> Leading companies want to build strong bases of loyal profitable customers who are also advocates for the organization. Advocates spend more, remain customers longer, and refer family and friends, thus increasing the

quality of the existing customer base and new acquisitions. (Heffernan and LaValle 2006, 5)

We predict that customer advocacy will be the new focus for business leaders. Customer advocacy will become the single most important initiative that cutting-edge, forward thinking companies will adopt. (Petouhoff 2006, 3)

Having identified the power of customer advocacy to influence the customer's own behavior and the behavior of others, the next challenge was to create and prove the effectiveness of a state-of-the-art research metric or framework for measuring and leveraging it.

So, customer advocacy, as identified by these consulting companies, could now provide organizations with many valuable business outcome benefits. This new consumer influence also meant that market research companies would need to evolve beyond historical methods of interpreting customer attitudes and determining how those attitudes could affect behavior to incorporate drivers of customer advocacy. Some new models were created, principally to evaluate emotional connection; however, in general, the market research industry has not embraced the new realities of customer decision making represented by customer advocacy.

Whenever senior executives are asked to identify their most important corporate and marketing priorities, they invariably include at the top of their lists issues involving the provision of optimized value to customers, linked directly with stronger business performance. For brand and customer researchers, the recurring challenge has been to provide their organizations with actionable, real-world metrics and diagnostics that link directly with customers' marketplace behavior. The most contemporary, actionable research approach for meeting this objective is customer advocacy.

WHAT IS CUSTOMER ADVOCACY, AND WHY SHOULD IT BE A KEY ORGANIZATIONAL FOCUS?

Advocacy plays an increasingly pivotal role in influencing consumers' opinions and behavior toward companies. Extensive customer research shows that B2B and B2C customers today are quicker to take action, make decisions to buy products and services, and express satisfaction or dissatisfaction with their experiences. With specific regard to the downstream impact of customers expressing themselves, consulting organization McKinsey has found that word-of-mouth is the primary factor behind 20%–50% of all purchasing decisions, and 50%–80% of word-of-mouth comes directly as a result of personal experience with a product or service (Bughin, Doogan, and Vetvik 2010, 2).

For purposes of analysis and action, customers can be divided into advocacy segments according to degree of kinship and engagement with a supplier, and this kinship has direct and explicit monetary translation. This is a key reason why creating advocacy is at the core of effective customer management. Put in bottom-line terms, advocacy represents revenue and profitability, plus a great deal more.

At the very low end of advocacy, our research has shown that there are customers who are indifferent or openly negative toward a brand or supplier. They identify themselves as being generally disinterested and uninvolved with that supplier, even becoming vocal "badvocates" if they have had unsatisfactory or unsavory experiences. For purposes of segmentation, we label these customers as alienated. At the other end, active advocates not only purchase the supplier's products or services at the highest level of all customer groups, but they are emotionally aligned with the supplier and its values, are engaged and closely bonded with the supplier in a long-term relationship, and reliably, voluntarily, and frequently speak to others about the supplier in a consistently positive and supportive manner.

THE UNDENIABLE POWER OF WORD-OF-MOUTH

Two books, Malcolm Gladwell's *The Tipping Point* (2000) and Ed Keller and Jon Berry's *The Influentials* (2003), considered together, provide an effective reference point for understanding the behavioral impact of word-of-mouth and social networks (also known as neural, peer-to-peer, informal, and viral communication). The significant increase in available information about alternative suppliers, combined with how customers now make supplier product and service selections, has put word-of-mouth front and center in the minds of marketers and organizations.

When the effectiveness and trust levels of traditional sources of supplier information—print and electronic advertising, print and electronic editorial, and word-of-mouth—are compared over time, word-of-mouth emerges as the dominant communication vehicle for influencing customer decision making and supplier selection. Customers use words like *trust*, *relevance*, *objectivity*, *integrity*, and *honesty* to describe why informal communication—that is, word-of-mouth—is the most reliable and behaviorally leveraging information source.

At the macro level, word-of-mouth produces societal influentials, those individuals (about 10% of the population, as identified by Keller and Berry [2003, 29]) who influence and guide the behavior of the rest of society. On a category influence basis, Gladwell (2000) has identified members of social networks who are mavens, connectors, and salesmen. Everyone knows people like these. They are product or service category experts in subjects like wine, sports, food, entertainment, computers, cars, and travel to whom others defer when making decisions in these areas.

Finally, there are specific brand influentials, or advocates. Advocacy, simply defined, occurs when customers select a single supplier from among all those they might consider, giving that supplier the highest share of spend possible, and telling others about how positive the relationship is and how much value and benefit they derive from it.

Advocates are the golden prize for any brand or supplier organization because they are customers who have minimized their consideration set, are extremely favorable toward "their" supplier, and are active, vocal, frequent, and positive communicators in behalf of that supplier.

As Figure 1.1 illustrates, advocates are happy to spread the word, whether off-line or online, about the brands and product and service experiences they favor.

Figure 1.1 An advocate (actually allegiant customer) spreading the word.

THE IMPORTANCE OF BRAND ENGAGEMENT AND FAVORABILITY

"Brand" and the "branded customer experience" are powerful components of customer advocacy. To begin, often even before the customer relationship has been initiated, or when a brand is endeavoring to build or expand on it, promises are made to the consumer in the form of (1) messages through advertising, packaging, and promotion and at the point of contact and (2) a set of performance and value expectations generated from peers and/or their own research, which will ultimately be derived from the customer's individual transactions, experiences, and impressions built on a longitudinal engagement basis. Increasingly, because of the impact of word-of-mouth and the availability of information, and especially where there is active competition within the same market space, the customer will hold the brand accountable for at least meeting (and hopefully exceeding) those expectations.

The degree to which expectations are met—through under-delivery, anticipated delivery, and overdelivery—has a great deal to do with the level of *trust* between the customer and the brand. Trust and its related elements (authenticity, objectivity, credibility, transparency, honesty, and relevance) help drive reputation, the emotional center of brand equity. The brand can also help its own cause by creating interest, involvement, and uniqueness.

There are great examples of building communities of interest and involvement. One is Apple, which for years built almost a counterculture of creative computer and laptop users, often developing its own software for Apple-owning peers to try. Another is Saab, which has a very close and authentic relationship with its owners through *Nines*, an independently produced owners' club magazine, and through annual conventions where owners can display their cars and attend seminars. Saab works very hard to make certain that dialogue is kept two-way.

Over the years, there have been many studies connecting levels of brand trust, engagement, and favorability with the financial value of the consumer. Satisfaction and loyalty are not enough. Simply stated, these studies invariably conclude that the deeper the emotional engagement and commitment, the greater the spend levels of individual customers.

It must be recognized that although highly committed and engaged customers represent key contributing elements to brand leadership and equity, these customers are not of equal value. Pricing, packaging, availability, attractiveness of promotions, and so forth can all work for or against a brand at different times. Like loyalty, customers can be engaged and committed to multiple brands. Word-of-mouth becomes the leavening element.

THE MARKETING VALUE OF CUSTOMER ADVOCACY

The conjoined elements of brand perception and word-of-mouth impact are definitely a "future trend" for companies that is here and now, one key reflection of the shift in decision-making influence to customers. This shift represents profound potential economic and strategic benefits, as well as risk, for companies. For instance, through research, a major worldwide consulting organization has determined that advocates can help a company grow at an average rate of 2.5 times their competitors (Marklein 2009). Conversely, in research with senior management of major companies by global PR firm Weber Shandwick (2009b, 35; 2009c), nearly 4 in 10 executives fear that a dissatisfied customer or critic will launch an online campaign against their company. Whether positive or negative, advocacy can be very powerful at leveraging decision-making behavior.

Our research has identified several specific advantages that are realized when companies make advocacy the focus and enterprise-wide objective of their customer management processes. By making certain that they deliver both functional and emotional/relationship benefits at a high level, these companies create a complete value package for customers that is strong enough that they will often give these suppliers their business on an exclusive basis.

First, customer advocacy is an excellent predictor of use levels with the supplier's products and services. Usage, recency of usage, and frequency of usage all typically increase as the level of engagement progresses from indifference to commitment and finally to active advocacy.

Next, advocates are significantly more likely (according to Weber Shandwick [2007], about 3.5 times) to forgive value delivery letdowns and to remain with preferred companies when they are in trouble.

Finally, share-of-wallet differences can clearly be seen among alternative products in the same competitive set when the customer relationship rises from indifference or negativity to active advocacy; advocates are significantly more likely to pay a premium for brands they support. These are the types of financial rewards many companies look for from advocacy, and it delivers.

Companies can help their own advocacy causes through such devices as loyalty and reward programs. These programs, when done well, are often proactive communication devices for creating stronger engagement and bonding with the sponsoring organizations. According to a study by the CMO Council (2010), there is evidence of direct and positive correlation between customer involvement in loyalty programs and their positive word-of-mouth and recommendation activity. Among the study's important findings were that program participants are 70% more likely to actively recommend the program and the company to others, and two-thirds of these customers will make that recommendation within a year. Important for marketers' relationship-building efforts, loyalty program members who have redeemed for experiential rewards, such as trips and concierge services, are 30% more likely to recommend the program than those who redeem for discounts.

So, advocacy has an array of marketing benefits, and these can be identified through research specifically designed to target important drivers of this behavior. When the effect of active advocacy is compared with such traditional research measures as high satisfaction and high recommendation levels, research proves that customer advocacy is a more accurate and stable barometer of customer management effectiveness. In a study conducted for one of our financial services clients, advocacy was more than twice as reliable and productive when looked at relative to high levels of either satisfaction or likelihood to recommend. This advantage of advocacy was sustained whether we were looking at recent or frequent brand usage or share of spend. Similar results, by the way, have been experienced in many other studies, irrespective of industry. As will be discussed in the next section, this includes B2B products and services as well as an array of B2C products and services.

CUSTOMER ADVOCACY FOR B2B PRODUCTS AND SERVICES

My colleagues and I are frequently asked, "Because of the importance of brand perception and word-of-mouth in B2C products and services, I understand how customer advocacy can provide highly actionable insights there. What about customer advocacy in B2B products and services? Does it exist?"

Extensive research into numerous B2B sectors has repeatedly shown that even with the tighter decision parameters such as pricing, regulations, and vendor qualification that may exist in B2B products and services, much of what drives initial and ongoing supplier choice is built around brand impression and peer-to-peer informal communication.

What creates and sustains top-end loyalty is, of course, excellent performance on "table stakes" tangible, basic value elements. Delivering at promised levels on pricing, completeness, accuracy, timeliness, reliability, and consistency is the minimum standard for building a foundation level of trust and helping to build the supplier–customer relationship. Proactive, personalized service that exceeds expectations, two-way communication, and engagement help bond the customer to the supplier. This is true throughout the customer life cycle, from initial supplier selection and purchase through cross-sell, upsell, and advocacy behavior.

B2B Advocacy Measurement: It's about Performance, Trust, and Relationships

Apart from procurement and pricing requirements sometimes encountered in B2B supplier selection and loyalty behavior situations, several factors contribute directly to perceptions and marketplace actions:

- Overall supplier brand impression/reputation—largely attitudinal, with some influence on purchase decisions
- Level of expressed commitment to supplier—largely attitudinal
- Overall performance satisfaction—influences purchase intentions
- Perceived service quality—influences both attitudes and purchase intentions

Service quality is a critical measure of organizational performance and a key condition of relationship quality. In turn, relationship quality links and contributes to the perception of satisfaction and trust, creating business outcomes of customer retention and advocacy. This is similar to the role of service in B2C product and service supplier selection.

Interestingly, although trust in employees is often a major contributor to B2C customer behavior, in B2B studies, employee trust is assumed and has been found to be less of a factor.

In a B2B analysis publication, a quote from Allegiance, a major consulting organization, reads: "Focusing only on the end customer in a B2B environment yields only part of your company's story. After all, your business partners represent your company and products to their customers. Therefore, you need to make sure your business customers are properly advocating your brand" (Carnick, Kumar, and Lowenstein 2010, 2). Even though B2B customer relationships are often higher-touch than in B2C customer markets, companies that depend only on anecdotal, qualitative information leave much insight uncovered. There must be a proactive, formal, and actionable advocacy-based research program to help stay ahead of the customer need curve.

Word-of-mouth, just as important in driving advocacy behavior, is critical in the B2B world. Word-of-mouth gets business decision makers to buy. According to a study by Keller Fay Group and Jack Morton Worldwide (2007), 53% of the 288 US business decision makers surveyed said that word-of-mouth from colleagues and friends would get them to buy and would contribute strongly to passing along positive comments themselves. This compares to 39% for sales representatives; 38% for meetings, events, and conferences; 37% for internet; and 37% for trade shows and exhibits. Direct mail, print, TV, and radio advertising were cited by between 22% and 32% as influencing work-related purchases.

How does that word get spread? In more than 17,000 conversations by business decision makers from June 2006 through January 2007, as monitored by Keller Fay, 75% were conducted face-to-face as compared to 19% by phone, the next most frequent communication medium. This proportion is much higher than it is for B2C consumers, who are more likely to communicate via the internet.

Other surveys have confirmed word-of-mouth's leverage in B2B marketing. Nearly half of the business respondents in a MarketingSherpa and CNET (2006) study said that peer-to-peer informal communication had the highest impact on buying decisions for technology and services. Word-of-mouth will only be positive if companies have been identified as creating strong brand impression and consistently outstanding, value-based customer experiences.

Capsule B2B Case Study: Computer and Peripheral Equipment Producer Drives Advocacy Behavior

Senior executives of our client, a major producer of computer and peripheral equipment, issued a mandate for their customer service operation: Be world-class, performing at such a consistently high and value-producing level that the service experience would positively drive downstream business outcomes. Customer advocacy research was conducted in 20 countries worldwide to identify likely behavior based on service experiences, irrespective of support channel.

Advocacy research results showed that knowledge, speed of responsiveness, and courtesy were insufficient to strategically and positively differentiate service. There was a need to proactively "take ownership" of the customer's service issue, to personalize it beyond the merely reactive and institutional response usually experienced by customers, thus creating a stronger bond and relationship. Knowledge, responsiveness, and courtesy were the expected "table stakes" elements of performance. This critical and highly leveraging finding was identified in all service channels, products, and countries studied.

Note: In previous research studies on customer service satisfaction conducted for this client, "taking ownership" was only one of an array of attributes where level of satisfaction was measured. Here, this single service factor was key to driving higher levels of downstream monetizing behavior resulting directly from the service experience.

Our client took several initiatives as a result of this research:

- Major overhaul of service processes, built around greater service proactivity

- Training/retraining of staff to go beyond the reactive basics of performance

- Staff incentive program based on "taking ownership" scores and overall research results

When follow-up advocacy research was conducted with this service population, there was a significant increase in the proportion of customers likely to purchase from our client specifically as a result of the service they had experienced.

Actual B2B Advocacy Research Results

A representative B2B customer advocacy study has been selected to share from the array of those we have conducted. Our studies for B2B companies represent the spectrum, types of results, and actionable insights provided for clients through our customer advocacy research framework. Here is one example.

Singapore SME Business Banking

Singapore is one of the most progressive financial and banking hubs in Southeast Asia. A study was recently conducted to determine some of the key drivers underlying customer advocacy levels toward banks, in particular among small and medium-sized enterprise (SME) customers.

A web-based survey methodology was used, and invitations were sent to business executives who had sole or shared responsibility in selecting banks and financial services companies for their organizations. Companies surveyed had yearly revenues of less than 100 million Singapore dollars. Three weeks of data collection yielded 175 survey responses.

In applying our customer advocacy research framework to the SME responses, only 12% of SME respondents were identified as advocates of their primary bank for all business transactions. The largest group of customers (38%) were allegiants. Allegiants are an "aspirational" segment: Building them to the advocacy level will increase their monetizing power for the primary bank. Close to a third (30%) of the respondents were in the alienated category (see Figure 1.2).

Although the consumption of banking products is generally not considered to be as emotional or relationship-based as that of consumer services and high-ticket products, our findings revealed that the emotional element of trust is instrumental in driving up the level of customer advocacy

	All banks	Lowest	Highest
Advocate	12%	5%	20%
Allegiant	38%	29%	51%
Ambivalent	21%	7%	29%
Alienated	30%	26%	39%

Figure 1.2 Business banking customer advocacy segmentation.
Source: Market Probe, 2010.

behavior. Advocate and allegiant customers tended to exhibit significantly stronger levels of trust, expressed in multiple ways, toward their primary banks, compared to ambivalent and alienated customers.

Results of our study showed that customer trust is cultivated through positive interactions with the banks. Two customer touch points that are key in establishing the trust of advocates are the account managers and customer interactions with general bank staff. More specifically, our research revealed that customers with high advocacy scores are generally those who are more satisfied with interactions with their account managers in terms of accessibility, promptness in response, empowerment to solve problems, and offering good financial advice.

In addition, it was found that these trust-building experiences with account managers have to be complemented by the overall interaction with other bank employees whom the customers encounter. Performance elements including friendliness, perceived competence, and the ability to render prompt and efficient service support the positive interaction. Results showed that it is critical for banks to present a positive, customer-centric culture that encapsulates their entire service offering through training and recruitment of the right people (see Table 1.1).

We also learned through the research that banking and financial products tended to be perceived as having better quality and more favorable pricing by the primary bank's customers identified as advocates.

Customer advocacy is very much alive and well in B2B products and services. Multiple studies have demonstrated that word-of-mouth and brand reputation are essential decision-making levers. If anything, due to the more critical nature of touch points, performance, brand perception, and relationships in B2B, advocacy may well be more important in this arena than in the B2C world.

Table 1.1   High scores (by group) on key measures.

Top 2 box rating (10-point scale)		Advocate	Allegiant	Ambivalent	Alienated
Image and reputation	Is a strong and stable bank	55%	46%	24%	14%
	Has a good reputation	55%	35%	16%	14%
	Has earned my trust and confidence	45%	15%	8%	0%
Transactional services	Waiting time to receive service at the branch	43%	14%	8%	8%
	Responsiveness of the staff	43%	21%	12%	13%
Banking staff	Staff makes me feel like a valued customer	36%	8%	20%	0%
	Staff follows up with information as needed	36%	14%	13%	0%
Account manager	Account manager is easily accessible	29%	19%	20%	4%
	Account manager is responsive to my questions and inquiries	29%	25%	20%	0%
Overall evaluation of the bank staff		**29%**	**11%**	**7%**	**0%**
Overall image of (primary bank)		**25%**	**11%**	**8%**	**2%**

Source: Market Probe, 2010.

CUSTOMER DISAFFECTION, ALIENATION, AND SABOTAGE

Although customer negativity in the form of disaffection, alienation, and outright, purposeful sabotage will be covered in depth in Chapter 7, for now we can briefly address this behavior as what happens with some customers—about 20% worldwide, according to research by PR firm Weber Shandwick and KRC Research (2007)—when they have had a transaction with an unacceptable result or a series of unacceptable results.

These customers will likely not purchase again from the source of the negative transaction or set of experiences. More viral and impactful, given the influence of word-of-mouth on customer decision-making behavior, they will say things to peers that detract from the brand's or supplier's reputation, post negatively on ratings websites, or advise others not to use that brand or supplier. In extreme cases, they will even set up contra websites as an electronic megaphone. Weber Shandwick calls these customers "badvocates," and it is a very appropriate term for their downstream behavior. As companies like Dell have learned, just a few mistreated customers can do great harm, both off-line and online (remember "Dell Hell"?).

The experience driver for a large proportion of customer disaffection, alienation, and sabotage is unsatisfactory support and service. In many companies, transactional processes, especially those related to service, have minimum flex, either in processes or in the behavior of employees. Certainly, they could not be described as either customer-centric or even customer-sensitive. This can be exacerbated by the lack of motivation sometimes found in frontline transactional employees. Since these employees' performance is often evaluated by antiquated metrics like "average handle time," a measure of efficiency, service providers are encouraged to complete the transaction with customers as quickly as possible, rather than focusing on the *quality* of dialogue with the customer, provided in as real-time a manner as possible and reaching an acceptable outcome.

Another misunderstood component of B2B and B2C customer behavior is complaints. There is often a tacit belief that customers with complaints will register them, either online or off. But the reality is that only a small minority will ever contact a vendor's customer support line or other contact channels. The remaining customers with a problem or complaint will speak to others, either directly or through blogs, review sites, or other social media. If an organization bases its improvement processes only on information received through complaint channels or short transactional surveys—ignoring deeper drivers of relationships, online "social voices" that can be evaluated through text analytics, and sources that can provide unsolicited feedback (website forums, online communities, e-mail messages, chat messages, and call center agent logs)—it is like hearing customers with only one ear. Companies such as Comcast and JetBlue have learned that when customers voice negatives or complaints through social media such as Twitter, they expect company representatives to quickly respond. Again, whether communicating directly or indirectly with a company, the survivors will increasingly understand that failure to rapidly react leaves them quite open to vocal customer disaffection, alienation, and even sabotage—"badvocacy."

THE FUTURE OF CUSTOMER ADVOCACY

As a management concept, advocacy has just begun to become mainstream. Over the past few years, advocacy and social media impact studies have been conducted by some of the leading management consulting companies, such as Gartner, Hitachi, Forrester, and IBM. McKinsey, for instance, has recently introduced a word-of-mouth marketing measurement tool.

Noted marketing professor Philip Kotler, of Northwestern University, believes that standout organizations are those that can most effectively optimize stakeholder trust, engagement, and perceived personal value. In a recent article, Dr. Kotler was quoted as saying that some of the most successful companies spend less on marketing than companies that have achieved lower success, building value through inclusion, engagement, authenticity, and stakeholder focus. Though it sounds counter-intuitive, Dr. Kotler said, "They use the word-of-mouth effect of unpaid advocates—truly loyal customers—to boost their reputation. Advocates will do your marketing for you if you mobilize them, listen to them and engage them" (Stern 2010).

Here is another example of how the power of word-of-mouth and advocacy is increasingly being recognized at senior marketing and corporate levels. Jaime Cohen-Szulc, president of the Goodyear Tire and Rubber Company Latin America region (and former CMO of Levi Strauss, Eastman Kodak, and SC Johnson), served as the keynote speaker at the Ad:Tech San Francisco Conference early in 2010. There were over 11,000 exposition attendees, and 1500 attended the conference itself (65% C-suite and senior marketing executives). In his presentation, Cohen-Szulc recommended that marketers stop focusing on loyalty and turn their attention to advocacy. "Loyalty is very passive," he said. "I may be loyal and buy products from a brand, but I don't go out and speak about the brand. Advocacy is active." He also spoke about including customers as a strategic entity and resource, by having them share views and help reinvent brand and corporate perceptions. He concluded, "It is not about selling a product. It is about being coveted and creating a consumer experience. It's about quality and consumer relevance of the core idea. It's about a holistic business view."

It's not at all an oversimplification to say that advocacy is essential to effective customer management. The reasons boil down to this: When companies create active advocates among their customers, they have succeeded in capturing the hearts, minds, wallets, and vocal cords of this group. These are customers who, through their personal, voluntary peer-to-peer communication and marketplace activity, will vigorously leverage more active purchase behavior among both other customers and noncustomers. The ultimate goal of every marketer and every company, therefore, should be to make every customer an active advocate while simultaneously reducing or eliminating customer indifference and negativity.

2

The History of Customer Advocacy and Sabotage

I seen a peanut stand, heard a rubber band
I seen a front porch swing, heard a diamond ring
(I didn't see that, I only heard
But just to be sociable, I'll take your word)

—Lyrics from *When I See an Elephant Fly*,
from the Walt Disney Film, *Dumbo*, 1941,
Oliver Wallace and Ned Livingston

Though, admittedly, this is an offbeat way to start a chapter in a business book, this interaction among the five crows who first saw Dumbo fly in the famous cartoon feature from over 70 years ago gives a lighthearted illustration of the willingness of one individual to believe another. It's at the core of trust.

Customer advocacy, principally the impact of informal communication in behalf of a brand or product—on others as well as the communicator—has been with us since there were organized societies. Before there was mass communication, largely in the form of print and electronic stories and advertising, seeking the advice and guidance of others, along with learning about the customer's own personal experience, was how most product and service selection decisions were made. Put simply, people trusted other people. And, they trusted other people much more than they trusted institutions such as corporations.

It's interesting to note (to me, at least) that the word *sincere* began to be used in France about 500 years ago. *Sincere* comes from the Latin *sincerus*, which means "without wax." In other words, when a transaction was concluded between a customer and a trusted supplier, no wax seal was necessary to represent legal proof of the transaction. There was sufficient openness and honesty, and often a handshake was all that was necessary. For the customer, that was often a transaction worth talking about.

A BRIEF CHRONICLE OF COMMUNICATION EVOLUTION THROUGH THE CENTURIES

Pre– and Post–Industrial Revolution

Though newspapers had been around for several centuries as a one-way communication device, throughout the 1700s and most of the 1800s there was still a healthy rural population in virtually all countries. Even in cities, much of the personal interaction was still localized, face-to-face in small groups or one-to-one. The same could be said of B2B and B2C commerce. Businesses and consumers typically worked with area tradespeople, and long-standing relationships, with trust between customer and supplier, were common.

Then came the breakthroughs that would forever change communication. Transportation saw the rise and spread of the railroad. Then, there were significant developments in automated two-way communication. Samuel Morse's telegraph patent was issued in 1849 (although there were working versions of the telegraph almost 20 years earlier). Regular home mail delivery (in the United States) began in 1863, brought about by the need for faster communication during the Civil War. Alexander Graham Bell (and Elisha Gray) invented the telephone in 1876, and Guglielmo Marconi successfully sent the first transatlantic radiotelegraph message in 1902.

The US Post Office, which had mostly used the railroad to transport mail between cities, staged the first airmail flight in 1918; by 1925, its planes were delivering close to 20 million letters and packages per year through regular airmail flight schedules.

One-way mass electronic communication was also being developed and was just a little behind the time line of the two-way communication devices. Owing much to Marconi and Nikola Tesla (who was actually the first person to patent radio technology), Lee De Forest's invention of the triode amplifier and the Audion made it possible to boost the electromagnetic frequency signals picked up by receiving antennae. De Forest was the first to use the term "radio." His work, especially the invention of amplitude-modulated (AM) radio, made it possible for a multitude of radio stations to broadcast and receive content.

Television followed a similar invention path. Though Bell and Thomas Edison had expressed the belief that the telephone could send images as well as sound, television as we know it was first introduced at the Paris World's Fair in 1900 by Constantin Perskyi (who was also the first person to call his device "television"). The "real" invention of what we know as modern television was by Philo Farnsworth, son of an Idaho farmer, in 1927. His device was called an "image dissector." His patent was licensed to Radio Corporation of America (RCA), but not much work was done on it until after World War II (although RCA did improve Farnsworth's design with something it called the "iconoscope"). Commercial television broadcasting was introduced at the New York World's Fair in 1939.

Presenting: The Transistor

The transistor has, almost without question, changed the world of one-way and two-way human communication forever.

De Forest's invention of the radio and Edison's lightbulb both depended on vacuum tubes, and there was no further technological advancement until about the middle of the twentieth century. In other words, vacuum tubes were acceptable for the purpose. However, vacuum tubes had major problems— leakage, huge power requirements, complicated circuits, metal-emitting electrons in the tubes burned out, and so forth— which led scientists to seek new, more efficient solutions.

Following World War II, Bell Laboratories (the research arm of AT&T) began looking for a vacuum tube replacement. Led by William Shockley, a team of scientists (which included physicists Walter Brattain and John Bardeen) developed the first transistor, and it was introduced in 1948. Though the transistor received relatively little attention when it was introduced, the three scientists were awarded the 1956 Nobel Prize in physics, for what has arguably been the most important invention of the last century. Figure 2.1 shows typical transistors.

Initially, transistors were used for the military and space exploration markets in the United States, which left the door open for further development in foreign countries during the 1950s and 1960s. Enter Japanese engineers Masaru Ibuka and

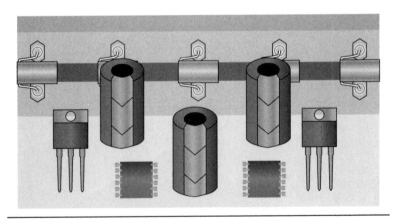

Figure 2.1   An array of transistors.

Akio Morita, the founder of Sony Electronics. Sony began producing small, inexpensive transistor-based radios for the general public. This mass production of transistors, and the ability to continue shrinking their size and apply them to small circuit boards, effectively opened up the information age, enabling communication to go from one pole of the Earth to the other in a matter of seconds.

Communication Sea Change for Marketers

The salad days for marketers began in the 1930s and lasted through the better part of the 1980s, with the growth of radio and television communication and commercials to go along with the newspaper and magazine advertising that had been around for a couple of hundred years before that. This represented the zenith of "push marketing," with marketers determining what to offer and when to offer and promote it, typically with little customer involvement at any stage of development or marketing. Before too long, consumers were being exposed to so many product-related messages—by some estimates, over 2000 per day—that absorbing fact from the clutter and distinguishing it from puff, hype, and fiction became a daunting task for any prospective or active customer. Then came the internet, handhelds (cell phones were invented by Martin Cooper of Motorola in 1976, with the first systems in the United States and Japan just a few years later), and smartphones, and with them arrived the exponential availability of product information—good and bad product ratings, positive and negative "buzz," and so on.

During the mid and late 1990s, the tide began to turn as personal communication and open-source media availability were seeing a dramatic increase and corporations were becoming notorious for executive and financial misdemeanors. The locus of product and service decision-making influence shifted quickly from the aforementioned push approach that companies had used for decades, even centuries, to a situation where the customers dominated, if not owned, the selection of suppliers.

Word-of-mouth influence began to be recognized as a marketing and customer decision-making force. Early on, this was seen in the entertainment industry. *The Blair Witch Project* (1999) was one of the most profitable films in history based on the initial investment. Made for approximately $50,000 and grossing over $100 million in the United States alone, the financial performance of this low-budget independent film over the major studio blockbusters instigated a wake-up call among Hollywood executives due in large part to the important role of the internet and word-of-mouth in the film's commercial success. While the mainstream film industry had already begun to create online-specific content, internet promotion and leverage were still considered to be supplementary to established media techniques. For *The Blair Witch Project*, however, the internet became the central medium for the film's promotion and its reception, as well as its marketing or "franchising," which began more than a year before the film's major theatrical distribution. In this sense, the web functioned in the 1990s for *The Blair Witch Project* in the same way that newspapers and magazines did in relation to the earliest commercial cinema in the 1890s by playing a primary role in the film's marketing program and its meaning for the audience.

In later years, word-of-mouth and the internet became instrumental in the effective marketing of "small" movies like *Sideways* in 2004 (for which Virginia Madsen and Thomas Haden Church were nominated for Oscars) and *Little Miss Sunshine* in 2006 (for which Alan Arkin won an Oscar for best supporting actor).

There are many other early B2C and B2B successes resulting from the application of word-of-mouth and use of the internet in marketing programs. One of the more publicized of these is Hush Puppies. Hush Puppies is a brand of casual, pigskin footwear that had fallen out of fashion over the years. In 1994, when sales of Hush Puppies were down to 30,000 pairs a year and Wolverine Worldwide was considering phasing out the brand, Hush Puppies suddenly became "in" shoes in the clubs and bars of downtown New York City, where teens and young adults were scooping them up at small shoe stores in sections of the city like Soho and Greenwich Village. In 1995, several famous fashion designers began featuring them in their collections. Relying on off-line and online word-of-mouth for marketing, Wolverine sold 430,000 pairs of Hush Puppies shoes that year, and four times that the following year.

The internet has become a great vehicle for creating product and service buzz, with a potential for making word-of-mouth truly global. A venture capitalist first coined the term "viral marketing" to describe the phenomenon of off-line and online interest-building when Hotmail was introduced in 1996. Hotmail created buzz so well in introducing its no-cost e-mail service that it was practically advertising itself for free every time the service was used. With the phrase "Get your free email at Hotmail.com," it was little wonder that Hotmail subscribers grew to 12 million in just 18 months, principally through word-of-mouth.

The internet has become the universal communications enabler and knowledge fountain, the visible source for creating both trust and distrust. It is the perfect place to harangue, extol, lecture, complain, and otherwise send personal missiles of opinion on virtually any subject, especially experiences with products and services. And, in this "need for speed," we've gone from internet connections dominated by slow-download dial-up to high-volume broadband in less than a decade.

Product review and rating sites, such as Usenet, Deja, Bizrate, Epinions, Yelp, and Planet Feedback, give consumers a level of empowerment, enabling them to share their views with other consumers by rating their product and service experiences. Some of the mercantile sites, such as Amazon, QVC, and eBags, also have evaluation systems. And, there are a lot more:

- Social networking sites, such as LinkedIn, Facebook, and MySpace

- Social bookmarking sites, such as Delicious and StumbleUpon

- Social news sites like Digg and Reddit

- Photo and video sharing sites, such as Flickr and YouTube

- Blogs—millions of them

- Microblogs, such as Twitter

One recent study from the Pew Reseach Center put the number of social networking sites at 250,000—already an enormous number, and one that is growing daily (Rainie, Purcell, and Smith 2011). Of course, some sites have only a small number of followers, and there are many niche sites that have content available for a more selective and targeted audience.

It has been estimated that, at any one time, over 150 million people around the world are logged in to Facebook, updating their status, interacting with friends, and interacting with brands. Barack Obama's 2008 presidential campaign used Facebook, MySpace, and other social networking sites to reach millions of supporters and raise nearly $1 billion in campaign contributions. Research from the same Pew Research Center study indicates that 10% of Americans (and 30% of Americans under the age of 30) used Facebook or other social networking sites to get information about the presidential election (Rainie, Purcell, and Smith 2011). The United States is increasingly becoming a minority online social media player. Data from the comScore World Metrix (2009) audience show that Russia has the world's most engaged social networking audience, with the average visitor spending 6.6 hours and viewing 1307 pages per month. China and Korea show even more potential in this regard.

Country notwithstanding, most of these sites generate so much content that it's both a major and sophisticated undertaking to search, collate, and generate high-quality information produced by the vast array of publicly available text material through online social media. As will be discussed later in the book, as important as social media has become, the overriding amount of word-of-mouth continues to be generated off-line. Text mining and analytics has become a major and thriving industry and has grown based on the need of B2B and B2C companies to interpret informal consumer dialogue as it affects their brands, products, and services. Irrespective of source, however, informal, voluntary peer-to-peer communication remains the most leveraging component on customer decision making.

The Reemergence of Customer Advocacy

Perhaps the pivotal moments in history when customer advocacy began to reemerge as a powerful marketing force came with Gladwell's book *The Tipping Point* (2000), followed by Keller and Berry's book *The Influentials* (2003) and several others that address similar subjects. In somewhat different ways, each of these books chronicles the ability and empowerment of individuals to influence the product and service purchase behavior of others through social word-of-mouth. At the core of each book's message is the need for companies to focus on relationship building and experience optimization with their customers. These books were followed by a flurry of volumes on the emergence of social networking, Web 2.0, consumer-generated media, and other major trends.

Much of customer advocacy (and sabotage) depends on the level of *trust* between individuals and related concepts such as objectivity, credibility and expertise, honesty, reliability, and originality in the online and off-line communication methods that they themselves have created. Advocacy recognizes that consumers were far less value-accepting before this new power they now have. Instead of being passive recipients of company offers and marketing messages, they now require more knowledge-creating, problem-solving dialogue and take more control of how value is defined, created, and delivered. Further, advocacy requires a more holistic and participatory relationship between supplier and customer. This relationship requires higher levels of trust, accountability, and transparency and a focus on experiences for organizations. These factors are explored in depth in the next chapter. What is important to keep in mind, though, is that the influence of word-of-mouth can be felt at any stage of the customer life cycle, which we have identified as suspect/prospect/new customer/retained customer/ at-risk customer/lost customer/recovered customer.

Many companies are focused on the dynamics involved in a suspect and prospect progressing to the new customer state. This is customer acquisition, which is typically where much of the push marketing and advertising content is directed. It's largely one-way communication.

At each stage of the consideration-to-purchase process, pictured in Figure 2.2, marketers are beginning to understand that their efforts will be more financially productive and time-effective if they engage in two-way dialogue with prospects, setting the table when the prospects are gathering information and initially considering supplier selection and purchase alternatives, and also endeavor to build advocacy behavior at each decision-making point.

An Example Chronicling 100 Years of Push Advertising and Promotion, and Communication and Positive/ Negative Advocacy in the Twenty-First Century

Since the second decade of the twentieth century, Camel cigarettes have been advertised and promoted to the general public. The arc and evolution of communication and media selec-

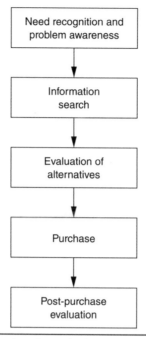

Figure 2.2   Consideration through the post-purchase process.

tion approaches, and the degrees of effectiveness through the decades, can tell us volumes about what works and doesn't work with leveraging purchase activity through traditional advertising and promotion in today's marketplace. It can also reveal much about how brands have had to adapt and morph their messages and communications arenas. In the case of Camel, the brand has experienced its share of both sabotage and advocacy.

Beginning around 1915, Camel became one of three major brands of cigarettes in the United States (along with Lucky Strike and Chesterfield). The brand sold for less than the other brands, which made it popular, and the camel, nicknamed "Old Joe," became one of the most recognized ad symbols of all time. By 1921, parent company R.J. Reynolds was spending over $8 million in advertising, principally on Camel cigarettes.

Around the same time, advertising agency N.W. Ayer launched the iconic "I'd Walk a Mile for a Camel" campaign, and Camel sales represented close to 50% of the cigarette market. Conveying messages such as freshness, taste, mildness, energy, and even calmness (!) as key product benefits, Camel remained highly popular throughout the 1960s. Celebrity endorsers, such as professional athletes, TV series comedian Phil Silvers, and movie stars Rock Hudson and Tony Curtis, were seen regularly in Camel ads during this period. Cigarette ads even featured endorsements by physicians and dentists.

Throughout the 1960s, the 1970s, and the early 1980s, the promotion and messaging for all brands of cigarettes were largely unregulated (see Figure 2.3). Though Camel continued to be an advertising leader by being a sponsor of NASCAR, Formula One, and Superbike racing series, other brands were building volume and share and Camel was no longer among the top three or even top five brands. Camel brand managers were looking for a radical change in positioning and messaging direction, and in 1987 R.J. Reynolds introduced "Joe Camel"

Figure 2.3   A Camel ad from 1973.

to mark the brand's 75th anniversary and actively used this cartoon figure to advertise and promote the brand with a new image (see Figure 2.4).

The Joe Camel character was almost ubiquitous, seen virtually everywhere and in all types of media after its introduction. Camel brand rode this tide of new popularity until, several years later, the prestigious *Journal of the American Medical Association* published two significant reports destined to call attention to the then-power of push advertising. These reports changed the brand's image and the brand's communication approach for a considerable period to come. The first study reported that 91% of five- and six-year-old children recognized Joe Camel, similar to the percentage who recognized Mickey Mouse or Fred Flintstone (Fischer, Schwartz, Richards, Goldstein, and Rojas 1991).

Figure 2.4 Joe Camel ads.

Benign enough, but the second JAMA-reported study in 1999 found that since the beginning of the Joe Camel campaign, Camel's share of the illegal under-18-year-old market had risen from 0.5% to 32.8%, worth over $400 million a year in sales (Goldstein, Sobel, and Newman 1999). At about the same time, the Centers for Disease Control (1994) in Atlanta reported through a surgeon general's study that smokers between the ages of 12 and 18 preferred Camel cigarettes, along with two other widely advertised brands (*Preventing Tobacco Use among Young People* 1994). Subsequently, the American Medical Association asked R.J. Reynolds to cancel the Joe Camel campaign.

These combined findings resulted in actively negative public word-of-mouth for Camel, and there began a negative advocacy campaign from both health and legal directions to restrict or ban all cigarette advertising. Then, there was an important chronology of events:

- In 1995, R.J. Reynolds said it would remove Joe Camel from all billboard advertising

- In 1996, President Bill Clinton made a public statement to the effect that advertising appeals such as Joe Camel entice children to start smoking in their early teens, and he made a pledge to eliminate all tobacco advertising and promotion to children

- On July 19, 1997, under threat from the Federal Trade Commission, R.J. Reynolds announced that it would eliminate Joe Camel from all advertising for the brand

This experience was "tough love" learning for R.J. Reynolds, even though the company continued to deny that the Joe Camel promotion and image were intended to target children (saying that the intended audience was 25- to 49-year-old males and current Marlboro smokers). In its next new product introduction, tactics and approaches underwent considerable modification. Although in 1998 the cigarette companies had agreed not to target adolescents and teens in their advertising (in part because of the popularity and visibility Joe Camel had generated), in 2007 Camel introduced its No. 9 cigarettes, featuring innovative feminine-oriented packaging with the image of the camel made smaller, and in pink. Partially, this was because Camel wanted to generate sales from a younger audience, but it was also because about half of adult smokers were women but only about 30% of Camel smokers were female. Camel was out to steal shares from its principal competitor among women, Virginia Slims.

The No. 9 cigarettes were clearly intended for teenage girls, with its updated camel package design and advertisements in trendy magazines such as *Vogue*, *Glamour*, *W*, *Flaunt*, and *Cosmopolitan* (although R.J. Reynolds insisted that its own studies showed that the vast majority of female readers of these magazines are over 18). The launch was punctuated by feminine advertising and such promotional giveaways as flavored lip balm, cell phone jewelry, purses, and wristbands. This time, traditional advertising and promotion were only the beginning.

To get around federal laws against cigarette advertising, R.J. Reynolds began a program of media ownership and channel innovation for Camel. This included creation of a lifestyle magazine (*CML*), use of in-venue events and alternative media (such as New York's *Paper Magazine* and the *San Francisco Bay Guardian*, which ran full-page ads and card-stock promotional inserts), point-of-sale, direct mail, and active promotion to charismatic "hipsters," young trendsetters ages 18–35 who serve as a style and cultural clearinghouse for what is socially cool and new.

Another new feature of the marketing of Camel No. 9 cigarettes has been the more deliberate and active use of social media to promote the brand and build customer relationships. For example, Reynolds created a new website, http://www.camelno9.com, with information about promotional activities and events. There has also been a tremendous amount of pro and con blogging about Camel No. 9, with younger blog-gers generally defending the product positioning and older bloggers decrying it.

CUSTOMER SABOTAGE ON STEROIDS: THE PIVOTAL INTERNET TRADEMARK CASE OF BALLY TOTAL FITNESS HOLDING CORP. V. ANDREW FABER

Decades ago, when I was employed as a market research super-visor for du Pont, my daily auto commute took me from the suburbs of Philadelphia to downtown Wilmington, Delaware. On the way into work, my notice would often be taken by a gigantic sign on the lawn of a house situated at the traffic sig-nal of a major intersection. At the top of the sign, in big block, black lettering no one could miss, was "I Hate Kenmore Appli-ances. Don't Shop at Sears," followed by a couple of paragraphs of explanation in smaller print. One day, curiosity about what was written on the sign got the better of me, and the impression made during the five-minute stop to read it has stayed with me for over 40 years.

Through research, PR firm Weber Shandwick has deter-mined that, worldwide, about 20% of customers are likely to be detractors, even saboteurs. The more critical finding of the firm's studies has been that almost half of corporate executives fear that a disgruntled customer will post negative things about their company on the internet (Weber Shandwick/KRC Research 2007). The following story illustrates one well-publicized man-ifestation of that fear.

In the late 1990s, Bally Fitness, a national chain of fitness centers, enraged members by having what amounted to an open-ended financial services contract when customers first joined. In other words, customers could sign up for member-ship on what appeared to be a month-to-month basis, only to find that the contracts could never be cancelled. Many customers ended up paying for years. Andrew Faber, one customer who had reached the breaking point with this arrangement, set up a contra, or "gripe," site so that members with similar experiences could be attracted to express their negatives on a community basis.

The contra site attracted visitors by the thousands and cost Bally millions of dollars in lost sales. Called "Bally Sucks," the website opened with the image of Bally's federally registered trademark "Bally," across which appeared the word "sucks." Immediately following were the words "Bally Total Fitness Complaints! Unauthorized." Faber, a professional website designer, neither sold nor offered any products for sale on this website.

Bally sued Faber to force him to discontinue this use of its mark and also, hopefully, to dismantle the negative site. In its complaint, heard in a federal court in California in 1998, Bally asserted that Faber's actions constituted trademark infringement, dilution, and unfair competition. The court disagreed, and on Faber's motion for a summary judgment, it dismissed the complaint. The court went on to conclude that the average consumer was not at all likely to be confused by the defendant's use of the "Bally" mark as to the source of the defendant's "Bally Sucks" website. Quite the contrary, the court held that the average consumer would assume that the site was not authorized by Bally and was put up by an unaffiliated party. Accordingly, Bally's trademark infringement claims failed as a matter of law. In *Bally Total Fitness Holding Corporation v. Andrew S. Faber* (U.S. District (C.D. Cal 1998)), the court concluded:

> Faber's site states that it is "unauthorized" and contains the words "Bally sucks." No reasonable consumer comparing Bally's official website with Faber's would assume Faber's site to come from the same source, or thought to be affiliated with, connected with, or sponsored by, the trademark owner. Therefore, Bally's claim for trademark infringement fails as a matter of law.

While this legal finding didn't open a floodgate of negative corporate sites—although quite a few rancorous ones were developed by angry consumers, including ones targeting Microsoft, Northwest Airlines, America Online (AOL), Walmart, Toys R Us, and GTE, to cite just a few—it opened the era of mass online negative communication and even introduced the threat of internet-based retaliation. Nike, for instance, has been the target of close to 10 negative sites over the years, criticizing everything from company personnel policies to running overseas sweatshop factories that employ underage children. In Faber's case, he simply felt that a website would be tougher to ignore than a stream of angry letters. As evidence of corporate recognition of the potential impact of these contra sites, many companies now assign employees to surf, and otherwise monitor, them for evidence of unhappy customers so that they can be contacted right away.

A 2009 degree-of-trust study conducted through the Nielsen Global Online Consumer Survey of over 25,000 internet consumers from 50 countries found that over 90% said they trusted recommendations and positive word-of-mouth from people they know. Personal peer-to-peer communication is the most impactful element of advocacy creation. This compared to much lower percentages for advertising through brand sponsorships (64%), television (62%), newspapers (61%), magazines (59%), radio (55%), and permission-based e-mails (54%). Approaches like search engine results ads had low trust (41%), as did text ads on mobile phones (24%).

We've now come full circle. In simpler times less dominated by speed and connectivity, people trusted other people more than institutions and their advertising and promotional blandishments. Today, in significantly more complex times, they do again.

3

The Importance of Experience, Authenticity, and Trust in Customer Advocacy

Billy Joel is one of my all-time favorite musical performers. In 1986, he recorded "A Matter of Trust," a great rock song in which the lyrics describe what can go right and what can go wrong in a relationship. A company's relationship with, and desire to capture the hearts and minds of, two of its principal stakeholder groups—customers and employees—is almost entirely built around belief and value, that is, perceived personal benefit. Largely, the loyalty behavior that companies get is a direct result of the trust and authenticity they create with these stakeholders.

The Free Dictionary (http://www.thefreedictionary.com) defines *trust* as "assured reliance on another's integrity, credibility, objectivity, veracity, and justice." *Sincere*, a related word, means "pure, real, honest, and free of hypocrisy." In the previous chapter, it was noted that *sincere* means "without wax." In earlier times, when a transaction was concluded between a vendor and a customer, it was so open and transparent that it did not require the usual seal of wax to complete the transaction or maintain the relationship. The vendor's reputation was sufficient to seal the deal.

Both sincerity and trust are at the heart of partnerships, contracts, relationships, and dealings between people and institutions. These two words and concepts, along with authenticity and openness, are central to optimizing stakeholder experiences and behavior. As Billy Joel wisely observed in his song, trust is "a constant battle for the ultimate state of control," which, too often, companies want to hold and not share. Then, customer trust becomes "a lie of the mind," in which neither customer nor vendor feels fairly treated. And, seeing the glass as half empty—"After you've heard lie upon lie, there can hardly be a question of why"—companies lose customer and employee support, favorability, and passion, leaving the door open for discontent and sabotage to occur.

Trust comes from deep within organizational rules and process execution, and it is built on the customer- and employee-related vision, values, and mission regarding transactional experiences and marketplace behavior, through communication and purchasing or service. Trust, externally, is best understood as reputation. It can be graphically represented by a "line of sight," the real continuum or connection that exists between customer management and experience creation through engagement processes and messaging, the customer's perception of relative overall value, and resulting in marketplace outcomes. It is often the consultant's role to help companies evaluate and improve *who they are*, *what they do*, and *what they get*. Figure 3.1 is a graphic illustration of line of sight.

CUSTOMER TRUST: NEED INTERSECTING WITH DELIVERY BELIEF

There are basics associated with trust, such as privacy, consistent delivery of essential elements of tangible value, and building and sustaining a proactive, positive, customer-centric reputation within the marketplace. Building trust in a customer–

Figure 3.1 The customer experience/behavior line of sight.

supplier relationship begins with meeting these essential customer needs and requirements. Briefly, the customer needs one or more elements of a supplier's product or service, resulting in that customer moving from prospective to engaged, "new customer" status when an initial purchase is made. Then, the relationship builds on emotional and rational/functional delivery of perceived value over time, comprising one or more components of the customer's "trust equation." If any element of trust is received in a less-than-desired manner (including a nonauthentic, deceptive, or otherwise negative experience), the relationship can be undermined, sometimes very quickly and sometimes with unattractive long-term consequences.

Trust has become an essential, differentiating element in creating customer loyalty behavior. In fact, trust may well be the only truly sustainable competitive advantage for an organization. It is necessary, for example, if the supplier is to learn from customers through a free and open exchange of information, off-line or online. It's essential in positive customer word-of-mouth and referral, in having customers be resistant to competitive offers, and in having them be tolerant of occasional value delivery lapses. Without trust and authenticity, companies can quickly find themselves back to square one with their customers, where everything they offer—price, design, convenience, service, and so on—can be easily replicated by competitors.

Many companies endeavor to attract customers and to build trust through a rather passive, commoditized, rational, and product-centric sales and marketing approach. Such companies often believe that high accuracy, delivery timing and completeness, and other tangible components of value will earn both differentiation and customer loyalty. As a result, they don't adequately determine the customer's real priorities and set of expectations, what the customer wants to hear (positioning), how the customer wants to hear it (preferred communication channel), or how they are going to say it (messaging). This is the traditional push approach to marketing, lacking authenticity and engagement. It often doesn't involve, or minimally involves, the customer in actual planning or dialogue. And if the company fails to deliver expected value—that is, not doing what it says it will do and not meeting basic commitments and requirements, even using traditional one-way communication techniques—the relationship will inevitably fail.

When tough economic times put pressure on customers, whether in B2B or B2C, optimizing relationships and perceived value becomes even more important. In studies by customer service software firm RightNow Technologies (2010), the most important factor influencing customer loyalty behavior has been determined to be quality of the service experiences. Close to 90% of customers in the RightNow studies said they would be likely to move their business elsewhere if they encountered poor overall service experiences. Even in difficult times, it's notable that almost 60% of customers said they would pay more for a better, more authentic service experience. Over 50% of customers said they would be encouraged to spend more and would recommend the supplier to other customers. Getting customers to pay for service is, however, not the typical approach used to maintain customer trust and loyalty behavior. What is required is close experience management through setting (or resetting) service levels so that they do not degrade from the customer's perception of value and, at the same time, not overinvesting (with capital, people, time, or technology) in competency levels not important to the customer.

Building trust does indeed take investment and effort. Companies that rely largely on brand pedigree—what they think is product or service uniqueness, pricing, or corporate recognition—are likely to be challenged. Why? Because these factors have been identified again and again as the least influential in customer purchase decisions. Further, while customers are often willing to provide feedback and do so, they also insist that companies take action on the input they have provided. Increasingly, customers are insisting on a sense of partnership with their vendors or suppliers. Thus, a "bank account" of trust and belief that the company is acting in the customer's best interest can be built. However, just as bank deposits can be made, so can withdrawals, in the form of expressed and unexpressed complaints. In the same RightNow customer experience impact studies, over 80% said that they would stop doing business with a firm as a result of bad experiences (and close to 70% said they would *never* return). Close to three-quarters have told others about poor treatment, and 20% have posted negative feedback online.

Once reputation is impaired, the "long tail" of negativism is difficult to recover. The next section details in monetary terms just how difficult this can be.

THE ECONOMIC POWER OF NEGATIVE CUSTOMER EXPERIENCES

ClickFox (2009) recently conducted a study in which the objective was to understand how negative customer experiences played out in economic terms. Respondents were first asked which kinds of companies they find most frustrating to interact with. Close to 27% said cable companies, followed by telephone companies (19%), healthcare companies (14%), and insurance companies and banks (both about 11%). Although dealing with rude or inexperienced reps and being kept on hold were among the main gripes, the principal complaint and frustration expressed by almost half the adults in the study was having to deal with multiple reps and starting over every time. Consumers considered this both a waste of time and a quick erosion of trust.

In this study, bad customer experience began a chain of economically unfortunate events. Over half the respondents had communicated with a supervisor, and almost that many said they would tell others about their experience and stop doing business with the vendor. Similar to the RightNow results, about 20% said they would post negative results online.

But the statistic that made negative customer experience ramifications so profound was length of time as a customer. Only 13% of those who said they would leave as a result of poor experiences were new customers. Most companies invest large proportions of their available resources to attract new customers, and endeavor to personalize experiences. When these customers are frustrated as a result of poor interactions, the organization is less sufficiently prepared to address these issues because they don't know these customers as well.

In the ClickFox study, the statistic that stood out was that 81% of the customers whose frustration was so high that they were determined to leave after having had a bad experience were "established." Losing longer-term customers means that the investment in cross-sell and upsell propensity would constantly be at risk because of poor value delivery.

WHEN TRUST VANISHES: A RESTORATION HOW-TO EXAMPLE

United Parcel Service (UPS) suffered staggering customer defection as a consequence of its 15-day Teamsters work stoppage in 1997. The result was that, even after its 80,000 drivers were back behind the wheel of their delivery trucks and tractor-trailers, many thousands of UPS workers were laid off. The company's reputation was in shreds. A UPS manager in Arkansas was quoted as saying, "To the degree that our customers come back will dictate whether those jobs come back" (Leumer 2007).

The UPS loss was a gain for Federal Express, Airborne, RPS, and even the US Postal Service. They provided services during the strike that made UPS's customers see the dangers of using a single delivery company to handle their packages and parcels. FedEx, for example, reported expecting to keep as much as 25% of the 850,000 additional packages it delivered each day of the strike.

UPS's customer loss woes, and the impact on its employees, was a very public display of the consequences of customer turnover. Most customer loss is relatively unseen, but it has been determined that many companies lose between 10% and 40% of their customers each year. Still more customers fall into a level of dormancy, or reduced "share of customer" with their current supplier, moving their business to other companies and thus decreasing the amount they spend with the original supplier. The economic impact on companies and the crushing moral effects of downsizing, rightsizing, plant closings, and layoffs on employees are the real effects of customer loss.

Lost jobs and lost profits propelled UPS into an aggressive win-back mode as soon as the strike was settled. Customers began receiving phone calls from UPS officials assuring them that UPS was back in business, apologizing for the inconvenience, and pledging that the company's former reliability had been restored. Drivers dropping by for pickups were cheerful and confident, and they reinforced that things were back to normal. UPS issued letters of apology and discount certificates to customers to help heal the wounds and rebuild trust. Face-to-face meetings with customers large and small were initiated by UPS—all with the goal of getting the business back.

These win-back initiatives formed an important bridge of recovery back to the customer. And they worked. The actions, coupled with the company's cost-effective services, continuing advances in shipping technology, and the dramatic growth of online shopping, enabled UPS to reinstate many laid-off workers while increasing its profits by a remarkable 87% in the year following the devastating strike.

UPS is hardly an isolated case. Protecting customer relationships in these uncertain times is a fact of life for every business. We've entered a new era of customer defection where customer churn is reaching epidemic proportions and wrecking businesses and lives along the way. It's time to truly understand the consequences of customer loss and, in turn, apply proven win-back strategies to regain these valuable customers.

CUSTOMER COMPLAINTS: GETTING THE WHOLE ENCHILADA

Along with performance and loyalty metrics gathered through customer research, complaints are one of the best sources of experience data a company can have, yet most organizations are getting half, or considerably less, of the complaints that exist. Their portion of the enchilada is the complaints customers post via telephone, fax, mail, and the internet. Suppliers need to have a compendium of complaints, available through basic research and analysis. And if they can't get complaints directly, either from customers or through customer inquiry, then they need to identify them through other sources, such as web scraping as posted via online social media.

Nothing is as effective as complaints in sinking a sales, marketing, customer loyalty, or customer management program or giving it new life. Complaints can be a positive or negative influence on customer word-of-mouth, as well as intention to remain loyal, to buy more, to recommend, or to defect. The challenge for companies is that they have to know about the complaints in order to do anything about them.

At a time when product and service loyalty continues to be more of an issue in many industries, consumer advocacy groups report that more than half of the buying public has problems or complaints with items or services they purchase. Yet, it has been estimated that only about 2%–10% of customers actually air their grievances to the supplier (Goodman 1999). Some industries tend to experience notably high levels of customer complaint silence: financial services, food and beverages, pharmaceuticals, and technology.

If not the vendors, then whom do these customers tell when they have a complaint? Their friends, relatives, colleagues—and the ether on the internet, through communities, blogs, forums, rating sites, and the like. It's been well documented why—principally for reasons of trust and perceived benefit—customers won't complain directly to the company:

- They're busy, and they can't or don't want to take the time

- They consider the complaint interaction process a hassle and an annoyance

- They see no direct value or benefit to them in making the complaint

- They don't think the supplier will do anything about the complaint

- They can get what they want from an alternative supplier, so they switch

Canadian marketing research firm Hepworth + Company (1999) found that over 40% of the companies in its B2B database that had a problem or complaint never informed the supplier about it. Their reasons for not expressing complaints were remarkably similar to those given by consumers. Other studies suggest that, depending on the industry, unexpressed B2B complaints may be as high as 80% or 90% of the complaints that exist, so this issue is hardly exclusive to B2C.

Even though the rate of expressed complaints is higher in the B2B world, the lost revenue potential of unexpressed complaints is significantly higher because of the lifetime value of each customer. Hepworth, for example, has estimated that the total amount of revenue at risk due to poor service and complaints is 10% of the entire sales base.

THE POWER OF UNEXPRESSED COMPLAINTS, AND A COMMERCIAL BANKING EXAMPLE

Several years ago, a major Midwest bank conducted a study of the loyalty leveraging effect of expressed and unexpressed complaints on its commercial customers. The bank found that about half of these customers had service complaints. Of those with a complaint, only about half had expressed them, despite ongoing contact between them and the bank. In other words, fully one-quarter of the complaint "enchilada" was missing.

When customers do complain—either through customer service operations like the Campbell Soup Company's Consumer Response and Information Center (which takes more than 300,000 calls a year) and the General Electric Answer

Center (which is open 24/7 every day of the year) or through traditional means or via outbound complaint solicitation—how the complaints are received and acted upon makes all the difference in their effect on customer trust levels and resulting behavior.

The potential for complaints to negatively affect customers' future purchase intent and recommendation likelihood should never be overlooked. In loyalty research for one of our clients, a major manufacturer of paper and related products, it was determined that 40% of its high-volume accounts had serious performance complaints. These complaining customers were 15% less likely to be positive about continuing to purchase from our client than those without a complaint. Other studies show similar negative loyalty effects of complaints.

Hepworth's (1999) own B2B research showed that only about one-quarter of the customers who complained felt their concerns had been successfully resolved, a very serious issue. Two reasons are that, in the minds of customers, resolution often either takes too long or requires too many interactions with the supplier, both areas of real frustration and trust-robbing. Hepworth has found, for instance, that it frequently takes two or three contacts beyond the initial one to get issues resolved. Customers experiencing inefficient or insufficient complaint resolution are not only less likely to repurchase from or recommend that supplier but also likely to spread their negativism— telling anywhere from 2 to 20 people off-line, and potentially limitless numbers online, about their bad experience. Poor service and complaint resolution are principal drivers of customer alienation and sabotage.

With numbers like these, it's little wonder that, left poorly handled or unresolved, complaining customers can, and will, sabotage even the most carefully crafted marketing or customer loyalty program. The incidence of poor customer service experiences demonstrated by many online and brick-and-mortar companies has been actively reported in the media. Angry customers will tell one another, post on rating sites, and even set up their own websites so that other upset and former customers have a forum for their negative experiences.

So, having seen how complaints can hurt, how can complaints complement, or even enhance, a company's customer trust-building and loyalty efforts? There are three ways.

First, actively encourage customers to contact the company with questions, comments, problems, or complaints, and make it as easy as possible. Further, make it an active, open, and honest dialogue between the company and the customer that everyone, including noncustomers and employees, can see.

Second, identify the root causes of all complaints, registered and unregistered, so that their sources (staff, messaging, or experience processes) can be addressed and corrected.

Third, enhance the effectiveness of problem and complaint resolution processes so that customers are given the most efficient and effective contact venues.

There is a fourth method to consider when approaching complaint generation and management. And it may be the simplest, most effective of all. Most companies, in their customer value and performance research, fail to *ask* about complaints, especially those that have not been registered. This needs to be supported. Complaints, after all, are a different category of involvement with a supplier than just low performance ratings. They're much more intense and personal. If we can identify unresolved complaints that have been registered, and those complaints that haven't been registered (and the reasons for nonregistration), we will have a complete inventory of customer complaints that will shed new light on the complaint processes and consequences. The specific potential impact of complaints on customer loyalty behavior can then be modeled for prioritized action.

Returning to the bank example, those commercial customers who registered their complaints—and then had those complaints handled in a positive manner by the customer service department—indicated a very high level of loyalty toward the bank. In what has come to be understood as conventional wisdom resulting from studies in many other industries, *the level of loyalty for those with complaints was actually higher than for those who had no complaints.* On the other hand, those customers who hadn't expressed a complaint (even though they actually had complaints when asked) had bank loyalty levels about two-thirds as high as those whose complaints had been expressed and positively resolved. And, the customers whose complaints had been handled poorly had loyalty levels only one-quarter as positive as those whose complaints had been handled well (see Figure 3.2).

The lesson here, as has been proved again and again, is that when customers are encouraged to engage in dialogue with suppliers regarding performance problems or concerns, that opportunity for enhanced value provision actually creates stronger, more bonded relationships.

Having a database of registered and unregistered complaints gives a company the entire spectrum of customer negativity, enabling corrective action to be much more focused and

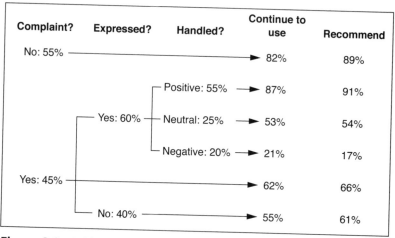

Figure 3.2 Midwest bank expressed/unexpressed complaints results. Source: Banc One, Ohio.

relevant. When this is combined with customer profile and contact data, an assessment of key rational and emotional elements of performance delivery, and metrics about intended behavior through targeted research, companies can be far more effective in optimizing customer experiences and behavior. That's the power of the whole enchilada.

REPUTATION, TRUST, AND ADVOCACY

Depending on how much a customer comes to trust a brand or company, it is possible for neural social communication, or word-of-mouth, to represent the propensity for that customer to act and also to influence others by telling about his or her experiences. If the experiences have been seen as positive, the customer can become an advocate for the brand or company. If the experiences have been negative, the customer can become unconnected and alienated, undermining—even sabotaging— the image and reputation the company is endeavoring to build with customers and prospects.

Extensive research into the drivers and results of advocacy behavior has revealed that active positive or negative communication to others highly correlates with the customer's own downstream behavior (known as self-perception), as well as directly and indirectly influencing the behavior of others. The media for communicating these impressions and opinions can be as sophisticated as online communities, blogs, or forums or as simple as off-line back-fence or water cooler chat.

Customer advocacy, built on trust achieved through individual experience, is a legitimate and strategic objective. It links closely with the number of companies or brands in a customer's consideration set, degree of favorability, likelihood to repurchase, and likelihood to recommend. Arguably, because share of wallet correlates so closely with advocacy level over time, it defines the relative strength of a brand or company's franchise within the marketplace.

On the positive side, a study by Kelly Hlavinka (2010) has found, for example, that engaged B2C customers who participate in loyalty programs of preferred brands are 70% more likely to communicate to others in behalf of that product, service, or brand compared to the general population. Further, those who are active in the loyalty program are three times more likely to create positive word-of-mouth than those who are passive members. Over two-thirds of those who are active informal communicators will actually recommend that brand or product to others over the course of a year.

Customers who have had negative experiences or considered the experience nonauthentic, conversely, may not voice their disappointment back to the company; however, they will voice their sentiments to others, both off-line and online. With the internet's reach as an enabler of these customers' disappointment and discontent, most companies in this situation will see further erosion of trust through cascading loss of customers.

Marketers are becoming aware that customers are inundated and overwhelmed with "push" messages and impressions, and the availability of product and service information in both print and electronic formats. As a result, they have gone in large measure to alternative, informal, and less traditional methods of helping them decide what and where to buy. At the heart of seeking sources for decision input is the desire for *trust* and *authenticity*.

Today, both macro and targeted advertising and marketing communication—indeed, most traditional forms of electronic and print messaging and promotion—receive low trust and believability scores in survey after survey of B2B and B2C customers. Beyond permission e-mail, supplier and brand websites, and the like, customer trust is consistently highest for informal, social word-of-mouth. How high? In a 2004 report, more than 90% of consumers said they trust word-of-mouth, compared to less than half that for most other forms of advertising and formal customer communication (Nail 2004).

While the aggregate influencing effect of electronic and print advertising has remained about the same for the past 30 years, word-of-mouth has doubled in leveraging power to the point where it is the dominant communication device in our society. Through these studies, Roper Reports (now part of GfK) has learned that more than 90% of customers identify word-of-mouth as the best, most reliable, credible, and relevant source of ideas and information about products and services. This is about the same percentage who find it the most trustworthy and objective source.

ADVOCACY STRATEGY AND TACTICS: MOTOR VEHICLES AS A METAPHOR

No matter how well companies believe they have created trust and how well they think they understand customers' needs and behavior on an individual basis, they must have programs that facilitate peer-to-peer communication. This means having an open channel from customers to the organization and back again, along with mechanisms for maintaining the flow of both information and advocacy creation. In this section, we'll explore how two different sectors of the motor vehicle industry have succeeded in creating and sustaining the trust that leads to customer advocacy.

H.O.G. Wild

Owners of Harley-Davidson motorcycles who are members of H.O.G. (Harley Owners Group) clubs around the world are very visible advocates for the brand (see Figure 3.3). For Harley owners, being H.O.G. members helps them live the branded customer experience. They not only buy the motorcycles but also actively accessorize with Harley-Davidson equipment for their rides, wear a vast array of Harley-Davidson logo clothing (at a rate more than 30% higher than average Harley-Davidson

Figure 3.3 H.O.G. chapter logo.

owners), and enthusiastically participate in Harley-Davidson events. Since starting with fewer than 50 members in 1983, H.O.G. has grown to having close to 1 million members, more than half of whom attend at least one Harley-Davidson event per year. They are also goodwill ambassadors for both Harley-Davidson and motorcycle riders, annually contributing major amounts to the Muscular Dystrophy Association.

How important is creating enthusiastic customer advocates to the company? Harley-Davidson does almost no advertising, relying instead on its worldwide community of owners to purchase both motorcycles and logo gear—and spread the word to others. Customer advocacy has an impact on virtually every area of company activity. As John Russell, managing director of Harley-Davidson Europe, said, "If it is important to the customer, if it's a good insight, if it's a good point of understanding and connection to the customer, it makes its way into business processes and becomes part of what we do" (Dourado 2005). This is an excellent example of how creating trust and partnering with customers result in enhanced value for the company.

Price Automotive Group, New Castle, Delaware

Every customer experience with an organization, no matter how seemingly small and insignificant, has the power to excite and reinforce trust, creating loyalty and advocacy. Unfortunately, each experience also has the potential to create dissatisfaction, disaffection, disloyalty, anger, and even sabotage. Companies are well advised to fully interpret and understand the potential loyalty impact of each transaction and experience—as well as the components of each experience—to take prescriptive action. This is especially true if the experience is identified as a contributor to customer risk or loss.

Dealing with auto dealerships, whether buying, taking delivery, or having a continuing service relationship, has all the potential for trust creation or trust destruction. Just about everyone owns a car, SUV, or light truck, and we have all gone through the often painful and exhausting experiences associated with vehicle purchase or maintenance. For many, such an interaction compares favorably with the anxious anticipation of a trip to the dentist or a visit with an IRS agent.

In the movie *Fargo*, there's an incidental scene in which an auto buyer is forced to pay more for a car than he had agreed to because the factory "automatically" applied undercoating (a $500 option), even though he had previously specified that he did not want the undercoating. Obviously angry, the buyer nevertheless takes delivery of the car but makes it abundantly clear to the dealer that he feels victimized and will never shop there again. And, it's implicit that he will tell everyone he knows to avoid the dealership as well.

This is an example of how *not* to manage customer trust and experience.

For lessons on how to do it right, enter Michael Price.

Michael Price is the general manager and executive vice president of Price Automotive Group. Based in New Castle, Delaware, a densely populated suburb of Wilmington, the seven-brand auto dealership chain focuses on creating optimized experiences and redefining what buyers and owners think of auto dealers. And, the dealership does it at least as well as many better-known best-in-class companies such as Nordstrom,

Wegmans Food Markets, Ritz-Carlton, Starbucks, the Container Store, and Southwest Airlines.

What Price has accomplished proves that companies of all types, sizes, and industries can optimize the loyalty behavior of both customers and employees. The achievements of his flagship location, Price Toyota, include:

- 67% of customers repeat or refer business

- 13.5 vehicle sales per representative per month

- 97% of customers have A or B credit scores

This represents real customer commitment to the Price Toyota dealership. Price has built a positive, customer-centric reputation in its market area and beyond. Each of these results is significantly above industry norms. For example, the industry average for monthly sales level per representative is 9.5 vehicles, meaning reps at Price Toyota sell about 50% more than typical salespeople.

Price's success is driven by closely monitored process management at each customer life stage. It begins at the prospect stage, and every step and interaction is done with the objective of optimizing perceived customer value. The process is built on a solid foundation of insight into customer needs and expectations, coupled with flexible, innovative approaches to delivering benefits. Further, and perhaps most important, the dealership is able to customize and value-enhance the individual and long-term experiences of each customer.

Several years ago, the Price dealerships switched to a "one-price" method of new and pre-owned vehicle selling, in which what they have determined as the best, most fair vehicle price is offered up front. Research on this approach revealed that customers tend to equate a long, drawn-out vehicle purchase transaction with personal vulnerability and the potential addition of unwanted expense. The research also showed that if the purchase process extended beyond two hours, both future purchase and recommendation likelihood scores declined rapidly (charted in 15-minute increments beyond two hours). In other words, the shorter and more straightforward the transaction, the stronger the experience authenticity and greater the customer's trust level in the dealership.

To address this, Price reduced the transaction time for most customers to under two hours. The financing and insurance, often the longest and most painful part of the transaction, has been compressed to less than 25 minutes. As a result, among the more than 75% of customers who complete their purchases within two hours, 100% plan to repurchase at the dealership, 97% plan to service their vehicles there (a desired dealer profit opportunity), and 67% have already referred others.

The dealerships now offer 15 high-perceived-value benefits to buyers, including a 72-hour buy-back/exchange policy, service and parts discounts, no-charge towing, and an additional $300 for their Price vehicle at trade-in. But the real differentiators are the approaches that create intangible, emotionally based trust and relationship value.

Price executives understand that, particularly at the beginning of the customer's life cycle with the dealership, the sales process—and resulting experiences for buyers—must be designed and aligned to address each customer's needs.

For example, sales reps are carefully trained to guide customers through the purchase process and to offer quick, responsive support. They are on salary rather than commission, so sales pressure is mitigated. The dealership has also defined the critical profit-driving linkage between employee loyalty and customer loyalty (which is covered in detail in Chapter 11). Accordingly, special emphasis is placed on making certain that sales representatives—and all Price dealership staff—feel that they are part of an integrated team, that they are directly contributing to the dealerships' successes, and that they are appropriately compensated without having to push customers for each additional dollar. As a result, Price dealerships have very low employee turnover, and customers get a consistent and authentic purchase experience.

Postsale communication and service transactions are monitored to identify any potentially neutral or negative situations that need to be stabilized or turned around. Price does some basic predictive churn modeling to help identify when customers will be ready to make their next vehicle purchase, and management actively believes in anticipatory customer engagement. They provide service reminders and otherwise customize the postsale communication for each customer to help maintain trust and continuity.

Price is also concerned about customer loss, so it invests in win-back. The chain identifies when and why a customer has stopped servicing his or her vehicle at the dealership and has methods in place to reestablish the relationship. Few other dealerships do this.

Trust is at the very heart of understanding how supplier and individual purchase decisions are made, and we view this as common to all customers. Created and sustained through positive experience, trust has to be continually earned and reinforced, and it can very quickly disappear if the experience is negative. This is particularly true if the product or service can be easily replaced, such as at a bank, retail store, or auto dealership.

THE RELATIONSHIP "LASAGNA" RECIPE FOR OPTIMIZING IMPRESSIONS, EXPERIENCES, TRUST, AND ADVOCACY

Why a cooking metaphor for creating customer advocacy? Good cooking requires the artful, sometimes scientific, blending of ingredients to create an appealing dish. The first objective of any supplier is to bring tangible and emotional elements of value such that it will create a solid longitudinal relationship with customers. Done well, delivery of these elements means that the customer will give a high share of wallet to that supplier, hopefully to the exclusion of others.

Just as lasagna has layers of cheese, pasta, sauce, and other assorted ingredients, the relationship is constructed on alternating layers of messaging through various media (including word-of-mouth) and experience through an array of touch points. This applies even when the experience involves little or no direct touch, such as with consumer goods, where a key objective is to create an emotional as well as a functional or rational connection. With care given to melding these layers so that they result in a positive, lasting impression, a masterpiece can be created, ensuring continued customer loyalty behavior. Without it, the customer may well go to another restaurant or kitchen, or to another product or service.

Much of the remainder of this chapter will center on bank marketing. Why? Because the kinds of relationships banks have—and don't have—with their customers can pretty much serve as a metaphor for what works and what doesn't work in crafting and balancing the value proposition and promise created by messages with the reality of actual customer experiences.

How does a bank, or any company, develop and sustain customer advocacy? It's really fairly straightforward. In all the messaging to customers and prospects, companies need to set and then reinforce the promise (and premise) for what will be experienced in touch points and in all experiences over the long term. Then, they need to deliver at a rate and level that at least meets, or preferably exceeds, what they have promised in the messaging.

Overpromise and Overdeliver

Business consultant and author Rick Barrera (2005) has hypothesized that progressive banks such as Commerce Bank (now a division of TD Bank, and taking the TD name) can create a brand that uniquely demonstrates high customer loyalty behavior in this sector. It has achieved this success in an industry noted for fairly antiseptic, passive customer experience creation. Where larger and better-funded competitors often fall short or fail by having a disconnect between promise and delivery, Commerce Bank has broken through functional brand promise clutter with value-added benefits and solutions that appeal to customers on an emotional level. Customers seem more than willing to trade lower savings account and CD rates, and higher loan rates, for these benefits. It's a winning strategy, but it takes focus and discipline (overall and at the branch level), plus a deep understanding of what resonates with customers. That understanding first gets applied to general and specific customer messaging.

Commerce, a regional powerhouse headquartered in Cherry Hill, New Jersey, is an easy banking example of overpromise and overdelivery. All of its communications to customers and prospects reinforce the bank's bold brand promise: "America's Most Convenient Bank." Its well-trained branch staff, seven-day and extended hours service, and local community retailing (nonbanking) orientation reinforce the message of overpromise through service overdelivery. Like T. Scott Gross's (2004) mantra of "positively outrageous service," now seen in places like Southwest Airlines' advertising, Commerce sets itself up to succeed or fail through higher-order promises not made by other banks. Then, Commerce succeeds by doing even more for customers, creating even more attractive experiences than intimated in the messaging. That's the ideal recipe for cooking up customer advocacy.

Begin with Messaging to Build Trust and Authenticity through the Brand Experience

Marketers have always been concerned about whether the chicken or the egg came first, or the cowboys or the saloons. When assessing the behavioral impact of experiences over an extended period, this evaluation needs to begin with the overarching message, that is, how the brand or product promise is initially communicated and received. Then, with each succeeding customer engagement and contact, the messaging must be there to reinforce, sustain, and hopefully grow the relationship.

Companies rightly believe that customers gain experience with their enterprises entirely through people, products, and services. It's the word "entirely" that's at issue here. As important as people, products, and services are, organizations often don't have enough awareness that what is communicated to customers—and how, when, and where it is communicated—has an equal, if not greater, behavioral impact. For notable companies like Wegmans Food Markets, the Container Store, FedEx, Amazon, Southwest Airlines, IKEA, and Zappos—organizations known for consistently delivering a positive "branded customer experience"—this concept is already well known. All have shining corporate reputations for customer centricity. For other organizations aspiring to deliver an out-of-the box, differentiated, and certainly noncommoditized customer experience, this is a critical pay-attention point. Layers of communication are about *consistency*, *relevance*, *authenticity*, and *trust*, key elements in how customers see the supplier.

As discussed, customers have grown increasingly skeptical about supplier messaging. When considering alternative suppliers or making final purchase decisions, it is now becoming well understood that the principal, previously neglected criteria are intangible, emotionally based relationship benefits, with much of what is tangible seen as one-dimensional, expected commodities. This absolutely requires that the meld between messaging and experience be as seamless as possible.

Why Fuzzy Value Proposition Messaging Doesn't Work

Like too many other B2B and B2C product and service companies, banks seem fixated and overfocused on tangible elements of value and underfocused on relationships. Relationships are where customers often make the critical distinctions of where they want their share of spend to go. Here's a straightforward example. The fuzzy value created by bank marketers and their affiliates in the mad scramble to lure consumers to their credit cards offers great insight into the imbalance between messaging and experience.

There's a great deal of money to be made through the extension of credit to qualified card users, so it's no surprise that there's so much competition to obtain them or steal them away from the cards they already have. It has been estimated that the average American household receives at least three credit card offers a week. That's over 150 a year! One online credit card search engine carries close to 350 different credit card offers.

Much of the sales messaging approaches from banks appear both similar and muddled, so both commoditized *and* confusing. That's a big part of what makes the real value proposition for these cards so indistinct for the customer.

The offer structure usually contains a low introductory APR (annual percentage rate) for new purchases or balance transfers from other credit cards. Then, they layer on services like high credit lines; 24/7 "relationship managers" available by phone, e-mail, or online chat; e-mail account reminders; online record keeping; travel insurance (life, automotive, and even luggage); concierge service; and on and on. There is also an array of hidden fees, such as for the "convenience checks" banks often send to encourage further card use, or bank and international transfers.

That's just the beginning. There are credit cards that provide a 1% or 2% yearly cash-back rebate on purchases. There are themed credit cards (university alumni clubs, *National Geographic* magazine, Bass Pro, Six Flags Entertainment, National Hockey League, US Ski Team, Universal Studios, World Wrestling Entertainment, etc.). There are frequent-flier credit cards, where a cardholder can earn miles on any airline, plus other assorted benefits. Then, of course, credit cards are offered by the airlines themselves. Alaska Airlines, Delta, USAir, Northwest, and British Airways have credit cards. Most of these travel-related credit cards charge an annual fee, but they have a fistful of "benefits" like anniversary bonuses, low-cost companion tickets, reduced blackout periods, class upgrades, bonus miles at sign-up, bonus miles at first usage, and a free subscription to their publication—just to add fuel to the confusion fire.

There are automobile company credit cards, such as the GM Card by General Motors, where cardholders can earn points on usage that they can apply to the purchase or lease of a new car or truck. Gasoline companies like Phillips 66, Citgo, Texaco, Exxon, and BP; specialty retailers like Barnes & Noble, Eddie Bauer, Home Shopping Network, and L.L. Bean; mainstream retailers like Macy's, Sears, Kmart, and Toys R Us; and even entities like *Reader's Digest*, Sony, and Star Trek (!) offer credit cards. Many grocery and supermarket chains have their own Visa and MasterCard programs. Most of these offer points or percentage rebates on purchases from these companies, plus lower percentage rebates from affiliated merchants.

The net result is that many economists believe credit cards to be the most complex form of customer indebtedness around. Often, customers can't tell what's real and what's not, and when they will see an unexpected benefit or unanticipated charge. So, *trust* in the credit card issuer is a constant issue. There are companies that have figured this out. Before being acquired by Bank of America, MBNA had become the second-largest issuer of credit cards in the United States (behind Citibank). Notable about MBNA was that its entire culture was built around getting and keeping the right customers. Recognizing that length of time as a cardholder is a critical marker for building trust, MBNA set about providing proactive and highly customer-sensitive service that permeated the organization. It also featured benefits that were appealing to customers, such as quick and easy credit limit increases and built-in over-the-limit protection. These benefits created a distinctive, differentiated value for cardholders. The result was that MBNA customers had higher debt outstanding but lower defaults, and they were also paying higher APRs. These profitable outcomes made MBNA the paradigm of an organization that knew how to provide customer value.

For companies that are not out-of-the-box thinkers like MBNA, the big question in the industry is, With this blinding array of so-called benefits, which benefits have customers identified as having distinctive value—that is, perceived personal advantages that will be enough to both attract and keep them? Or, as is more often the case, by what process, divine or otherwise, have the card issuers decided which combination of benefits to offer and how to communicate them?

Royal Bank of Canada: Delivering the Trust Lasagna

Here's an example of a banking organization that evaluated its line-of-sight competencies and, through this assessment, identified the most effective strategic approaches to providing customers with positive, compelling value delivery through messaging and experience. The organization has profited in many ways from both this examination and the resulting program.

Research conducted by our success example, Royal Bank of Canada (RBC), revealed that customer perception of the bank's value proposition was not well understood. Building on that important insight, RBC set out to identify what hindered a customer from having a stronger, more engaged relationship with the bank. The bank learned that clients didn't feel that RBC was proactive in their behalf and, about as damaging, showed little personal interest in them. RBC was seen as often providing bank-branch high-tech gadgetry while forgetting to develop any kind of an emotional bond with customers. This was a classic case of presumption, stagnation, antiseptic relationships, and benign customer neglect.

Through its customer management assessment and focused research program, RBC determined that stronger customer bonds create real, sustainable value for customers, and this led to a remodeling of bank involvement with customers at all points of interaction. The bank dramatically repositioned its relationship and engagement perspective with customers, and it refocused employees around the creation of greater customer intimacy through centralized service and branch contact, especially on understanding customer needs and personalizing the engagement. Customer centricity became a stated company vision, shaping processes and initiatives across the entire enterprise.

The results of this revamped "customer first" approach have been strategically and financially attractive from many perspectives. As one key initiative, RBC has microsegmented its customer base around dollar level, degree of engagement, receptivity to receiving information about specific bank programs, and demographics and lifestyle characteristics. The goal of this element of customer relationship management is aimed at building a culture of trust between RBC and its customers.

There are now close to 20,000 identifiable customer microsegments (from only three segments a decade ago), enabling tightly targeted messages and more personalized, consistently positive experiences. Profits have increased substantially, averaging 25% per year for the past several years, in part because marketing programs have become more efficient. For instance, marketing cycle time has been reduced by 60%, and most of RBC's direct marketing programs average over 49% response. That's a clear reflection of how the effective interweaving of messaging and experience has achieved greater harmony and a higher order of relationship building over the long term.

As a result of the assessment and actions taken, each customer's needs and wants are better understood. And with this deeper level of insight, new products and services can be created and launched with much greater speed and effectiveness, and customers are significantly more responsive to RBC's promotional efforts and other communication programs. Though RBC might state its customer trust results differently, it has cooked up and delivered a great advocacy lasagna.

THE LESSONS AND OPPORTUNITIES OF STRONG REPUTATIONS AND CUSTOMER TRUST

Companies that have succeeded in building excellent industry reputations and also in earning and sustaining customer loyalty and trust understand that these are active, valuable states in a relationship. They require an emotional as well as a rational connection to the company through all possible touch points: product experience, customer support and other employee interaction, advertising and promotion, and formal and informal social word-of-mouth communication. While functional and rational components of value are important as must-have deliverables, it is the emotional bank account—the level of trust that has been earned—that keeps the customer, or not.

Loyal customers have endured. They have overcome the relationship and value skepticism so prevalent between customers and suppliers today. Customers know more than ever before, they are less patient than ever before, and they expect more than ever before. The advocating customer has come to expect and believe that the supplier will deliver the best overall product or service experience. As will be demonstrated in succeeding chapters, the trust that companies are careful to build and sustain creates advocacy that has real monetary benefits. It also has cultural and cohesiveness benefits for the company creating it. Companies work to build and keep trust from the inside and from the outside through employees and community visibility so that, in every way, they can be known for providing differentiated, personalized customer value.

4

The Business Case for Creating Customer Advocacy (and Eliminating the Potential Negative Impact of Alienation and Sabotage)

The worldwide economic meltdown experienced during the second half of the millennium's first decade directly contributed to a major shift in business decision making and asset allocation. A word we hear more than ever before is *accountability*.

There's an ancient Persian proverb that is particularly apt for this subject: "Thinking well is wise; planning well, wiser; doing well wisest and best of all." Companies have two major areas where customer advocacy and the utilization of advocacy-based research and metrics to improve performance and guide decision making are essential. One is management of the customer life cycle, or customer life stages. The second involves the customer service and support function, critical for delivering value promises and maintaining continuity and perceived value among customers. Both customer life-cycle management and customer service optimization have critical areas of accountability and limited resource allocation, essential for planning and execution of the customer experience. As this chapter unfolds, the business case for both will be revealed and put forward in detail.

In the previous chapter, we covered the importance of customer experience and trust in building advocacy behavior. There is a definite linkage between execution of optimum experiences and trust building among customers such that customers become advocates, and the financial accountability that companies require for disciplined and rigorous customer management. Some companies have sought accountability mnemonics or single-number metric approaches (such as customer satisfaction, recommendation, or a loyalty index), hoping to create high correlation between key elements of performance and actual business results. In most cases, these have proved to not be very reliable (see Chapter 6 for a thorough discussion of the positives and negatives of recommendation as a core metric), because they don't correlate well, on either a lead or lag basis, to real marketplace outcomes realized through customer behavior.

Most companies, however, don't put all their accountability eggs in a single measurement basket, and they report utilizing multiple metrics to guide decisions. In an August 2010 survey conducted by the American Marketing Association and Duke University's Fuqua School of Business, in the panel of respondents (88% of whom were corporate vice president level or above), it was found that B2B Services companies utilized an average of 3.2 metrics to help in decision making. This, as it happens, was low among the organizations studied. B2B Products companies utilized 3.9 metrics, B2C Products companies utilized 7.4 metrics, and B2C Services companies utilized an astounding 10.4 metrics. This represents a true "Tower of

Babel" level of disconnect and minimal correlation between performance indicators and actual business results.

Employing the kinds of single- and multiple-number metrics thus far available to management has made disciplined accountability an unattainable goal. Still, organizations understand that the metrics and key indicators they apply, the value proposition of the products and services they offer, and the need for fiscal and resource accountability must be conjoined.

MANAGING THE CUSTOMER LIFE CYCLE TO DRIVE ADVOCACY BEHAVIOR

Customer Behavior and Life Stages: A Tale of Two Bakeries

The recent findings of Argyriou et al. (2009), of the Chartered Institute of Marketing (CIM)—namely, that less than 1 out of 10 British adults believe that relational marketing gives them more value than the suppliers providing the benefits, and that they also don't want these organizations driving the relationship—shouldn't surprise many.

Customers are savvy, fickle, demanding, and value-directed. They're certainly intelligent enough to know the difference between a program with components that create genuine value and one that's little more than a giveaway or an old-fashioned snake-oil repeat-sales pitch.

Most companies don't look at the complete spectrum of a customer's life and how relationships have to be built and sustained to drive top-end loyalty behavior. Just as relatively few companies have developed algorithms and processes for estimating lifetime customer revenue value, so also have few companies looked at how experience management programs have to be modified depending on the customer's life stage.

Companies in industries like banking, telecom, wireless, and automotive, for instance, are still rather notorious for devoting large proportions of their marketing budgets to new customer conquest and then treating those customers pretty passively once in the fold. This is just as true for B2B and B2C companies. More recently, we've witnessed the furious and expensive prospecting for new customers among e-commerce companies (see the next section), only to lose them through poor follow-up and service at an almost equally furious pace. Research companies like Jupiter and Forrester have noted how attraction activity contrasts with the low level of service these customers tend to receive after coming on board. Argyriou et al. (2009) also noted that less than 20% of internet customers in their study felt that messaging personalization was important, a technique that some marketers believe is "the answer" in relationship marketing. These are clear breakdowns as customers move through their life stages.

Experience management and advocacy behavior creation should be viewed as never-ending double-barreled processes that embrace mutually beneficial and value-producing relationships for all customers (past, present, and potential, and internal, intermediate, and external), creating not only enticements to become customers but also barriers to exit or churn. The RightNow Technologies/Harris Interactive (2008) series of customer relationship studies show that good customer experiences lead to customer acquisition, namely, that over half of customers would communicate positively about their experiences, recommend, and spend more with the supplier providing the positive experience.

Conversely, bad customer experiences lead to lost business, both among current customers and potential customers. The 2008 RightNow/Harris studies show that over three-quarters of customers who have had negative experiences would stop doing business, and two-thirds would *never* return. Three-quarters of these same customers would tell others about their poor treatment, and one-quarter have either posted negative feedback online or will at some point. In addition, there is an operational burden associated with bad experiences. Almost two-thirds of those with negative experiences have complained directly to the company, and one-third have returned products. Both of these statistics are dramatically higher than the cross section of customers in the base.

Clearly, there's a lot to gain, especially from a financial perspective, in managing customer experiences for optimized advocacy behavior. It makes perfect sense (at least to us) that companies have insufficiently defined either the components of their relationship programs or the elements in their overall experience and transactional activity plan that address each customer's life stage.

As we see it, there are three major phases of a complete customer life cycle: targeting and acquisition, retention and loyalty, and lost and won-back. This translates to seven stages of a customer's life with a supplier:

1. Suspect

2. Prospect (active/developmental)

3. Customer (new/recovered)

4. Retained/Loyal customer

5. At-risk customer (attrition/pre-defection)

6. Defected/Lost customer

7. Recovered/Won-back customer

Here's how the life stages work. Taking a town with two bakeries as an example, the suspect stage would begin when a potential customer first desires baked goods. That desire may come on its own, or it may be encouraged or stimulated by one or both of the bakeries advertising or promoting their wares.

The potential customer then becomes a prospect, going through a screening process and sorting through perceptions of each bakery's image and reputation, array and quality of desired products and services, awareness of prices, and other information, such as referrals, advertising, or promotional materials. The prospect is considered either active or developmental, depending on how strong the purchase desire for baked goods is at this stage.

Then, the bakery selection is made, and the prospect becomes a new customer. The bakery's complete value proposition—personalized service and communication, product quality and range, and price, to cite a few key elements—creates a level of emotional commitment within the customer. If that commitment is strong enough, the new customer will make repeat purchases over time and become a retained/loyal customer. Frequency and volume of purchase will mark the customer's long-term value to the bakery.

If any negative perception develops regarding an important aspect of value—product quality, price, communication, or service—the new customer or the retained/loyal customer will enter an attrition mode and become an at-risk customer. This is where the bakery should be most aware of customer perceptions, because the undermining of perceived value is the strongest contributor to exit or churn.

Should the customer's problems or complaints with the chosen baker not be resolved, or if the problems or complaints become stronger than the benefits provided, then the customer is lost or defected, most likely to the other bakery in town, if the desire for baked goods is still strong.

Assuming the bakery is like most companies, once the customer has been lost, rather minimal resources or effort will be devoted to either understanding the reasons for the customer's exit or winning the customer back. According to Kirkby et al. (2003), 95% of companies know why customers defect, but not until it is too late. Roughly 60% of customers who leave will never come back. Let's be positive, though. Let's say the bakery *does* know the customer, *does* make an effort to know why the customer left, *does* have a customer relationship management (CRM) and recovery process to win the customer back, and *does* succeed in getting the customer to return. Then, the customer could be considered recovered or won-back. During this win-back process, the customer might be viewed as a prospect again, especially if the value proposition needs to be completely reexpressed.

Most bakeries, again like most companies, typically set their experience management goals around increased spending and purchase frequency, and increased profitability and market share. They do this by offering something of presumed positive value so that the customer will have a stronger emotional relationship and identification with the products and the bakery itself. But that's where the majority of customer experience programs begin and end. They tend to be rather one-dimensional, often benchmarking against other companies in the same industry—in this case, the other bakery in town.

Experience management programs should also function as brand-building, referral, and word-of-mouth vehicles to attract new customers. This can happen in two ways. The first way is that the new customer or the retained/loyal customer will offer positive word-of-mouth to suspects and prospects—for example, friends, colleagues, and relatives. The other way is that what the bakery offers in products or experience is so strong and attractive that noncustomers learn of it and are drawn in. Their experiences, assuming they're positive, then serve to repeat this process.

How does the bakery's experience program respond when the customer becomes at risk? If it's an organic program, the bakery will have collected and interpreted insights during its customers' earlier life stages. If service or product problems surface, the bakery should be able to have intensified contact and communication with these customers to stabilize the bond and commitment. The bakery may also offer some type of value incentive to the at-risk customer to help reestablish the relationship.

Relationship dynamics when the customer has been lost or has defected are quite different than when the customer is active. At the point of exit, the customer has become emotionally detached from the bakery. There is no longer sufficient value in the product or service for the customer to remain. Once the customer has been identified as lost, the bakery has to do two things (especially if the customer had high volume or frequent purchase activity): (1) find out why the customer left, and (2) have relationship management techniques and processes in place to recover the customer. If the root cause of departure is a product or service issue, restating the value proposition and offering some "please come back" incentives may be enough to reestablish the relationship, although this may take some time and effort to accomplish. If the customer has moved, had a lifestyle change (such as going on a diet), or been lured away by lower prices, any recovery effort will probably not be worthwhile or successful. If won back, the customer is recovered.

Focusing on customer segmentation by life stage necessitates that companies have a single, integrated view of customers that's enterprise-wide. Do they? A recent study by Forrester Research showed that while 92% of companies say this is critical (44%) or very important (48%), only 12% of companies say they have it fully (2%) or somewhat (10%) (Nail 2004). So, for most companies, having a relationship and experience program that flexes to accommodate each stage of a customer's life will be a challenge at a minimum. For even more companies, having a relationship continuity program that includes lost customers is virtually nonexistent.

Companies' relationship-creating and relationship-building programs tend to focus principally on attracting new customers or rewarding customers who are new or who spend a lot or spend frequently, mostly in the short term. That's fine and completely appropriate, but it makes secondary many customer groups and life stages that may offer attractive revenue and profit opportunities. It may also completely bypass some customer groups—notably those who are at risk or who have defected.

Several centuries ago, Takeda Shingen, a samurai general in medieval Japan, wrote: "A person with deep far-sightedness will survey both the beginning and the end of a situation, and continually consider its every facet as important." We believe the same kind of thinking should be applied to CRM and customer life stages. Every life stage represents attractive potential revenue and profit, as well as the opportunity to learn which stages affect the other stages. Smart companies should not miss the opportunity to build (or rebuild) customer relationships, irrespective of stage.

Customer Acquisition: Ready-Fire-Aim or Ready-Aim-Fire?

Stating that all customers are not created equal is hardly an oversimplification. But just like the pigs in Orwell's *Animal Farm*, some customers are more equal than others. No company has unlimited resources to equally service or support all its customers. Repeat buying power and the willingness (even desire) to speak about experiences, two bases of customer loyalty behavior, are everything. Some customers are worth a great deal, some may become more valuable over time, some may be valuable for a brief period but may be easily lured away, and some are likely to never become valuable.

At a minimum, companies need to segment their customers so they can determine how much longer that customer will remain with them, how much revenue each customer will contribute, how much and what kinds of services the customer should receive, and what efforts will be needed to keep the customer, whether he or she is new, at risk, or even already lost. Also, if a company is changing its product or service focus—such as beginning a new customer management or frequency marketing program—decisions will have to be made about which customers to retain.

Just as companies are becoming smarter about keeping the customers they want, or "firing" less attractive customers through stepped-down services, they have to invest more up front to learn which potential customers will be the most valuable over time. This goes beyond segmentation. It is almost pre-segmentation.

The business of gaming in Las Vegas and Atlantic City and on numerous riverboats and Indian reservations and offshore is built not on a house of cards but on a house of numbers. Take the Rio Hotel and Casino in Las Vegas. It has 100,000 square feet of casino floor, 2375 slot machines, a buffet that feeds 10,000 people, and 4 pools. The Rio serves 50,000 cocktails a day. The 5200 electricians, slot technicians, laundry haulers, blackjack dealers, show performers, and custodians, toiling in three shifts, make the Rio run like a plush yet high-tech gaming factory.

The Rio's purple and teal colors are everywhere, and there is an around-the-clock carnival atmosphere. Almost 7 million customers per year play poker, slots, craps, pai gow, baccarat, keno, roulette, and blackjack. But the real game at the Rio is how it uses data to attract and keep the customers it wants.

In an industry like gaming, where the level of customer migration is very high, it is imperative that casinos not only keep the players they want but also put extra effort into targeting the right customers in the first place. They do this in a number of ways, including geodemographic profiling for their acquisition. For the high rollers they've lost, many of the casinos make an extra effort to get them back as well.

Advanced companies have begun applying sophisticated acquisition research and targeting models, seeking customers who:

- Need less direct motivation (incentive) or indirect motivation (promise of support and committed resources) to purchase

- Have demonstrated more resistance to claims and attempts to lure them away

- Are less price-sensitive

- Are more accepting of occasional value delivery lapses and are less likely to accept alternatives if their brand/service is unavailable

- Will demonstrate more positive attitudes about "their" brand

If these characteristics seem quite similar to those of a customer advocate, it's no accident.

In the retail automotive industry, for example, potentially loyal new customers take less time to make their purchase decisions, consider fewer dealerships, are less price-driven, and rely less on magazine articles and other media and more on previous experience and personal peer recommendation.

Noted customer experience management expert Professor Adrian Payne (2005,147) has conducted studies among marketing executives showing that 80% of companies spend too much of their marketing budget on customer acquisition (Acquirers). About 10% spend too much on retention (Retainers), and about 10% are Profit Maximizers, who balance between acquisition and retention. Tough economic times demand that all companies better allocate their budgets so that they not only get customers but get the "right" customers—those who are the most profitable and the best fit for their business.

CUSTOMER SERVICE AS A KEY DRIVER OF ADVOCACY BEHAVIOR

Customer experience is supposed to be about creating and optimizing relationships with customers; however, experience and support initiatives, frequently through service operations, are typically almost all about the technology: software systems, sales contact management, data warehousing, and so on. Apart from that, in this era of steadily shrinking resources, the emphasis has also been on tight budget controls, doing the most with the least. People, especially customer-facing staff in the service and support operation, have largely been an afterthought in experience and strategies.

Customer service representatives (CSRs) across the United States handle an average of 2000 customer interactions each week. If CSRs are not aligned with the overall experience strategy—indeed, are not *directly involved* with creating and executing the strategy—this can represent 2000 opportunities to put customers at risk or lose them.

"It will not suffice to have customers that are merely satisfied. An unhappy customer will switch. Unfortunately, a satisfied customer may also switch, on the theory that he could not lose much, and might gain" (Deming 1986, 141). W. Edwards Deming made this statement close to 30 years ago in his book *Out of the Crisis*. Though an expert in total quality processes, he well understood that it is *customer experience*—formed by interactions with employees, augmented by systems and processes, and supported by a company's messaging and other communication—that creates success. He concluded: "Profit in business comes from repeat customers, customers that boast about your product or service, and that bring friends with them . . . profit in a transaction with a customer that comes back voluntarily may be 10 times the profit realized from a customer that responds to advertising and other persuasion" (141).

Placing the customer first and having a complete focus on customers, two clarion calls of customer experience optimization, have a hollow ring if strategies aren't drilled down and reduced to a point where CSRs' daily efforts can have a positive impact on customer loyalty. These centers of customer contact now represent the principal touch point with customers, and, beyond technology, they have the capability to generate and manage a continuous flow of customer information and to increase customer loyalty.

Nowhere is this more true and evident than in high-tech industries such as computers, software, printers, telecom products and services, and complex entertainment products and services. Recently, major consulting organizations such as Accenture, McKinsey, Allegiance, and Forrester have examined what drives success, defined as leveraging customer loyalty behavior in high-tech customer service on a global basis. In addition, RightNow Technologies, a customer support technology solutions company with over 1900 customers worldwide (mentioned earlier in this chapter), recently conducted the latest in a series of annual customer experience studies in the United States (through Harris Interactive) addressing many of the same service impact subjects. In this review, I will present results from these studies and how they contribute to understanding the importance of service and how the insights they offer can make service more effective.

OVERALL KEY FINDINGS AND IMPLICATIONS OF SERVICE-BASED EXPERIENCE RESEARCH

Accenture's research (as cited in Campbell 2009) consisted of two simultaneously administered online global surveys—one for providers and the other for customers. The surveys explored the state of business customer service in the communications services, communications equipment, and electronics and high-tech industries, querying more than 650 senior executives from 11 countries.

The research revealed that 70% of business customers said that it's possible for a provider to create an experience that "locks in" their future business. At the same time, 70% of providers said that improving the overall customer experience and customer satisfaction ranked as their main business priority for 2009. Over 80% of customers agreed that superior customer support increased their likelihood of making subsequent purchases from the same supplier.

Respondents were asked to explain in their own words what they considered to be the main characteristics of a superior, differentiated customer experience. Their responses fell into several categories, the top three of which were knowledgeable staff and accessible support (32%), efficient and timely problem resolution (26%), and proactive, personalized solutions (21%). The research also found that compared with customers in Europe or Asia, those in North America were more loyal to their providers and were less likely to switch providers or consider doing so.

And if North American communications and high-tech companies deliver a distinguished and superior customer experience, they have a 20% better chance than European and Asian companies of generating more customer service revenues from the same customers. McKinsey's research (Braff et al. 2003; Georgiadis et al. 2000) focused on what market researchers would call "thresholding," or finding the correct level of support in multiple areas. The yardstick McKinsey uses for making this determination is estimated customer lifetime value. It has determined that companies either overspend on service levels, hoping to reach a level of customer delight, or underspend, hoping that customer satisfaction won't be affected. In its studies, McKinsey has found that while most executives think compromising service levels is a mistake, they still struggle with identifying necessary investment levels while addressing pressure on revenue and costs. The companies that are best at this have rigorously applied customer experience analytics, matching survey responses to intended or actual behavior and then evaluating correlation and causation to the extent possible. Principally, the most sophisticated companies, McKinsey found, figure out what matters most to customers, eliminate investments that don't matter, and finance the ones that will help them survive and thrive.

Interestingly, 58% of customers in the 2010 RightNow study said they would always or often pay more for a better customer service experience, even in a down economy. Further reflecting the revenue implications of service, almost 60% said they were at least somewhat likely to make a purchase during a service engagement, and 24% had already made a purchase based on an agent's recommendation during service.

IMPACT OF NEGATIVE EXPERIENCES

Accenture's (2006) research uncovered a critical outcome of poor service. Nearly 30% of business customers surveyed are considering switching to another provider because they are dissatisfied with the quality of customer service they receive. With their current providers, each of these customers spends, on average, $15 million on products and customer service per year. When asked why they are challenged in delivering superior service, providers most often cited a lack of supporting technology (selected by 30% of respondents), followed by a dearth of trained resources (29%) and nonexistent definitions of support processes (22%). According to providers and customers, the quality and competence of service agents and their ability to address customer concerns on the first phone call or e-mail rank as the two most important factors in delivering a superior, differentiated service experience.

In related research conducted in the United Kingdom, Accenture (2006) learned that 60% of all high-tech customers would be willing to switch providers for more reliable or better service, while 31% indicated that a company's unwillingness to take sufficient action to meet their needs had a strong impact on their decision to stop patronizing that company. Over 42%, for example, have encountered service representatives who were unable or unqualified to solve their problems, contributing to future negative behavior.

Even more serious, RightNow (2008) learned that 84% of customers who experienced poor service would communicate that result to others (up from 74% in 2007 and 57% in 2006), and 87% said they stopped doing business with a company because of a negative service experience.

PROFITABLY MANAGING COMPLAINTS FOR LEVERAGING CUSTOMER ADVOCACY

One of the key, yet relatively misunderstood, aspects of customer transactions and experiences is complaints. In many ways, complaints are more serious than just poor or negative customer experiences, especially with respect to their potential to affect downstream customer behavior. Multiple research studies have identified problems or complaints coming out of roughly half the experiences and transactions of both B2C and B2B customers, and they are a prime contributor to customer alienation and sabotage. In the previous chapter, we covered the impact of complaints—especially those that are unresolved from the customer's perspective or unsurfaced by the organization except by research, and the potential behavioral damage and advantage they can create. To state that complaints represent both challenge and opportunity, as well as an extended area of business accountability, is quite appropriate for building customer advocacy. Why? Because, handled proactively and well, complaints represent openings to improve the relationship and bond between company and customer through the positive perceptions and trust they create. Handled reactively, grudgingly, or poorly, complaints detract from the customer–supplier relationship and result in negative downstream behavior.

Companies must regard every complaint they receive as "gifts," according to business authors Janelle Barlow and Claus Moller (2008, 20–23). Organizations are constantly seeking ways to identify and build downstream loyalty behavior among their base of customers, and complaining customers offer organizations the high-value opportunity to recover from a problem or a failure, to make restitution, and to build on the repaired relationship. Each complaint can be leveraged to create customer benefit. For the company that has a proactive approach to identifying and resolving complaints, they can be an advocacy-creating differentiator.

Let's look at some of the facts about complaints. TARP Worldwide, a customer service consulting and research organization, has been studying the business impact of complaints around the world for decades. John Goodman (1999), of TARP Worldwide, found that on average, and across all industries studied, 50% of B2B consumers complain to a frontline person and 75% of B2C consumers complain to a frontline person; however, only 1%–5% take this complaint to a service operation or to management. He also found that customers who complain and receive positive, rapid resolution are, on average, almost 10% more loyal than those who did not have a problem. This is not dissimilar to the banking complaint example presented in the last chapter. These customers are, in turn, more likely to tell their friends, colleagues, and relatives about how the company addressed and resolved their complaint.

One of the world experts on the impact of customer complaints is Dr. Bernd Stauss, professor of business administration and service management at the Ingolstadt School of Management, Catholic University of Eichstatt-Ingolstadt in Germany. He refers to the acknowledged high percentage of noncomplaining customers (in Germany, for example, an empirical study of noncomplaining customers placed the percentages at 68% for banks, 83% for hardware and home improvement stores, and 94% for investment fund companies) as "the annoyance iceberg" (Stauss and Friege 1999, 351; Stauss and Seidel 2008). As Stauss notes, few B2B or B2C complaints are articulated and registered, and many organizations continue to see complaints as a threat because they are regarded only as a cost factor.

Again, the vast majority of complaints are like icebergs lying below the surface of the sea, articulated but not registered ("hidden") or nonarticulated ("unvoiced")—at least so far as the company is concerned. Companies that are successful in discouraging dissatisfied customers from complaining often point to decreasing complaint rates and reduced customer care costs. What they miss is that the decline in complaint rates may be accompanied by increases in customer churn and negative off-line and online buzz. And reductions in complaint processing costs will almost always be significantly outweighed by the increased loss due to customer defection.

Stauss believes that instead of trying to suppress complaints or grudgingly and reactively handling them, companies should be engaged in active complaint stimulation—that is, customer complaint maximization—by having complaints come to the firm in any way customers desire (verbal, written, telephone, or electronically) and in as user-friendly a manner as possible. Given a major finding by Goodman (1999)—namely, that twice as many people are told about bad complaint resolution compared to good complaint resolution—it's essential to both generate these issues and resolve them in a consistently positive manner.

As shown in Figure 4.1, complaints, whether expressed or unexpressed, resolved or unresolved, are an accountability sub-

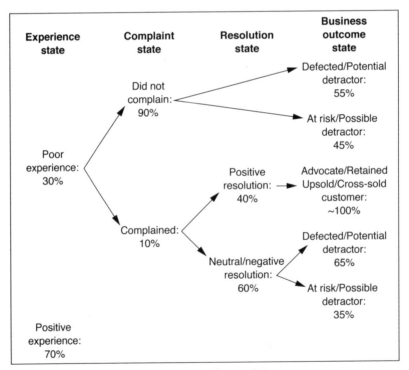

Figure 4.1 Hypothetical true cost of complaints.

category of customer service, and they should be considered as such for the long-term profit or loss they represent to the organization by virtue of the array of future behaviors that disaffected or angry customers can represent.

Though some might argue with the allocation of percentages for each complaint state, the facts behind them are irrefutable: It's essential for companies to calculate and control complaints and to account for their true effect on business outcomes. The impact of complaints on customer advocacy is so profound that failing to be thorough in identifying complaint rectification priorities can put an organization at considerable risk. In their book *Complaint Management: The Heart of CRM*, Stauss and coauthor Wolfgang Seidel (2004, 28) outline an eight-step research-based method for how complaints and their impact should be identified and managed:

1. *Determine the number of annoyed customers*—This can be identified with normal satisfaction or relationship tracking surveys simply by asking customers if they have issues or reasons to complain. Assuming the research is cross-sectional, this percentage can then be extrapolated to the entire customer base.

2. *Determine the number of complainants*—In the same surveys, customers can be asked whether they have complained. This number can also be extrapolated to the customer base.

3. *Determine the number of noncomplainants*—This can be determined by subtracting the number of complainants from the number of annoyed customers, or simply by asking whether customers have complained.

4. *Determine the nonarticulation rate*—This is the number of nonregistered complainants divided by the total number of complainants.

5. *Determine the number of registered complainants*—This is simply the number of customers who actually made complaints that were received by the company.

6. *Determine the number of nonregistered complainants*—This number is reached by deducting the number of registered complainants from the total number of complainants in the database.

7. *Determine the nonregistration rate*—Comparing the number of nonregistered complainants with the number of complainants yields a nonregistration rate. The higher the nonregistration rate, the greater should be the organizational concern.

8. *Determine the evidence rate*—This is the number of registered complainants against the number of annoyed customers, obtained through research and projected to the entire customer base.

Stauss and Seidel illustrate in Figure 4.2 the calculation of these complainant figures, which they describe as a "customer annoyance iceberg."

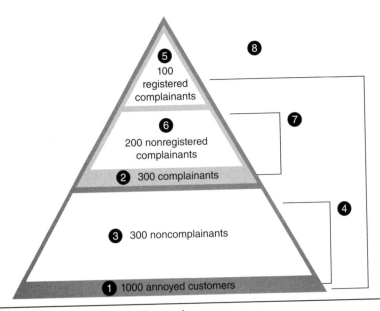

Figure 4.2 Complainant hierarchy.
Source: Stauss and Seidel, 2008.

These data are enormously important. Nonarticulation of complaints points to the urgency of analyzing the specific reasons for not complaining and what steps the company can take to encourage complaints where they exist. Further, the organization can evaluate elements of complaint nonexpression by specific customer segments or groups to determine whether there are either customer group or issue patterns.

Nonregistration rates tell companies what needs to be done to improve complaint intake and processing. A high nonregistration rate immediately says that the majority of complaints addressed to the organization are unknown to customer service, and so they can't serve as a basis for improvement priorities. Companies must conduct in-depth analyses of interaction and communication processes to identify reasons for nonregistration and correct them.

Again, annoyance is a customer state of mind that is considerably more serious than just commoditized, passive, plain-vanilla customer experiences. Stauss and Seidel (2008) conclude that "all companies should investigate the size and structure of the annoyance iceberg by complaint evidence controlling. This is the basis to get a realistic picture of customer annoyance and a clear information fundament for quality improvements and measures to stabilize endangered customer relationships."

DRIVING CUSTOMER TRUST AND ADVOCACY THROUGH SUPERIOR SERVICE

Accenture's (2006) service studies have revealed that trust and credibility are critical to continued purchase and recommendation, and 45% of customers in its UK and US high-tech customer service research said that they would be positive because they have grown to trust the company's products or services. But, Accenture notes that trust can easily be broken—such as when a company solicits feedback from customers on how to improve products or services but fails to act on the input given. In fact, 30% of respondents said such a lack of credibility has played a strong role in their decision to stop using a provider.

Service as a key brand differentiator is evidenced in customer likelihood to recommend the company to others, and also to escalate their own share of wallet. RightNow's 2008 study, for instance, showed that 58% of customers identified receipt of outstanding customer service as the number one reason they would recommend a company to someone else, higher than either pricing or quality of products and services. This was an increase from the 51% of customers giving this same response in 2007.

Even more compelling, in 2009 research by the Consumer Forum, nearly two-thirds (61%) of respondents said that "a personal response to their issue" was most important, while 44% cited speed of service as an important factor. Close to 100% of respondents said that a good customer service experience would increase their brand loyalty, and a similar percentage said that experiencing bad customer service would compel them to take their business elsewhere.

Capgemini, reporting on the Genesys (2008) (contact center software and enterprise efficiency and collaboration) Global Consumer Survey results, concluded that most high-tech customers are regularly frustrated by service-related issues such as long hold times, interactive voice response (IVR) systems with too many options or incorrect options, and having to repeat information already provided. These issues undermine the relationship.

Successful companies are, as Capgemini sees it, transitioning to make the service operation a "customer experience center." Customers today are looking to benchmark their experiences against the greater sophistication of Web 2.0 technologies, and they are coming to expect multichannel support and an integrated experience. Companies have failed to keep pace with these expectations due to poor customer segmentation, underinvestment in (or poor design of) technology solutions, silo-based organizational structures, and poorly designed processes and agent training. What customers actually want, and what companies need to deliver, is *trust*, that is, a perception that service processes and technologies are designed to optimize their relationship with the company.

To build the kinds of service and support capabilities that can help companies achieve high performance during and after the current economic crisis, Accenture (2009, 17) recommends six actions:

1. Enhance the content on the service and support portal

2. Invest more in training and developing customer service agents

3. Enhance the knowledge of each provider's installed base

4. Improve first-call or e-mail resolution

5. Improve the overall customer experience of self-service, not just reduce costs

6. Implement analytical and diagnostic tools

Forrester has looked at the broader landscape of what companies can do through service and support to help optimize the customer experience. Megan Burns (2008), of Forrester, has identified six operating "laws":

Every interaction creates a personal reaction—Experiences need to be designed for individuals, customer segments must be prioritized for tiered service, customer feedback (in the form of debriefing and research) needs to be central to designing superior experiences, and employees need to be empowered so they have latitude to accommodate the needs of key customers.

People are instinctively self-centered—Customers care about their own needs, not how companies are organized. Therefore, companies must make certain that processes and procedures are streamlined, easy to understand, and helpful to customers.

Customer familiarity breeds alignment—Companies need to have a clear view of what customers need, want, and dislike so that they can align decisions and actions. It's vital that employees at all levels have access to customer feedback and how that insight drives response to customer requirements.

Uncommitted employees don't create committed customers— From Disney to the Service Profit Chain (discussed in Chapter 11), it's well understood that employees are core to optimizing customer experience. If employee morale is low, for example, providing superior service is a challenge. So, training must be a priority. In addition, companies should communicate inclusively, provide enabling technology, and coach approaches that help customers. Finally, measure employee commitment.

Employees do what is measured, incentivized, and celebrated—Metrics that are tracked, activities that are rewarded, and actions that are celebrated are what drive employee actions. Customer experience needs to be the primary focus of metrics tracking, and this must be communicated in a nonambiguous manner; otherwise, employee behaviors may be counter to desired outcomes.

You can't fake it—Employees, as well as customers, can sense if experience optimization isn't a top priority. So, irrespective of the amount of money spent on advertising and brand building, companies have to be strategically committed to this course in everything they do. For example, advertising should reinforce, not create, positioning. Otherwise, it may be better not to start at all.

Bob Thompson (2008), CEO of CustomerThink, used the professional, collaborative resources of his company to prepare a guide (sponsored by RightNow) to achieving customer focus and centricity: *Accelerate Your Customer-Centric Journey.* Much of what he discovered, particularly in the area of customer relationships through service, to improve both strategy and execution could be reduced to four precepts: (1) Staff front lines with friendly and competent people, (2) understand and experience what customers experience (in CustomerThink's 2008 survey, only 8% of executives thought their organizations fully mapped customer experiences and identified interactions likely to influence customer loyalty behavior), (3) see your customers from all sides (i.e., make certain that everyone, irrespective of function, shares the same customer profile and research data), and (4) build genuine relationships through collaboration, such as using social media to share ideas, solve problems, and co-design new products and services.

AN OVERVIEW OF SERVICE IMPLICATIONS FOR DOWNSTREAM CUSTOMER ADVOCACY

Service is a key behavioral driver, especially when customers perceive their experience as negative. For example, due to poor service, in one year 60% of customers canceled accounts with banks, 36% changed insurance providers, 40% changed telephone companies, 35% changed credit card companies, and 37% changed internet providers.

Service can represent either strategic, positive differentiation or the opportunity to undermine perception and loyalty among current customers.

Technology providers, especially, have been challenged with the convergence of solutions in a single device—causing customers to potentially interact with multiple vendors to find a solution.

Service providers have become swamped as they cope with rapid adoption of PCs and mobile technologies penetrating the mainstream consumer market.

Customer sentiment (dissatisfaction) with service short-falls has gone global—and public—with internet adoption. Firms struggling to focus on "ease of use" and to identify the root cause of technical difficulties often miss the larger emotional elements of service.

Firms attempting to cope with burgeoning support demand via IVR systems have seen further depression of customer satisfaction as human interaction is eliminated—and websites created to tell customers how to "hijack" the IVR systems have extended this challenge.

Internet communication and social networking continue to amplify poor service performance, which leads to customer share and market share erosion.

Most recently, we have all seen a shift to web-based self-help as a component of integrated touch-point options for support.

Poor training and implementation of outsourced care simply generate more problems and result in collateral damage to customer relationships.

Companies are now entering a "rebuilding" period as customer care moves to the number one position in buying criteria. Better human interfaces on devices, intuitive controls, and personal assistants or diagnostic programs are being embedded in new product designs.

Growth of Service Technology

As technology becomes mainstream, service and support offer an opportunity for differentiation, making mishaps very visible when they occur. Companies such as Dell have reacted to the highly public and negative attention to customer support challenges and have increased the number of representatives, set up internal service advocates with special e-mail addresses, and now offer a "fee for service" for customers desiring greater support priority (or desiring communication with an English-speaking rep).

Current trends in best practices tend to focus on two major areas: technology innovation and a refocusing on the human element as a dominant and impactful component of support.

Opportunities to leverage positive phone experiences to a self-help environment empower employees to make decisions within a predetermined bandwidth, and opportunities to leverage technology through the customer database will enable frontline employees to reach "first-call resolution" more often.

Focus on the human element: McDonald and Aron (2011) have found that 92% of all customer contact is still through the contact center. And, it's been reported that 70%–90% of what happens with customers is driven by *human nature*, having nothing to do with technology. State-of-the-art technology is certainly a necessity today, but it is meant to enable human endeavors, not to disable them.

As the contact center takes on a more central role in the business, the volume of interactions it handles grows, and the number of agents and sites expands to match.

Technology and Virtualization

Virtualizing contact centers solves the issues that arise from this expansion by (1) improving the efficiency of call allocation around multiple centers when it comes to scaling to meet peak demand, (2) making it easier to allocate calls across different agent skill sets, (3) handling emergency closures of individual call centers, and (4) improving visibility of call and customer data from across multiple centers to make better strategic decisions.

Recognize that technology and virtualization have multiple benefits: Business continuity is improved by implementing mirror sites; staff morale is increased with flexible work schedules and locations; skills-based routing ensures that the call goes to those best qualified and available to answer the query; scalability is enhanced to handle peak demands by drawing on staff across multiple locations; hours of operation can be extended around the clock using centers in different time zones; intelligent routing to the most appropriate staff, wherever they are, cuts transaction times and enhances productivity; dynamic control of call routing strategies allows the contact center to respond to changing circumstances quickly and effectively; management workloads are cut; and the entire contact center can be managed from anywhere through a web browser.

Employees

Many firms are focused on leveraging service personnel to cross-sell within the support environment—blurring the roles between service and sales. This trend is not limited to phone-based service. Web-based and self-service environments are designed to enable cross-selling opportunities as well. Service representatives need to seamlessly move from addressing a problem or concern to proactively advising about or even recommending a new product—further supporting the customer while raising the profitability of the enterprise.

Investing in the team: Literature focuses on training and empowering support personnel to maximize the value of customer interactions. Investment promises to elevate the value of the customer care group with an enterprise, aligns the activities of the service organization with stated business objectives of the organization, and tightens the linkages among sales, marketing, and service.

Customers

Align customers with overall strategic goals. Some customers may be too demanding, reducing your ability to serve those who are more easily satisfied. Customer segmentation is key here, and customers can be categorized by a variety of parameters (lifetime value, technology, sophistication, etc.). Approaches can also be used to identify those individuals most likely to be amenable to a shift to web-based or self-care solutions.

SUMMARY

The contact center, and its handling of customer transactions, problems, and complaints, is the heart of organizational centricity and advocacy creation. Studies by Feinberg, Trotter, and Anton (2000), of Purdue University's Center for Customer Driven Quality, have shown that the branded customer experience, especially as realized through company service agents, has a profound effect on future behavior:

- 85% of customers create their opinion of a company and the level of trust in its brands based on the experience they have with contact center agents

- 63% of customers said they would never buy from a company again because of a negative service center experience

- 87% of customers will follow the opinions of their friends, colleagues, and family; if they have a bad contact center experience, they tell everyone, utilizing both online and off-line means to spread negative word-of-mouth

Business strategists such as Michael Porter (1998) have observed that organizations can, potentially, differentiate themselves based on core products and services, price, and the strength of the customer relationship. The first two, he notes, are virtually impossible to execute or sustain today. At this writing, for example, the Apple iPad has had a banner sales year. Despite its success and its attraction as the latest and greatest electronic gadget, there's a groundswell of resistance to it—at least for immediate purchase—among many. It's too expensive (the price will continue to drop); it doesn't have a camera, now a must-have for many (Apple has indicated it will add a webcam in future versions); it can only handle one task at a time; iPhones are more convenient; the broadly touted touchscreen isn't a game changer; it lacks storage space; and it doesn't really replace laptops or notebooks.

As Jim Barnes noted in his book, *Secrets of Customer Relationship Management: It's All About How You Make Them Feel* (2001, 6), emotional responses to the B2B or B2C customer experience are extremely important, even critical, in shaping downstream behavior: "Value, in the customer's mind, is created every time they are made to feel welcome and important." Putting the customer first, and driving customer advocacy through people and processes, has significant strategic profit implications.

In their books on how to align enterprises to advocate for the customer (so the customer will advocate for the enterprise), Glen Urban (2005) and Rajendra Sisodia and coauthors (2007) have articulated the true business case for customer centricity. It has been borne out by such organizations as Zappos, Wegmans Food Markets, and Southwest Airlines—companies that are customer-centric and advocacy-focused. These companies tend to share several common characteristics:

- A single view of the customer across the enterprise through master databases that are continuously cleaned and updated and made available to all employees

- Employees, especially in customer touch functions, who are brand ambassadors focused on optimizing customer experiences and mitigating or eliminating negatives wherever they exist

- A sense of company-wide customer proaction, for generating optimum value delivery in every touch point, transaction, and experience

- Engagement of, and dialogue with, customers in all key decision areas, and utilizing their real-time feedback and guidance, especially where innovation and product/ service enhancement are concerned

- A focus on branded customer experience throughout the organization, making certain that trust and reputation are emphasized and that there is a direct linkage between promises communicated and value realized, overdelivering where possible

Customer advocacy can have a profound effect on the operating performance and competitive position of virtually any organization. Figure 4.3 shows the impact of advocacy level on retention rate and share of wallet for one of our clients. The y axis shows share of wallet and retention, and the x axis shows increases in retention rate (solid line) and share of wallet (dashed line).

Changes in rates of retention and share of wallet as advocacy rises have been found in industry after industry and company after company. These kinds of outcome results are only the beginning of the business case for customer advocacy. As discussed in several chapters of this book, word-of-mouth and brand trust are core elements of advocacy and significantly affect business outcomes. CEO Steve Wynn, creator of Mirage, Bellagio, Encore, and Wynn Las Vegas hotel/casinos, said in an interview, "We need word-of-mouth. It's the most powerful force in marketing. Marketing is about getting people to

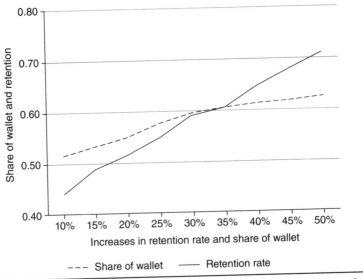

Figure 4.3   Impact of advocacy level on retention rate and share of wallet.

Source: Market Probe, 2010.

trust us. Telling the public what to think never works" (Wynn 2009). When positive brand perception and downstream word-of-mouth effect are added into the equation, it's clear that there is no more powerful force or basis for judging business performance excellence than advocacy.

5

Measuring and Monetizing Customer Advocacy

Virtually every company and market research professional aware of Net Promoter Score (NPS), whether they actively use it or not, would agree that the metric provides some degree of value and guidance to organizations. The principal challenge to its more universal acceptance has been that NPS, claiming to be a forward-looking measure linked to business outcomes, has often been found through further research to have tenuous connections to such key marketplace proofs as revenue growth.

Consultants and academics seem to be on an endless "holy grail" search for a single-item loyalty metric that will correlate more directly with business outcomes and corporate growth. Recently, another metric has emerged—the Customer Effort Score (CES), in which customers rate on a scale of 1–5 the effort they must exert to get their needs met by a brand or at a company. Its creators, presenting their results in a *Harvard Business Review* article, claim that this metric outperformed both customer satisfaction and NPS in terms of customer service initiatives (Reichheld 2003). Note, however, that their definition of customer loyalty includes positive word-of-mouth, which they take to be a downstream outcome (only) rather than both a decision-making factor and an outcome. Another newly introduced metric (2010) identifies "attitudinal equity," a method purportedly linking rank (between brands in a consideration, or evoked, set) with share of wallet, based on the brand's ability to meet a customer's needs *regardless of whether the customer had ever used this brand.* Amazing.

What if customer and brand researchers, marketers, and C-suite executives could have a simple, proven, contemporary, and consistent framework for identifying near-term and downstream customer behavior? And what if that framework could provide enhanced actionability around a recommendation score?

Advocacy, the highest expression of customer loyalty behavior, will be the standard for successful brand and corporate performance going forward. Consulting organizations such as Hitachi certainly believe this to be true. In a 2005 study it concluded: "We predict that customer advocacy will be the new focus for business leaders. Creating the customer experience via customer advocacy will become the single most important initiative that cutting-edge, forward thinking, innovative companies will adopt" (Petouhoff 2006, 3).

As covered in earlier chapters, advocacy occurs when customers select a single supplier from among all those they might consider, giving that supplier the highest share of spend possible, and informally, voluntarily (without any form of compensation), and often frequently telling others about how positive the relationship is and how much value and benefit they derive from it.

Advocacy incorporates opinions formed from customers' transactional and other contact experiences, but it is built on a foundation of strategic, positive purchase and communication behavior. This level of behavior results when the customer is favorable toward a supplier and not only purchases consistently from that supplier over others but also actively tells peers about the personal value and benefit received from the relationship.

How is advocacy different from satisfaction or loyalty (or even recommendation or referral), which so many companies use as key measures of performance and effective customer management?

Satisfaction, as explained in Chapter 1, depends principally on attitudes and recent customer transactions, as well as the tangible, rational, and functional elements of value. As a result, it doesn't correlate very well with actual customer behavior and bonds with suppliers or with key monetary measures like share of spend. It tends to be a minimum, passive standard for a relationship with a brand or supplier.

Loyalty, though it tends to represent a longer-term relationship and more active purchasing from fewer suppliers or a single supplier, often doesn't take into account the genuine influence of peer-to-peer communication, now determined by multiple studies (including a recent one from McKinsey) to leverage 20%–50% of brand and supplier decisions. Nor does it usually consider depth of brand impression and perception. Advocacy not only considers the likelihood to have an exclusive purchasing relationship but also incorporates both strong, emotional, aligned brand kinship and active, positive, and voluntary communication about, and in behalf of, the chosen supplier.

A BRIEF HISTORY OF CUSTOMER LOYALTY BEHAVIOR MEASUREMENT

Advocacy explains the strength of a brand or a supplier's brand franchise, enabling a company to confidently plan or modify marketing, services, communication, and other important initiatives. In brief, results from advocacy research *monetize*, offering definitive, highly actionable guidance for companies on how to optimize loyalty behavior. By examining how customer research has changed over the past few decades, we'll identify how and why we've arrived at this conclusion.

We can depict research approach evolution by a range of dates—or, more accurately, a continuum of approaches—for how researchers have looked at customer attitudes and behavior and endeavored to take action with the findings over the years. As shown in Figure 5.1, this explanation of how customer

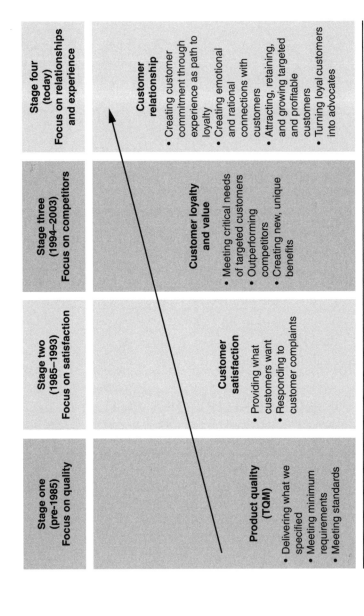

Stage one
(pre-1985)
Focus on quality

Product quality (TQM)
- Delivering what we specified
- Meeting minimum requirements
- Meeting standards

Stage two
(1985–1993)
Focus on satisfaction

Customer satisfaction
- Providing what customers want
- Responding to customer complaints

Stage three
(1994–2003)
Focus on competitors

Customer loyalty and value
- Meeting critical needs of targeted customers
- Outperforming competitors
- Creating new, unique benefits

Stage four
(today)
Focus on relationships and experience

Customer relationship
- Creating customer commitment through experience as path to loyalty
- Creating emotional and rational connections with customers
- Attracting, retaining, and growing targeted and profitable customers
- Turning loyal customers into advocates

Figure 5.1 Evolution of the quality/satisfaction/loyalty movement.

behavior measurement has morphed began in the late 1970s and early 1980s, with the focus on total quality management (TQM). It has since gone through two intermediate stages to reach the most contemporary understanding of the attitudinal and behavioral impact of customer relationships and experiences.

Stage One: Focus on Quality (Pre-1985)

Although customer research has been conducted in one form or another for close to a century and really began to see more active usage after World War II, the first formal stage and period we can identify is the late 1970s, consistent with the worldwide focus on product and service quality. The emphasis at this time was on the delivery of basic, mostly tangible and functional elements of value such as meeting standards and other foundation performance requirements. Many organizations still emphasize their total quality efforts, and it is not unusual to find companies with active Six Sigma initiatives.

Research during this period began as an effort to assess perceived quality, but it soon morphed into a connection with customer satisfaction. Noted TQ (total quality) consultants were quoted as saying, "Customer satisfaction is the key to quality" and "High customer satisfaction is an indicator of perceived quality." This perception remained virtually unchallenged until the mid-1990s; however, customer satisfaction became the dominant research tool for articulating and endeavoring to understand customer behavior.

Stage Two: Focus on Customer Satisfaction (Mid-1980s to Mid-1990s)

One major factor behind the growth of customer satisfaction was its inclusion in well-recognized measurement systems for corporate performance, such as the Malcolm Baldrige National Quality Award, initiated in 1987. The need to capture "voice of the customer" data was (and continues to be) a core element of TQM. Known as VOC, gathering the customer's voice meant putting in place a core metric to evaluate essential needs and wants. In a *Harvard Business Review* article, Professor David Garvin (1991, 80) observed, "The Baldrige Award not only codifies the principles of quality management in clear and accessible language, it goes further: it provides companies with a comprehensive framework for assessing their progress toward the new paradigm of management and such commonly acknowledged goals as customer satisfaction and increased employee involvement."

TQM expert Noriaki Kano, reflecting on the prevailing views of business at the time, defined his concept of building customer satisfaction into measurement systems: "Total Quality Management is exercised under the philosophy that the best way for a corporation to expand sales and make a profit is to provide its customers with satisfaction through its products and services" (Kano et al. 1984, 39). So, while there was some concern about the real relationship between quality initiatives and customer behavior, during this period almost no one was questioning the quality-satisfaction-business performance linkage.

But, does satisfaction, as a method of explaining customer actions, really *satisfy*? One of the principal challenges with satisfaction as a key or sole research metric is that it is about customer *attitude* rather than customer behavior, or intended behavior. During the late 1980s and early 1990s, studies began to emerge that questioned the results orientation of TQM programs and the connection of satisfaction to marketplace action. Christopher Fay (1995, 1) of the Juran Institute, a noted TQ consulting organization, wrote: "The tacit belief is that as a customer grades a supplier with an increasingly higher satisfaction score, so should that customer increase share of spending on that supplier, pay a price premium, refer new prospects, and so forth. In point of fact, this assumed correlation between what customers say and what they do has been disproved in the vast majority of business studies." However, to give the concept of customer satisfaction fair reporting, it has been well proved that transactional and longer-term experience *dissatisfaction* can lead to customer risk and defection. Trying to optimize customer *satisfaction*, however, doesn't have the opposite effect on actual behavior.

Peter Drucker (2001, 18) has been quoted as saying: "To satisfy the customer is the mission and purpose of every business." But is it really the *right* goal? Is it one that, if achieved, will drive behavior? In other words, does satisfaction *monetize*? And if so, does this occur on a reliable, regular, and predictable basis? As marketers and customer experience managers, we want and need only the most actionable and real-world tools and techniques for identifying and measuring how customers behave. The following paragraphs will demystify customer satisfaction—identifying why satisfaction, longevity, and true loyalty represent different constructs. Then, more contemporary and action-centric methods of determining what truly leverages loyalty behavior will be offered.

First, here's a short history lesson (within the broader history lesson) addressing the myth of customer satisfaction. For a long time, it had been assumed that satisfaction and loyalty research were identical, or at least very similar, methods for understanding customer behavior. Almost two decades ago, Fred Reichheld (1993, 71) reported in a *Harvard Business Review* article: "While it may seem intuitive that increasing customer satisfaction will increase retention and therefore profits, the facts are contrary. Between 65% and 85% of customers who defect say they were satisfied or very satisfied with their former supplier. In the auto industry, satisfaction scores average 85%

to 95%, while repurchase rates average 40%." Reichheld later performed a statistical analysis of the satisfaction score annual change for 300 major companies and compared those findings with the sales annual growth change for those same companies and found no correlation (R^2 of 0.00, for the quant mavens) between the two sets of results.

Here is an example of support for this finding from our work at Market Probe. We asked current active customers (those making 10 or more purchases a year) of a major B2B products company to rate service quality and product quality on a five-point scale of satisfaction. At the same time, we asked formerly active frequent buyers who hadn't purchased anything from this company in the past year these same questions (see Table 5.1).

As is easily discernible, their scores were almost identical. Clearly, the client involved in the study would have gotten little or no direction from these data if satisfaction were the principal or only basis for success or failure—as related to a customer's life cycle with the company. If customers who were at risk, or who discontinued purchasing as in our example, were as satisfied with the client's products and services as those still buying, other underlying drivers for risk and defection behavior must have been at work.

Table 5.1 Excellent quality satisfaction ratings (5 on a 5-point scale of satisfaction).

	Overall quality of service	**Overall quality of products**
Active buyers (10+ purchases in past year)	88%	79%
Inactive buyers (formerly active, not in past year)	84%	76%

Stage Three: Focus on Competitive Set, Customer Loyalty, and Value (Mid-1990s to Mid-2000s)

In moving beyond customer satisfaction, companies began to focus on somewhat more robust and advanced measures of performance. The first of these was *customer retention*. While customer retention has certainly proved to be more actionable than satisfaction (in part, because it measures behavior rather than attitude), it still has some basic, fundamental weaknesses. The customer may continue, for instance, purchasing from the supplier (even for a long period of time), but this alone tells us nothing about the level or frequency of purchase or the motivations for this activity.

In the early and mid 1990s, there was a series of articles, and later a book, that keyed on an upgraded approach to understanding customer needs and the features, benefits, and solutions companies could provide—which, ideally, were better than those offered by competitors. The focus was on creating customer loyalty and value, essentially defined as creating barriers to exit from the current, preferred supplier.

One of the related approaches and set of measures during this era was customer value analysis, or CVA. CVA, which was an outgrowth of customer satisfaction measurements associated with the Baldrige Award, essentially looked at where competitors were perceived on a price and performance continuum. Thus, it always considered rational performance, constructed around price, as the sole determinant of what customers want, where (competitive) suppliers were performing well or where they were not, what product or service improvements to make, and even how to shape communications as the means to define customer *value*.

As customer researchers have continued to evolve their own learning around both the rational (tangible and functional) *and* emotional (principally relationships, built around touch-point contact, brand perception, and trust) elements of customer experience and value, more limited and insular approaches such as CVA have declined in application.

Stage Four: Focus on Customer Experience and Advocacy (Today)

We believe that the most actionable "code" for understanding committed customer behavior at any life stage is quite straightforward. It consists of defining the emotional and rational elements and bonds that make up a supplier's value proposition—the sum of each customer's set of experiences and perceived benefits associated with the supplier's products or services. The emotional elements are based on trust, a customer's sense of personal assurance in purchasing and benefiting from using a company's products or support. Service experiences, for instance, play a big role here. Rational, or tangible, elements are those things that we associate with cost and functionality: original price, cost to maintain, accuracy, completeness, reliability, and the like. For us, rational performance *is* satisfaction, the table stakes necessary to help create a more strategic and deeper relationship between customer and supplier, but little more.

Advocacy, which we can define as the active expression of commitment, is seen in such attitudes and actions as strong, frequently personalized brand favorability, but most particularly in positive, frequent, and voluntary informal (or word-of-mouth) communications in behalf of the preferred supplier. Similar to commitment, level of advocacy also monetizes, with true advocates giving significantly higher spend share to their preferred brand compared to those customers who are less enthusiastic, neutral, disaffected, or outright negative.

Advocacy not only brings into play word-of-mouth, customer-generated media, and peer-to-peer interaction (social media, wikis, and blogs being the new language of this trend) as marketing strategies, but it also incorporates viral approaches to push and pull marketing. Viral marketing is a recent addition to the arsenal of behavior-based techniques that companies are using to drive interest and activity. And actually, it is not a marketing term at all but a term that was invented by venture capitalists in the late 1990s to describe the success of Hotmail. It depends on social networks and media to facilitate and encourage people to pass along messages. Viral and neural approaches have now become essential tools for many B2B and B2C companies in their efforts to create awareness, favorability, a narrowed consideration set, and customer referrals. Though word-of-mouth marketing is still rather embryonic, researchers are relying on new techniques, such as advocacy measurement, to gauge the impact word-of-mouth creates in decision making.

Results of advocacy are highly correlated with actual wallet share and related to other elements of customer behavior. We are not measuring word-of-mouth per se but are identifying customers who demonstrate this behavior, in both positive and negative ways. We have even developed a multivariate approach that we identify as "swing voter" analysis, for identifying how to drive advocacy behavior—stabilizing those customers who are ambivalent and "bootstrapping" those who are allegiant (generally positive but largely silent) (see Figure 5.2).

In brief, swing voter analysis enables us to determine and prioritize which rational and emotional relationship attributes drive both positive and negative advocacy behavior.

By focusing on advocacy (and mitigating or eliminating alienation and even sabotage), companies are able to strategically and positively differentiate their value proposition while simultaneously creating optimum levels of desired customer behavior.

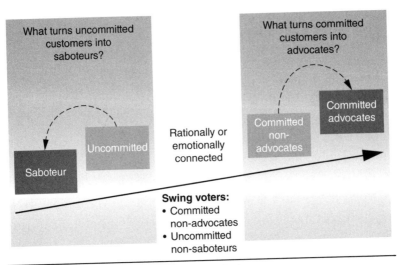

Figure 5.2 Advocacy swing voter analysis.
Source: Market Probe, 2010.

Much of customer advocacy (and alienation) depends on earned levels of *trust and openness* between individuals, and between brands and companies and their customers, as covered in the previous chapter. It also incorporates related concepts such as objectivity, authenticity, belief, credibility and expertise, honesty, sincerity, reliability, and originality in the online and off-line communication methods that they themselves have created. Advocacy represents the highest level of customer involvement and loyalty behavior achievable: interaction with suppliers on an individual and emotional level well past the typical functional, passive relationship between supplier and customer, and having customers proactively and voluntarily convey their experiences to friends, relatives, and colleagues.

Active advocates are fully committed, with an emotional connection well beyond the typical relationship of customer and supplier. They are the customers with the highest level of involvement—active, vocal, and proud. They are the crème de la crème: the people who "live" the brand that they regularly use and who help build or sustain its reputation. Their lifestyle often mirrors that offered by the brand, and they are active in talking about their experiences.

Further, and most important, advocates have demonstrably more powerful and sustainable behavior than most customers. The proof of this will be presented in this chapter in the form of B2B and B2C research from multiple sources.

Advocacy can be both measured and leveraged, and at a higher and more consistent level than earlier approaches to understanding customer attitudes and behavior. Brands and marketers are more aggressively using social word-of-mouth, both online and off-line, to activate purchase intent and related positive behaviors.

Advocacy is not merely a different spin on gaining insight about customer purchase, referral, and communication behavior. Arguably, because the name of the game is value optimization, learning about how customers perceive suppliers, brands, and products or services and then having them carry their experiences and consideration forward and communicating as active advocates is, or will become, the only way to think about them.

What are the specific benefits to sales, marketing, and customer service associated with understanding and leveraging customer advocacy? There are several, and all are vital:

- It helps companies identify emerging trends, image, service performance, their reputation relative to competitors, expressed and unexpressed problems, and complaints; response to new product or service ideas; and even rumors and back-fence internet digital, and off-line, gossip can affect customer behavior

- It is a means to understand and address the strength of the customer franchise and how it will differ by segment within the base

- It helps companies determine the amount of momentum behind the franchise and whether competitors are undermining it

- It identifies exactly why and how these perceptions have developed so that companies can act, both tactically and strategically

To meet this set of goals, it is essential that level of advocacy be identified through research. Better still, if the advocacy level can be developed through a standardized framework, then any company can apply it to enhance sales and revenue.

MEASURING CUSTOMER ADVOCACY

Today, there are many customer feedback measurement models. All attempt to explain and anticipate loyalty behavior. Most focus only on customer attitudes or outcomes of behavior rather than the behavior itself. Some have multiple elements, and others contain only a single element. None have consistently correlated with actual business outcome, and so users of each model are continually pressed by senior corporate management to guarantee accountability.

We have created a new research model—or more correctly, a framework—that blends attitudes with behavior, such as evidence and frequency of positive and negative word-of-mouth. Our framework represents the most contemporary, real-world thinking, writing, and study by leading academics and consulting organizations (McKinsey, Hitachi, IBM, Forrester, Capgemini, Accenture, Gartner, etc.) into what drives customer decision making and supplier bonding. It reflects the decline in trust in corporations (resulting from the highly publicized misdemeanors of such companies as Global Crossing, Tyco, and Enron), and also in their advertising and promotion. At the same time, it recognizes the impact and influence of off-line and online social, neural, voluntary, and peer-to-peer communication of opinions and feelings.

Our framework, simply stated, operationalizes positive and negative word-of-mouth and brand impression based on customer experiences. It helps organizations build a proportion of advocates within the customer base that, in turn, helps a brand grow in the marketplace. The framework itself is quite simple and straightforward, consisting of only three questions:

- Overall favorability or impression of the supplier or brand (based on personal experience)

- Consideration of the brand or supplier for future purchase

- Evidence (and frequency) of positive and negative word-of-mouth in behalf of the brand or supplier

The respondent's answers to the questions are used to segment and classify the respondent into one of the following four groups:

- *Advocate*—Characterized by strong personal involvement and a relationship with the brand, and high loyalty behavior in the marketplace, including active purchasing, limited consideration set, and frequent, positive, and voluntary communication in behalf of that brand.

- *Allegiant*—Positively disposed toward the brand compared with other customers, but inactive communication, broader consideration set, and relatively modest emotional connection, relationship, or communication.

- *Ambivalent*—Mixed disposition and consideration toward the brand, low emotional involvement and desire for connection or a relationship, broad consideration set, and greater willingness to switch to competitor. Little positive or negative communication in behalf of the brand.

- *Alienated*—Weak disposition and even anger toward the brand that ranges from mild disaffection to outright sabotage. Will likely not consider the brand in the future. Frequent negative communication about the brand.

Leading into the next section, it can be stated that advocates can, and do, positively influence business outcomes in multiple ways:

- They buy more, and more frequently, and give the preferred brand a greater share of wallet

- They have a propensity to continue the relationship even after experiencing a product or service problem

- They are more willing to try brand or line extensions and new products

- They make frequent and consistent purchases and usually cost less to serve

- They are less price-sensitive

- They do not churn when faced with competitive offers

- They have narrowed brand consideration, or evoked, sets for new purchases

- They have a positive, bonded, longitudinal relationship

- They communicate voluntarily and frequently about their preferred brand, and in a very positive manner

Again, by setting up a stable framework for understanding and leveraging customer advocacy (and alienation) behavior, companies are able to target and leverage scarce marketing resources to best effect.

MONETIZING CUSTOMER ADVOCACY

Beyond operational, marketing, and communication impact, the direct financial return for creating active advocates is both real and substantial. Studies in many industries have found that, compared to customers who were highly satisfied or even highly likely to recommend (as those who promote this metric as the single number that can be used to understand the drivers of growth), those who are true brand advocates have used products more recently, more frequently, and with higher share of spend than customers with high satisfaction and high downstream likelihood to recommend.

Further, as seen in Figure 5.3, from our retail bank customer advocacy study (to be discussed shortly), significant changes in level of monetization—notably, share of spend—can be identified at each level of advocacy; that is, as the level of engagement rises from negative (alienation, disaffection, and sabotage) to passive and indifferent, to positive, and then to real advocacy, share of spend dramatically increases.

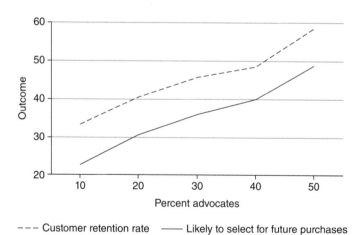

Figure 5.3   Money curves—customer relationship.
Source: Market Probe, 2010.

As a management and customer relationship concept, advocacy has just begun to become mainstream. Over the past few years, advocacy and social media impact studies have been conducted by some of the leading management consulting companies, such as Gartner, Hitachi, Forrester, and IBM. McKinsey, for instance, has recently introduced a word-of-mouth marketing measurement tool.

Noted marketing professor Philip Kotler, of Northwestern University, believes that standout organizations are those that can most effectively optimize stakeholder trust, engagement, and perceived personal value. In a recent *Financial Times* interview article, Dr. Kotler said that some of the most successful companies spend less on marketing than companies that have achieved lower success, building value through inclusion, engagement, authenticity, and stakeholder focus. Though it sounds counterintuitive, Dr. Kotler said, "They use the word-of-mouth effect of unpaid advocates—truly loyal customers—to boost their reputation. Advocates will do your marketing for you if you mobilize them, listen to them and engage them" (Stern 2010).

As stated, we believe that, going forward, advocacy will represent the standard for performance, and profitable, excellence. It's essential, then, to have a measurement model or framework that identifies, as much as possible, advocacy levels within the customer base.

EXAMPLES OF ADVOCACY MEASUREMENT AND MONETIZATION: B2C RETAIL BANKING IN THE UNITED STATES AND THE UNITED KINGDOM

Our advocacy framework clearly shows that retail banks have many opportunities for organic growth by building their portfolio of advocates in key segments. It is no secret that organic growth is more profitable than new client acquisition. In an IBM Global Business Services report, the issue is accurately addressed:

> As mergers and acquisitions become less attractive, leading financial institutions look increasingly to their existing customer base for growth. Critical organic growth measures—cross-sell, attention and new customer acquisition—dominate nearly every retail bank's agenda. (Lieberman and Heffernan 2006, 1)

We completely agree. However, the economic crisis of 2008 and the shrinkage of demand for financial products and services have put added pressure on customer retention.

In mid-2010, our company conducted the groundbreaking National Retail Bank Customer Advocacy Study (*National Advocacy Monitor*) among 7000 adult respondents in the United States. This research featured the application of a unique framework specifically designed to identify the most actionable, real-world attitudinal and behavioral drivers of customer decision making. The core of this framework is the determination of customer advocacy levels and the degree of kinship with, favorability toward, and trust of brands; but, principally, advocacy identifies the downstream customer communication and marketplace behavioral effects of word-of-mouth based on personal brand experience.

As noted, consulting firms such as McKinsey have determined that word-of-mouth drives 20%–50% of customer decision making, so our framework represents a valuable, contemporary technique for evaluating the impact of transactions as well as strategic brand strength based on peer-to-peer communication and brand perception.

The results of our UK bank customer advocacy research showed a dramatic difference in the demonstrated share of wallet—over twice the level of investable assets—between

bank customers characterized as advocates and those identified as alienated. In addition, whether we were examining
relationship-based performance attributes, such as trust and
confidence, or functionally based attributes, such as breadth of
accounts available for customers, advocates were significantly
more positive when compared with alienated customers. This
same result was seen among US bank customers.

In addition, for both the US and the UK bank customers,
perceived problems were quite high among the alienated group.
Worse, a high percentage of the alienated group with problems
saw them as unresolved. As reported in many customer studies,
unresolved problems are perhaps the single largest contributor
of defection, so this is an important issue.

Frequency of negative communication was extreme among
UK retail bank customers tagged as alienated. Alienated customers reported having close to 10 negative conversations
about their banks with others during the six months prior to the
survey. Conversely, advocates had about 8 positive conversations over the past six months. And, given that word-of-mouth
is so highly leveraging of the behavior of others, both numbers
are significant in their potential impact (see Table 5.2).

In the United States, where advocacy performance of the
nation's top 15 banks was evaluated, there was a dramatic
spread between the best performing and the worst performing of these organizations in terms of both the creation of
advocates (see Figure 5.4) and the creation of alienated
customers (10% for the best-performing bank, 25% for the
worst-performing bank).

Many studies conducted in the retail banking industry over
the years have determined that there is a fair amount of inertia
(i.e., willingness to remain with the present bank) among customers, almost irrespective of perceived performance. More
recently, likely as a result of the perception of greater instability within the industry, there has been a marked increase in

Table 5.2 Very high-level profile of UK retail bank customers—advocates versus alienated.

	Advocate (%)	Alienated (%)
Percentage of customers	12	19
Behaviors		
Share of wallet	73	37
Retention	98	1
Positive word-of-mouth	7.5	2
Negative word-of-mouth	0	9.5
Attitudes		
Trust and confidence	81	2
Reliable service from staff	71	3
Breadth of accounts	62	1
Problems		
Reported problems	3	33

Source: Market Probe, 2010.

propensity to switch banks in both the United States and the United Kingdom. Given that half of retail bank customers in both of our banking studies were identified as either ambivalent or alienated, this is a major concern for bank marketers and executives.

Our most important research conclusion in these studies was that advocacy monetizes at a stronger and more consistent rate than other key customer research measures in active use. For example, as shown earlier in the results, customers whom our research framework identified as advocates can contribute to significantly higher share of wallet growth for a bank than alienated or ambivalent customers.

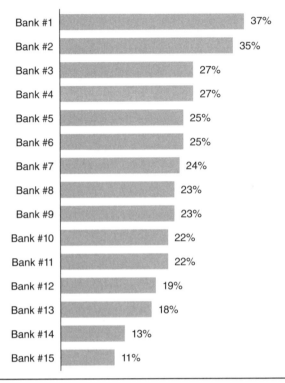

Figure 5.4 US banks vary in their ability to cultivate customer advocacy.

Source: Market Probe, 2010.

Alienated customers similarly added products and services at competitive banks at several times the rate of customers who were advocates of their primary bank.

For financial institutions—indeed, virtually any organization—it means that the odds of selling a new product to advocates (versus losing these sales to competition) are five times higher than the odds of selling a new product to alienated customers. This type of actionable polarity in findings between customers who are alienated and customers who are advocates sustained whether we were evaluating overall performance, trust and relationship, touch points (tellers, service representatives, etc.), functional elements such as ATMs, or key monetizing elements such as future purchase likelihood.

Among other key findings from our *National Advocacy Monitor*:

- The top two banks, in terms of the percentage of their customer bases identified as advocates through our framework, had three times the percentage of advocates of the bottom two banks (37% and 35% vs. 13% and 11%)

- One-quarter of the customers of the two lowest-performing banks were classified as alienated, that is, they are negative toward these banks and are disaffected communicators

- Emotional elements (trust and confidence) and satisfaction with key touch points (bank staff, account manager, service culture, branch, and live rep) are highly correlated with overall bank advocacy levels

- Advocates (of their primary bank) are significantly more likely to have strong belief and emotional connections to their bank compared to alienated customers. Polar results examples: "Always treats me fairly," 84% versus 2%; "I feel like I belong," 70% versus 1%

- Advocates have a strong willingness to explore new products from their primary bank—50% will consider versus 5% of alienated customers who will consider

- Advocates are virtually certain to have a continued relationship with their primary bank compared to alienated customers, who are virtually certain of not continuing

In addition, our analysis showed that transactional experience and overall experience were extremely important contributors to bank customer advocacy:

- Frequency of interaction is a definite "marker" of customer advocacy. Customers with 10+ interactions per month were almost twice as likely to be advocates as those with 1 or 2 interactions, and four times compared to those with no interactions.

- Customers who had no problems or issues with their primary bank were four times as likely to be advocates as those who had experienced a problem. Also, one-third of the alienated customers who had identified a problem or complaint said that these issues had not been resolved, and this is a cause for service-related concern.

- Having a business banking account with their primary bank was another "marker" of advocacy, as well as an opportunity to build profit and deepen the relationship. Twice the percentage of customers with business accounts were advocates, compared to customers with no business accounts.

Our advocacy results were also consistent with metrics typically applied in most bank strategic and transactional customer research, except that these findings were invariably much more polar and directional, thus yielding greater insight and actionability for organizations using these data.

6

Recommendation and Referral: The Hype and the Reality of "One Number"

The philosopher's stone, "philosophi lapis" in Latin, is a legendary substance that supposedly could turn inexpensive metals such as lead into gold and/or create an elixir that would make humans younger. It was a longtime "holy grail" of Western alchemy.

—WIKIPEDIA

The philosopher's stone was first mentioned in the writings of Zosimos of Panopolis, a third-century mystic and alchemist. Eventually, the philosopher's stone was thought to represent the force behind the evolution of life and the universal binding power that unites minds and souls. The lore of its amazing properties has captured imaginations ever since and became the basis, parenthetically, for the first Harry Potter novel and film—*Harry Potter and the Sorcerer's Stone.*

The search for a marketing holy grail—a measure that would attach real behavioral and business outcomes to sales, communication, and promotional programs—has also been with us for quite some time. Decades ago, marketers began using single-number scores, such as attention and interest level, in an attempt to understand the effectiveness of print and electronic advertising. More recently, the concept of a single-question

135

metric, which uses recommendations given to a product or service to predict future customer behavior, has been widely endorsed and promoted as a latter-day marketing philosopher's stone.

Just as it's unlikely that a stone can have magical superpowers, there are flaws, application inconsistencies, contradictions, and challenges with the thesis that referral and recommendation, or a metric created from them, can consistently decode optimum customer loyalty behavior. Few can doubt the appeal of ultimate simplicity in the idea of a single measure, but businesses should instead be asking, "Look, is increasing recommendation *really* the best way to drive business success? Is it going to have more of an impact than reducing customer loss? Is it more powerful than increasing customer volume, cross-sale, or share purchased? Is it the best way to go—and in all situations and circumstances?"

In large part, because the one-number metric concept was embraced by a phalanx of C-suite executives when it was introduced in 2003—principally because of its claim to represent a simple, direct means of monitoring the strength and growth potential for an enterprise or brand—the approach has found ready acceptance. Other companies have not accepted the premise from the outset, have reviewed the body of scholarly research that contradicts the one-number positioning as a philosopher's stone, or have moved beyond it. These companies prefer the proven benefits and the consistency with real-world market and customer situations of an index, a framework, or a model to uncover and create actionability around drivers of relationship health.

Many marketing scientists, having themselves determined that the one-number approach has limited usefulness and application, even when compared with other, and often more antecedent, customer metrics, went on record that (1) they doubted companies would take this technique seriously and (2) companies that did adopt the metric would abandon it once they saw that it didn't work as claimed. But the fact is that neither of these things has happened. Major corporations have not only on-boarded the technique as a foundation for understanding and predicting customer behavior, but also built entire performance infrastructures around it. Either by not understanding its limitations or by disregarding them, they have bought into the claim that the one-question metric is "the single most reliable indicator of a company's ability to grow" (Reichheld 2003, 54).

THE GOOD, BAD, AND UGLY REPRESENTED BY ONE NUMBER

The Good, the Bad and the Ugly—the famous 1966 Sergio Leone film starring Clint Eastwood, Eli Wallach, and Lee Van Cleef—can serve as a useful metaphor for the single number metric's qualities.

As will be discussed in this section of the chapter, the single number is well intentioned enough; however, its very simplicity and method of calculation have characteristics that can create negative, even unattractive, consequences for companies that depend on this metric as a sole key performance indicator.

Recommendation: The Good (That Is, What Is of Value)

One of the chief values of the one-number metric, and a benefit upon which many can agree, is the attention and focus it has brought to having a key experience and relationship performance indicator that is, at least hypothetically, stronger and more actionable than a metric like customer satisfaction. Its creators have argued that traditional market research is too complex and resource-consuming and can produce results that take companies in the wrong direction. The single number has face validity in that it yields advantages versus disadvantages and shows at least some linkage to business outcomes. It is a popular measure that facilitates scoring comparisons with other companies. Its simplicity and elegance are compelling to corporate leaders, and its thesis is easy to grasp. Among other things, it has created a recognition that:

- Companies need to set clear loyalty and business outcome goals as a means of creating organizational focus and action

- Customer loyalty is more than customer satisfaction, customer retention, and repeat purchase

- There should be at least a modicum of linkage between customer measures obtained through a survey device and actual business outcomes

- Customer data beyond the merely anecdotal should be shared within the organization, as this can create greater focus

- Results from this research can be used as a basis for performance comparison with industry peers

Even some of the technique's harshest and most vocal critics within the market research industry have credited the company offering the one-number approach with getting the attention and acceptance of senior management, and then solidifying the position of recommendation question results as a corporate rallying point.

Recommendation: The Questionable or Bad (That Is, What Is of Continuing Debate and Concern)

Since the one-number technique was introduced, numerous market researchers have weighed in with salient arguments about why it is, at best, a flawed approach. In the interest of broad, hopefully even-handed, and nonemotional exploration of their objections, they are presented here in no particular order of importance:

- Extensive research has shown that the one-number technique is not universally applicable; that is, it cannot be used in all industries and purchase situations. Its results cannot be applied to other areas of marketing decision making and effort, such as branding and positioning, product and service assessment, or loyalty program development and refinement. Further, it gives no guidance around customer life-cycle issues such as targeted customer prospecting and acquisition, customer risk mitigation, and recovery of financially attractive former customers.

• Marketing scientists have questioned even the scale used by the developers, because the question doesn't really ask about negative or detracting behavior. The "propensity to recommend" question uses an anchored 11-point scale (where 0 = not at all likely and 10 = extremely likely). For instance, Schneider et al. (2008) suggest using a fully labeled seven-point bipolar scale as a way to make the recommendation question more accurate, for example, "extremely likely to recommend against" at the bottom and "extremely likely to recommend" at the top. These researchers found that out of four scales tested, the 11-point scale advocated by the single-number developers had the lowest predictive validity of the scales tested.

• Others have taken issue with the calculation methodology, claiming that by collapsing an 11-point scale to three components (but only evaluating two of them), significant information is lost and statistical variability of the result is increased. The validity of the single-number scale's cutoff points across industries and cultures has also been questioned.

• It asks users to believe that causation and correlation are the same thing. For example, the rise and fall of yogurt sales may correlate with fluctuations in the economy or the stock market, but one does not cause the other. So, the interpretation of correlation between measures of customer behavior and making statements like "Remarkably, this one simple statistic seemed to explain the relative growth rates," as was done in the original one-number article (Reichheld 2003, 50), infers causation and is offered as the means to enhance business performance.

- It's an oversimplification of customer behavior leading to business outcomes. Even its creators now concede that more information, that is, detailed diagnostics, must be made available beyond the single number to help understand the "why" behind the recommendation level, at a minimum, what drives the recommendation result. Follow-up questions with open-ended responses are essential to facilitate higher actionability. For example, respondents in the one-number studies are rarely asked the reasons for their level of recommendation. This will be further addressed in the next section.

- Though the idea of recommendation is intuitively powerful and is held up by its creators as *both* the measurement tool and the means for understanding customer behavior, extensive research has shown that the single number is not considered a guide to the future health of a brand or an enterprise. Thus, it has real decision-making support limitations. It provides no direction about what to do or how to do it. A criticism voiced by many marketers is that the single-number recommendation score reveals nothing about a company's product or service line, innovations and new developments, pricing, or other key elements of value; nor, as noted earlier, does it offer guidance to companies on customer life-cycle-related issues. If, for example, a company's products had high recommendation scores but outlandishly high prices, very few would buy them; the high prices would attract few new customers and might also cause extensive losses. As a result, and closely related to the lack of detailed decision-making guidance represented by the recommendation question score, marketers can honestly ask, "So what?"

- As will be discussed later in this chapter, it is entirely possible to obtain the same net score using multiple scenarios: If Brand M has few low scores but also few high scores, it many get a net result of +10%. The same result could be achieved for Brand S, with a large proportion of high scores but also a large proportion of low scores.

- Related to this is the inability of the technique (because it is a difference score rather than a classification score) to distinguish between the meaning of gaining detractors and losing promoters, or endeavoring to analyze the effect of so-called neutral customers wave-to-wave in tracking research. For example, there might be a consistent +10% net result, but it would have been achieved by shifts in promoters (a decrease) and detractors (an increase) and an increase in the middle group, which the technique identifies as "passives." So, although the technique detects the shift, it provides no insight about the nature of the shift and offers little guidance to management for taking action.

- Many who use or have used the single number recognize that it is an aggregate macro number; that is, the low numbers are subtracted from the high numbers to get a net score on a grouped or company level, making it impossible to conduct analyses building up from individual customer responses. There has been little evidence of the one number being used on a micro basis, such as evaluating how a company's degree of growth can vary with the single-number metric results over time.

- The single-number approach is not discriminating; that is, there is ample possibility for a customer to recommend multiple brands or companies in the same sector. So, it doesn't really offer guidance as to what drives true loyalty, which includes narrowing of evoked, or consideration, sets. A customer can use many banks, supermarkets, or insurance companies and recommend them all at equal levels. A benefit of customer advocacy, which is addressed throughout the book and is also covered later in this chapter, is that advocacy behavior is often accompanied by reduced consideration, or evoked, sets of the product, service, or supplier in question.

- Another criticism heard in marketing circles, and an additional "so what?" issue, is divining what a good or bad recommendation score actually means, especially when compared with scores of other companies in an industry. Given the questionable actionability of the score in the first place, the fact that it performs worse than simpler antecedent measures such as "satisfaction" and "liking" (which end up being better predictors of recommendation than "likelihood to recommend," according to Schneider et al. [2008]), and its lack of correlation to other elements and gauges of performance, better or worse scores can be significant red herrings. Factors that determine recommendation are also related to the brand/firm that customers have chosen to do business with, but the inability to isolate the importance of these factors in driving those decisions is considered by many to be a weakness, which compromises the touted positive value of the measure's simplicity.

- Even the question used in the one-number approach has been challenged by some practitioners. For instance, the question asks, "Would you recommend . . ." rather than "Will you recommend . . ." or "Have you recommended . . ." The latter two variations are considered superior, since in the "Will you" variation the question calls for respondents to have greater certainty, and in the "Have you" variation there is actual evidence of having taken action, that is, actual behavior. Credibility of the respondent answering the question is also an issue. Results of research containing the single number make no distinction as to whether the individual answering the question is active or dormant, frequent or infrequent, or whether the individual has ever been a customer.

One particular challenge to the credibility and value of the single recommendation question is that repeated scholarly research studies and articles (Henning 2009; Hayes 2008; Keiningham et al. 2007; Morgan and Rego 2006; Anderson, Fornell, and Mazvancheryl 2004; Fornell et al. 2006; Grisaffe 2004) have found that older antecedent measures—such as customer satisfaction as produced by American Customer Satisfaction Index (ACSI) survey results, and future purchase intent—are actually as good as real business results, such as growth. Further, the one-number approach has been found to be statistically insignificant and weak in its ability to explain market share changes or predict future sales. Other metrics, derived from long-accepted central customer-perceived value elements (reputation, performance, quality, price, etc.), are much more effective in explaining changes in market share.

Other research has shown that traditional loyalty measures, such as likelihood to repurchase, are, at minimum, comparable to the one-number technique at predicting business performance outcomes such as cash flow. There is growing evidence that single-number-using companies, seeking more correlation with actual financial performance, have moved beyond the recommendation score by utilizing loyalty indices based on rational and emotional models that are close to 20 years old. Because the ability to identify drivers of marketplace outcomes is so important in decision making, the one-number approach may cause managers to focus on the wrong issues. This can result in strategy errors or ineffective resource allocation.

Some of these scientific, peer-reviewed studies have pointed out that the claims of superiority made by developers of the one-number technique have never been supported by published empirical evidence. Others have demonstrated customer management actionability flaws in the approach, such as the potential (and even the likelihood) for nonpositive, nonnegative at-risk customers to defect. Namely, the single-number technique would miss opportunities aimed at stabilizing customers with high likelihood to switch.

Many of these other techniques, which are older and more basic approaches to understanding customer behavior, actually facilitate more effective closed-loop dialogue and communication approaches with customers who give poor ratings to performance and relationship, who have complaints, or who perceive declining performance over time. Part of the now-accepted benefits of positive problem and complaint response, for example, is higher loyalty behavior, and the one-number approach simply cannot identify the value in quick response and resolution protocols.

Finally, several of these studies have identified potential research bias in the single-number approach because its developers have never presented the analysis that supports the claims (and refutes the published scientific research that questions their methods) that their technique is superior. This, critics state, results in mere marketing and sales puffery rather than proof that is underpinned by actual evidence.

Rather interestingly, authors of the peer-reviewed and published contra studies have been criticized by devoted users of the one-number technique. Even though the original one-number research had not been subjected to such scrutiny or rigor, the authors of contra research were subjected to claims that their data were wrong. In addition, the single-number savants have claimed that "the good outweighs the bad" and that, despite evidence to the contrary, the one-number technique is still an indicator of a company's ability to grow (Fou 2009; Keiningham et al. 2008).

As a capstone, there has been something of a "flat Earth" response to the contra studies by the one-number creators and users. Developers of the single-number technique believe, and have published statements to the effect, that market and customer researchers dislike the approach because it is too simple and because it threatens their ways of interpreting data from satisfaction, relationship, and loyalty studies. Proponents of the one-number approach claim that the score's benefits as a motivator for an organization to become more focused on improving products and services for customers outweighs any negatives. The contra study authors have concluded that data from their research showing that the single number has significant flaws and limitations, despite claims to the contrary and attacks by users of the technique, can stand on their own merits. The results, they say, "are what they are." Case closed.

Recommendation: The Ugly

The very first issue of *Mad* magazine, which was actually a comic book, featured a story called "Blobs," set in the year AD 1,000,000. People had evolved into little more than blobs of flesh with large heads and oversized brains, fitted into vehicles for life. The story centers on the abiding fear expressed by Alfred to his friend Melvin that the world is being run by machinery and that people are doing none of the hard thinking. Alfred exclaims, "And the heart of our whole civilization is that master monster machine that holds the complex mechanism that controls our whole existence. The machine without which we would be lost. Do you know what that means?"

Among other things, as applied to our discussion of a single number as the holy grail of customer loyalty behavior, dependence on this measure as the machine for producing profitability and growth means that there has to be an ultimate level of confidence and a no-fail belief that this question, and only this question, will reveal all to guide companies through the customer behavior wilderness. Further, there has to be a concomitant acceptance that few or no other questions are required to provide either desired answers or paths to answers. Companies subscribing to this line of thinking often state, in a rather Luddite view of customer research (or intransigence to not move beyond status quo in terms of generating more actionable markers for behavior), that not doing so would be a "distraction" to initiatives, and the piles of analysis, built around the single-number metric.

Readers of the original *Harvard Business Review* article, the popular "ultimate question" business book, and successive white papers touting the myriad "philosopher's stone" claims of the one-number metric approach could easily assume that the technique is the be-all and end-all, a "one size fits every situation" measure. A Bain & Company report states that "subtracting the percentage of detractors from the promoters yields a bank's . . . single simple number that yields powerful results" and that it "is a key that helps banks unlock organizational changes that most bankers would otherwise struggle to achieve" (du Toit et al. 2010, 3). From these statements, one would presume a finding of stunning results. The developers of the one-number approach have also consistently claimed that it is "the single most reliable indicator of a company's ability to grow." The fact is, however, that users of the one-number approach, while anticipating results that are a powerful potion, often get results that are little more than weak tea.

Here is a prime example. While du Toit et al. (2010) found that the average number of referrals from the top recommending group was more than 6.3 times that of the bottom recommending group (3.8 bank referrals compared to 0.6), the top recommending group owned only 25% more bank products compared to the bottom group (3.0 compared to 2.4). Again, connection to recommendation propensity and actual behavior is very weak and tepid tea indeed.

Despite years of backfill by its developers that this single-number recommendation metric isn't really the "only question you'll ever need" and that additional questions are invariably required to provide added insight around the single question, an ancillary issue is that many market and customer researchers using this technique have seemingly forgotten how to ask basic questions. Though its creators proffer the technique as a simple, universal, easy-to-understand metric, making it easy and inexpensive to track, there is a significant "What do I do now?" element behind the need to increase the number of customers making recommendations. This is one of the principal and most powerful criticisms leveled against the one-number approach—namely, that more detailed diagnostics and customers' views are needed to guide business decisions. While many of the senior executives who endorse the approach may not, per se, require the detail, those individuals making resource allocation decisions certainly should be exposed to real consumer perceptions and attitudes.

One of the most important shortfalls, or conceptual challenges, of the single-number recommendation approach is that it is an aggregated metric, as introduced in the last section. Companies looking to make decisions based on the lifetime value of customers cannot do so using the one-number technique. This is not an obtuse distinction, and it is potentially quite dangerous. If companies are going to be disciplined about using lifetime customer value as a basis for sales, marketing, service, and other areas of the business where resources need to be allocated, then the linkage must be at the individual customer level. It affects every aspect of the customer life cycle— attracting and converting prospects, retaining customers, cross-selling and upselling to optimize wallet share, mitigating customer risk, and even recovering attractive customers who have churned. Customer-level information simply links loyalty behavior to key indicators of performance (sales, profits, tenure, buying patterns, etc.), and though the one-number recommendation approach has been cited by its developers as having the promise for doing this, it cannot.

ONE-NUMBER CREDOS AND CLAIMS VERSUS REAL-WORLD CHALLENGES

Recommendations are a key goal, but are they the main goal? Most customer management research practitioners argue that while recommendation and referral are important (as is an unwillingness to recommend or refer), much more needs to be understood about customer decision and behavior dynamics.

Recommendation is undeniably one of the principal outcomes of loyalty behavior, but certain pundits seem to be preaching from bully pulpits that recommendation is a prime indicator—in fact, the only predictor—of the construct itself. There are numerous serious limitations to this oversimplified approach. It should be quickly recognized and understood that it's possible, for example, to incentivize customers and that they will refer, once compensated and rewarded to do so. If companies, in effect, buy referral and recommendation—and it can easily be done through viral marketing agencies specifically organized to create buzz through referral—what happens to the value of the metric? It's very, very strongly compromised.

There are many more problems with putting too much emphasis on recommendation and referral. One problem is that if other information is available about customer behavior, as it often is through targeted research, the overfocus on a single number suggests that these insights will receive less consideration and relevance. For example, if a company discovers that it has a high incidence of unresolved customer complaints, this serious loyalty-leveraging situation can get brushed aside as executives seek to create ever-higher positive recommendation levels.

Another claim of the single-number approach is that it "can make your employees accountable for treating customers right" (Reichheld 2003, 54). Really? This is a classic case of pushing responsibility without guidance as to what is required to optimize the customer experience. Focus groups conducted among frontline employees of companies using the one-number metric have yielded tales of pressure, in part through the metric being used as both an incentive apple and a behavior whip, to continually improve this singular result, often producing both anxiety and negative morale.

Also, companies using a single net recommendation score should understand that it can be obtained in multiple ways. In other words, a 40% recommendation score could be the result of a 65% positive recommendation minus a 25% negative recommendation or a 45% positive recommendation minus a 5% negative recommendation. Yet, these two net scores represent entirely different customer referral scenarios. Though the first scenario might create some cause for concern because of the level of negative recommendation, the second scenario is far more serious because of the lower level of positive scores, suggesting that many customers are potential candidates for churn.

Additionally, the use of alternative customer research methods to identify key drivers of loyalty—such as multiquestion indices and models and probability allocation (assigning probabilities to events, including purchase activity or informal communication)—has been found by numerous customer loyalty research methodologists to correlate much more closely with actual customer behavior than willingness to refer or recommend. While it is understood that these approaches lack the appeal of one-number simplicity, they represent far greater accuracy and actionability.

Finally, we've evolved to a place where most marketers live in a one-to-one customer communications, measurement, and management world. Linkage must be made between individual customer-detailed expressions of loyalty and customers' estimated lifetime value. So, perhaps the biggest challenge with a net recommendation score is that it's usually presented on a grouped or aggregated basis rather than on a specific customer basis. Customer-level information systems can help leverage profile and loyalty research data, enabling marketers to understand behavior on an individual basis, but an aggregated score such as net recommendation offers no such flexibility. At the end of the day, this may be one of the measure's most serious drawbacks.

COMMUNICATION-RELATED DOWNSTREAM ACTION TAKEN BY CUSTOMERS RESULTING FROM A PRODUCT OR SERVICE EXPERIENCE

There is an intersection among customer experience with a product or service, informal peer-to-peer communication about that experience, and downstream customer decision making. We designed consumer research to help evaluate the incidence and effect of both Web 2.0 social interaction media and off-line communication (where the strong majority of information sharing continues to take place).

The core intention of this research was to develop well-validated perspectives and trends relating to loyalty behavior that was influenced by experience and word-of mouth in selected industries, and to learn what types of downstream behavior take place following that experience.

Working through a major international polling research firm, we conducted a study early in 2009 among over 2000 adults ages 18 and over in the United States. Our qualification criterion was whether the respondent had a product/service purchase experience or a service experience over the past two months that stood out in his or her mind. Of the study respondents, 1404, or approximately 60%, could recall such an experience. By product/service category (with approximately 100 or more eligible respondents), these were as follows:

Healthcare services—206 (9%)

Restaurant dining—197 (8%)

Entertainment, such as seeing a movie or attending a sporting event—168 (7%)

Travel, including hotels, airline, rail, and rental cars—168 (7%)

Automotive vehicles, parts, or service—123 (5%)

Entertainment products, such as televisions, DVDs, and so forth—115 (5%)

Technology products, including cameras and computers—102 (4%)

Financial services—98 (4%)

Once they identified a memorable product purchase, use, or service experience, respondents were asked to describe what downstream actions they had taken. Almost 79% reported taking some form of communication-related action.

A total of 72% had taken positive action; among that group, 79% communicated about their positive experience to others, while 56% specifically recommended that someone make a purchase. Further, recommendation was significantly less likely to occur among automotive, healthcare services, and, especially, financial services (identified by only 4% of these respondents), while technology products respondents were much more likely to recommend (80% of those taking positive action). *Note*: This is yet another instance of where communication to others about the product or service is more likely to occur than actual recommendation, and the results also demonstrate a high degree of variability by category.

Additionally, 41% of respondents said they communicated directly back to the vendor or supplier, and this was significantly lower among entertainment respondents (18%). Of those respondents who had communicated directly with the vendor, about 70% were looking for some type of issue resolution; among those respondents, about 78% had their issue resolved in a positive manner. Close to 19%, however, were reporting still-unresolved issues, and this was particularly high among financial services respondents (38%). Of respondents who communicated directly with vendors, this was more likely to occur among older customers—baby boomers and matures—and less likely among echo boomers and Generation X respondents.

When specific action taken is broken out by product and service category, communication to vendor is strongest in automotive, followed by telecom products and services, financial services, and healthcare. Only in restaurant dining, entertainment products, technical products, and telecom products and services was positive recommendation stronger than positive communication. And in categories such as healthcare, automotive, and financial services, propensity to positively communicate was significantly higher than likelihood to positively recommend. Also, it should be noted that in some categories (such as restaurant dining), it was more likely that no communication-related action would take place at all.

The data in Table 6.1 are generally consistent with findings by Keller and Fay (2009), namely, that two-thirds of all brand-related conversations are positive, while less than 10% of the time they are negative.

Table 6.1   Downstream communication action as a result of product/service experience.

Within the past two months, have you experienced buying a product or service that stands out in your mind?*

	Communicate to vendor	Communicate positively	Positively recommend	No communication
Automotive	43%	46%	20%	21%
Telecom product/service	38%	27%	16%	38%
Financial services	37%	32%	30%	29%
Healthcare services	35%	45%	22%	19%
Travel	32%	39%	29%	31%
Technology products	27%	39%	44%	25%
Entertainment products	25%	40%	42%	25%
Restaurant dining	18%	30%	31%	41%
Entertainment	12%	43%	30%	34%

(Continued)

Table 6.1 Downstream communication action as a result of product/service experience. Continued.

As a result of your purchase or service experience, what action(s) have you taken? Select all that apply.**

Action(s) taken	Total	Generation			
		Echo boomers (18–32)	Gen X (33–44)	Baby boomers (45–63)	Matures (64+)
I communicated directly to the vendor/supplier	41%	28%	35%	48%	57%
Positive action (net)	72%	77%	80%	72%	57%
I communicated about my positive product/service experience to others	57%	56%	65%	59%	48%
I recommended someone purchase the product/service	41%	49%	39%	39%	30%
Negative action (net)	14%	15%	11%	14%	16%
I communicated about my negative product/service experience to others	11%	12%	11%	10%	11%
I recommended against purchasing the product/service to others	6%	6%	3%	7%	7%

*Base: Variable.

**Base: Had memorable purchase or service experience and took action. Multiple responses accepted.

RECOMMENDATION IS NOT— REPEAT *NOT*—ADVOCACY

Thesis of the One-Number Developers

Creators and sellers of the single recommendation question as surrogate for profitability and growth also, increasingly, appear to be asking the business community to accept the premise that *recommendation = word-of-mouth = advocacy*. This thesis, though the usually unchallenged annexation of the concept of advocacy has audacity, fails on a number of bases.

First, recommendation can be purchased. As identified earlier, some companies can, and do, directly incentivize customer referrals, and there are viral marketing organizations whose sole business proposition is to use recruited and compensated individuals who will communicate their endorsement of selected products and services to others. This makes the referral scores for those products and services go up, of course, though the reasons for this increased recommendation are artificial.

Next, recommendation is clearly only one of several downstream communication and action behaviors that can take place after a transaction or an experience. Off-line and online word-of-mouth between peers is one of them, and this behavior is certainly not coequal with either recommendation or advocacy (which also requires strong brand favorability). As the previous section demonstrated, based on national polling results, customers can also communicate with the vendor or service provider involved, and this can take place in an array of ways, again both off-line and online. Because the creators of the one-number approach favor very short surveys, it is unlikely that the technique would ever generate diagnostic information that leverages the type of downstream communication or other behavior taking place as a result of experiences and transactions.

Also, customers can be completely silent after a transaction or experience. This very lack of postevent communication has an impact on their future behavior (known as "self-perception theory" in academic circles), and all the while their failure to communicate has no influence on the behavior of others. Even though generally silent on their preferred brands, these customers, which we identify as allegiants, also demonstrate fairly strong loyalty. If companies can identify ways to build and bootstrap these quiet loyalists into more vocal supporters, the positive financial impact will be significant. Recommendation, as a single metric, cannot do this.

Another shortcoming of recommendation as a stand-alone measure, discussed somewhat earlier in the chapter, is that the same customer can, and often does, recommend or refer competitive brands, services, or suppliers in the same business sector. Nothing in the one-number technique requires a customer to narrow the consideration set or justify why he or she might recommend one or multiple brands or firms offering the same product or service. Because customer advocacy is more rigorous, connecting as it does on future purchase intent, and driven by brand impression and evidence of positive or negative word-of-mouth in behalf of the brand or company, there is often a natural reduction of consideration sets.

Customer advocacy behavior has been extensively discussed throughout the book; however, as it compares to individuals or customers who positively recommend, advocates are the deeply connected and brand-involved, energized, positive, and vocal de facto sales force within a company's, product's, or service's customer base.

Customer advocacy can, in part, be defined as the degree of kinship with, favorability toward, and trust of brands; but, principally, advocacy identifies the monetizing downstream customer behavioral impact of informal communication by individuals on a voluntary, active, peer-to-peer basis (and as it influences their own downstream behavior [i.e., the self-perception effect] as a result of personal experiences). Inclusion of the "personal experiences" qualifier is critical because it represents a depth of individual knowledge unidentified in the one-number recommendation approach. Consulting firms such as McKinsey have determined that word-of-mouth drives 20%–50% of customer decision making, so it is extremely important and every bit as leveraging as recommendation. Again, recommendation isn't word-of-mouth, nor is it advocacy behavior. It should be added that, just as recommendation isn't word-of-mouth or advocacy, neither is it customer loyalty (and it can't give management much guidance for creating loyalty or pinpointing motivations for individual purchase choices); however, as discussed throughout this book, much of true customer loyalty behavior can be identified in drivers of customer advocacy.

When considered as a core measure or metric of customer loyalty and business health, advocacy can be expressed as a combination of two key constructs: rational (tangible and functional) and emotional (service and brand impression) value perception of a brand, product, or service expressed through preference and a narrowed consideration, or evoked, set; a high share of spend; and positive, frequent communication behavior in behalf of the preferred company, brand, or product, principally through off-line and online word-of-mouth. As presented throughout the book, this approach, or framework, is far more robust, rigorous, and actionable when compared with the single-number recommendation metric, and the willingness to refer or recommend can be considered one *outcome* of loyalty or advocacy behavior, rather than the behavior itself.

Again, advocacy behavior isn't the same as promotion, nor is promotion the same as advocacy behavior.

The accuracy of the statement just made has been proved in multiple research studies. In a 2010 national study among customers of the 15 largest US banks (with full results presented elsewhere in this book), it was found that 90% of the customers identified as advocates were in the highest category of customers when the single-number recommendation metric was applied, while only 56% of these high single-number-metric customers were found to be advocates. In the same study, results showed that the highest group of single-number customers was 1.8 times more likely to open new accounts at their primary bank compared to the lowest group of single-number customers; however, using the advocacy framework, the advocates were 2.8 times more likely to open new accounts when compared to the antagonists, the lowest-performing group of advocates.

Thesis of Another, Nonresearch Company

Another organization, this one focused on helping companies design and maintain customer loyalty programs, has added more ingredients to the terminology confusion stew. In October 2008, it conducted a consumer research survey to identify the connections between customers who participate in loyalty programs and their word-of-mouth activity regarding brands, the programs themselves, and product categories. The study was thorough enough—about 3600 US consumers and 3600 Canadian consumers subdivided into specific demographic segments and word-of-mouth behaviors—and from it, the organization created its own breakouts and definitions of behavior.

The organization challenged the one-number approach and definitions by saying things like the single-number metric is "essentially a measure of customer satisfaction, and every market researcher knows that satisfaction scores are at best imperfect measures of customer behavior. We can reasonably expect at least some evidence of a say-do gap in [the single number score], as those customers who self-identify themselves as Promoters nonetheless fail to do any actual promoting. In these cases, [single number score] becomes the marketing equivalent of a tree falling in the forest with no one around to hear it" (Ferguson and Hlavinka 2009). The organization also created a new scoring system based on the following definitions and logic:

- *Advocates*—Consumers who are likely to recommend a product or service to other people in the next 12 months

- *Connectors*—Consumers who say they often have conversations with others about the products and services they use, and often, or always, recommend products or services they like to others

- *Champions*—Consumers who are both Connectors and Advocates (based on top two box scores to both questions, which were on a 10-point scale)

A dissection of these definitions reveals multiple challenges. First, the developers of this approach criticize the one-number approach and then utilize it as a core foundation of their technique and definitions. Second, there is absolutely no recognition of the strength or weakness of the consumer's own anticipated future purchase behavior for the product, service, or brand. Third, there is no identification of the role and impact of brand equity—the trust and relevance factor—in the consumer's behavior.

While their study report presents some interesting findings about the connections between word-of-mouth behavior and loyalty program activism, the simplistic thesis and definitions for advocacy and champions, though well intentioned, are less than edifying.

MAGIC VERSUS ACTIONABILITY

Objective critics of the one-number score, hoping to guide users, detractors, and those considering the technique, have made statements (in a LinkedIn group dialogue) like:

- "It is simply an indicator. It must be accompanied with a lot of additional information to really be helpful. You need to know why people will or will not recommend."

- "The approach is incomplete at best and potentially misleading at worst. Rather than simply accept the (technique) as a panacea for customer retention and business growth, executives must critically and objectively evaluate the merits and risks associated with this measure."

- "It is a red herring without backup questioning. What good is having a score if you can't explain what the score means?"

- "As a measure, it is cycloptic as it does not account for those who say they will recommend but will cancel the relationship when faced with a better, cheaper offer."

- "It doesn't work because it obsesses on the dynamics between two different groups while ignoring their velocities over time. I have seen a company lose 40% of sales in the same time period that the (one-number recommendation score) increased by 25%. Quite simply, the company lost a lot more detractors and neutrals than promoters, causing the equation to slope upward as sales caved."

So, marketers must truly understand which brands and products customers would consider within a category (known as the evoked, or consideration, set), what they're currently using, what their level of favorability is, and what their likelihood of saying positive and negative things about the product is. And if they then build recommendation into that kind of construct, they will have a framework that's more actionable: *customer advocacy.*

Here's the bottom line. A single metric is attractive, but its analytical limitations can be very dangerous. Marketers want to know more about their customers' perceptions and actions. They need to understand *why* levels of loyalty behavior are occurring, not just *what* is occurring or what the indicators are, on as subsegmented and individual a basis as possible. Again, referral and recommendation are important outcomes of loyalty, but they are not the end goal, or the holy grail, in and of themselves. Magic and potions may work for Harry Potter; however, marketers must understand customer behavior in the real world, and this must incorporate the leveraging effect of brand impression and positive and negative word-of-mouth.

Though many market researchers have been dismissive of the value of the recommendation question, expressed as net positive or net negative, they admit that it has created attention and acceptance. It has continued to endure due to the vacuum created by the absence of a better way of understanding customer behavior. Now, there is a better, more real-world, more actionable, consistent, and monetizing way. It is *customer advocacy*, the central theme of this book, and its benefits to corporations and decision makers are covered and explained, hopefully in sufficient and convincing depth.

7

The Other Side of the Coin: Negative Word-of-Mouth, and Customer Alienation and Sabotage

Daiji wa shoji kara: *Serious disasters come from small causes.*

—FEUDAL JAPANESE PROVERB

T he polar opposite of an advocate is a saboteur (or a "badvocate," as coined by leading PR firm Weber Shandwick). Saboteurs are the extreme of what we label as alienated customers, whose assessment of a supplier can range from mildly annoyed and disaffected to outright, revenge-seeking anger.

In B2C situations, more than half of customers report problems with one or more elements of their transactions with suppliers. These are customers who, having had a bad experience, will typically not tell the company about it (and there are multiple, well-documented reasons why so few customers actually complain) but will tell many of their friends, colleagues, and relatives through off-line and online means. This is "badvocacy," the alienated flip side of customer advocacy, which may be 20% or more of the consuming B2C and B2B public (as estimated by Weber Shandwick), varying by product, service, or supplier.

Alienated customers share many of the same characteristics as advocates, just in opposite ways in regard to their attitudes and behaviors. They are individuals who have poor opinions of certain organizations, brands, and products, and they speak or act as critics and detractors of these organizations, brands, and products. They communicate negatively to friends and families. They communicate negatively in their neighborhoods. They communicate negatively at work. They communicate negatively online, through chat rooms, rating sites, and blogs. Some may communicate negatively to small circles of friends, relatives, and acquaintances. The most motivated badvocates and saboteurs will go so far as to set up elaborate contra websites and encourage open griping from any and all about bad experiences.

Much of customer alienation and sabotage behavior, both B2B and B2C, has been spawned by frustration and disappointment over service and product experiences, and the feeling that brands and companies don't share their customers' concerns, leaving them unheard. Poor customer service experience is often the breeding ground for negative communication.

As will be explained later in the chapter, the dynamics of expression, both positive and negative, saw a major change with the rise of the internet. Initially, people went to websites to conduct their own research on brands, products, services, and organizations. Before too long, websites like Amazon and eBags were offering online customers the opportunity to rate products and services that they bought and used. Customers were also able to conduct pricing and performance comparisons and to offer opinions on their own experiences.

One key result of this online information accessibility was the realization that customers now had significantly more influence and power over product and service choice behavior (their own as well as that of others) than ever before. In fact, the pendulum for B2B and B2C customer decision-making influence had shifted away from companies. Consumers now owned the influence and could endorse or criticize companies, along with their products and services, both off-line and through online virtual soapboxes such as contra websites, podcasts, blogs, and communities. And, as will also be discussed in this chapter, sabotaging employees used many of these same online media to virally undermine their employers.

POTENTIAL BUSINESS IMPACT OF NEGATIVE WORD-OF-MOUTH

Studies conducted by academics and research organizations around the world have determined that negative social word-of-mouth, though less frequent than positive word-of-mouth, is at least as impactful on brand choice. For example, a 2006–2010 retail customer study among adult shoppers in the United States and Canada showed that of those experiencing problems, only 6% had contacted the company (in part because 46% of those who had a problem felt they would experience the same issue in the future), but 31% went on to tell friends and family. Of those, 8% told one person, 8% told two people, and 6% told six or more people (Baker Retailing Initiative/The Verde Group 2011).

Further, the study found that of 100 dissatisfied customers, a retailer would lose between 32 and 36 current or potential customers. Companies, as a result, need to monitor all negative communication, whether it appears online or off-line, and take steps to manage it. Otherwise, they may see financial consequences similar to those in Table 7.1.

Figures like these will get the attention of anyone in marketing, customer service, sales, or corporate management. Negative word-of-mouth, a principal component of alienated advocacy, can have a powerful bottom-line impact. This plays out, for instance, in further study results from the Baker Retailing Initiative and the Verde Group (2011). In addition to the negative communication resulting from bad experiences, almost half of

Table 7.1 Negative customer word-of-mouth can be expensive.

Lost customer	
1 unhappy customer who spends $200/month	$2,400 revenue lost/year
Lost business due to negative word-of-mouth	
1 unhappy customer	1
1 unhappy customer tells on average 11 other people	11
These 11 people each tell 5 others	55
Total number of people now negative	67
Assume 25% of those 66 people will not do business with you	17
Amount of lost opportunity from 17 people who spend $200/month	$40,800 revenue lost/year
Total business forfeited	
Due to 1 lost customer and associated negative word-of-mouth	$43,200 revenue lost/year $432,000 revenue lost over 10 years

those surveyed (48%) said they have avoided a store after learning of someone else's problems there. For those who had had a problem themselves, about one-third said they would "definitely not" or "probably not" return, and half felt they would probably experience the same problem or problems in the future.

Toyota Motor Corporation directly experienced the consequences of poor and reactive communication following the parade of recalls (over 8.5 million vehicles worldwide) and public airing of its quality problems (accelerator gas pedals and braking systems) in 2009. This included a 1% share of the US market (to 16.45%, according to Edmunds), and Kelley Blue Book stated that Toyota's resale value had declined $200–$500 for recalled models (a decline of 1%–3%). A 2010 US national quality perception study among prospective buyers showed that Toyota had fallen to seventh place among 36 brands, down from second in 2009 (BrandZ 2011). In the meantime, Ford has moved into sixth place in quality perception and into second place in US market share, at 16.57% of the market (behind General Motors' 18.12%), as identified by Edmunds' research ("Toyota Resale Value" 2010).

ADVOCACY AND ALIENATION BUZZ

A 2007 study among almost 600 adults by public relations firm Weber Shandwick found that a customer, after having an experience with a product or service, is more likely to forward negative information, on average, than positive information: 54% of those with a negative experience send information to others about their dislikes, compared to 45% of advocates who send information about products they like. Weber Shandwick has determined that these negative customers take their communication responsibilities even more seriously than advocates, feeling that they have a duty to protect, influence, and caution others. This is another reason why companies should actively monitor what is being said about them.

As mentioned earlier, RightNow Technologies has been conducting studies on the downstream impact of customer service for a number of years. In its 2008 study, for example, it found that while consumers are willing to recommend organizations and companies to others because of outstanding service, they are almost twice as likely to tell others about poor treatment. In addition, blogging about a negative customer experience is on the rise: 22% of consumers this year have posted negative feedback about a company versus only 13% in 2007.

This has enormous damaging potential, both among customers and those acquaintances they are likely to influence through off-line and online social word-of-mouth. The internet as negative viral enabler will be covered in the next section.

Weber Shandwick, as noted, has determined that 20% of the world's adult population is likely to be negative toward one or more companies and to express that negativism to at least 14 people each. Two of the industries most often singled out for frequently venomous off-line and online criticism are automobile manufacturers and airlines, which have been victimized on trip-planning sites and on Facebook and Twitter. General Motors has social media teams that regularly monitor comments on the internet, tweet and retweet, post on Facebook, and post on automotive blogs. Other automotive manufacturers have set up their own blogs and regularly meet with automotive bloggers to express their points of view (although, in the Weber Shandwick [2009c] *Risky Business* study, only 10% of executives surveyed felt that this was an effective method of protecting corporate reputations). American Airlines reaches out to people on social networking sites and posts information on lost luggage and canceled flights on its Facebook site, often before consumers have a chance to complain or criticize.

It should be recognized that companies can be criticized—both online and off-line—very quickly after a customer endures what is perceived as a negative experience. In Weber Shandwick's and KRC Research's 2007 study, *The New Wave of Advocacy*, one of the key findings was that, on average, nearly one out of two adults (45%) will express their dissatisfaction within one week after the experience. This is particularly important because, in the same study, Weber Shandwick and KRC Research found that, globally, 63% of consumers were making brand, product, and service decisions more quickly than a few years ago, with US consumers taking slightly longer. This puts more pressure on companies to monitor buzz and be prepared with measures to quickly counter or leverage it, depending on its negative or positive nature.

As an example of the impact of the speed of viral communications, in mid-November 2010, a Qantas pilot safely landed a jet in Asia after an engine had caught on fire. Close to 500 passengers were on board. Unlike the story of the "miracle on the Hudson" in 2009, when US Airways pilot Chesley "Sully" Sullenberger gained fame after landing his A320 in the river on the west side of Manhattan, Qantas didn't begin getting its story out for 12–18 hours after the incident. This wasn't soon enough to overtake the negative reports on Twitter that there had been a crash, and Qantas was forced into damage control rather than basking in the glory it really deserved.

THE INTERNET AS CUSTOMER ALIENATION AND SABOTAGE ENABLER

Although the majority of B2B and B2C purchase and relationship decision influence continues to come from off-line informal sources, the internet has had an undeniably pivotal role in creating, or undermining, consumer trust. For example, the 2010 *Decision Influence Index*, an international study co-generated by Fleishman-Hillard and Harris Interactive, shows that in some countries, consumers trust the internet more than they trust friends, family, and print media (McRoberts et al. 2010).

This study, conducted in France, Germany, the United Kingdom, Canada, China, Japan, and the United States (representing 48% of the global online population), found that the internet is becoming a critical medium for decision-making support, in addition to being a reliable research and communication tool. Internet users tend to look at many sources— search engines, corporate sites, blogs, review sites, chat rooms and forums, online communities, and so forth—when seeking information, suggesting that truth and trust come as a result of distilling material from multiple locations and perspectives.

The *Decision Influence Index* study found that, while there is some concern about too much information sharing on the internet (by about one-fifth of internet users), consumers generally are able to find blogs, sites, and boards that are credible and linked to their interest. An average of 39%, or twice the rate of those who expressed concern about this, believe it is safe to communicate with others online.

It must be recognized that for those seeking information online or who are communicating themselves, the lack of authentication and validation of individuals on social networking sites can be an issue. For example, in 2008, two researchers successfully impersonated Marcus Ranum, a security expert, on LinkedIn (Ranum did not have his own profile there). Within 12 hours, they had 42 connections to the phony profile and then joined several LinkedIn security networking communities to build credibility. Connection requests came from the CSO of a security firm, a former CSO of a Fortune 100 company, and even Ranum's own sister! The point here is that social networking sites like LinkedIn, MySpace, Facebook, Plaxo, and HighFive are all vulnerable, because they are open, "blind trust" social networking sites.

Internet users have a tendency to use multiple sources of information—credibility and trust in information are largely a function of the ability to locate and retrieve information from a variety of trustworthy sources and cross-check among them. They place strong trust in conversations with people they know, and they are also relatively trusting of comments posted by others. However, though the information may not be completely reliable, users will reference postings from others when making a decision. As an example, only 21% of internet users in the United States trust the comments of others, but 46% find the comments useful. This pattern—the gap between trust and usefulness—is also seen in Germany, France, and Canada.

Many of these comments occur on blogs and microblogs. Microblogging on sites such as Twitter has high awareness as an online communications medium (78%), and the *Decision Influence Study* found that one-third of aware consumers have a microblog account.

It should be noted that even though the number of blogs and microblogs is growing at a tremendous rate—and gaining influence on consumer decision making, news, and general information—trust and confidence drop significantly if the blog/microblog authors are identified as having been paid or having received free samples as a result of their postings. In the study, 82% of consumers reported being either skeptical or not trusting if they learned of the blogger having been given a free sample from a company he or she blogged about. If the blogger had been paid by a company he or she blogged about, there was a similarly reported low level of trust. The conclusion here is that credibility must be earned and sustained.

When making purchasing decisions, an average of 64% of internet users in the study considered online research to be either essential or very important. Though most users said the internet helped by giving them information to compare options, finding advice or support from other people, acting faster, saving money, and acting with more confidence were also prominently cited. Search engines were most frequently cited as a starting point, but decision aids on some products, such as those for children and packaged goods, were often comments from other people (about 70%). Other sources actively referenced were blogs and social networks, as well as company-sponsored websites and product/price comparison sites.

Overall, close to 40% of study respondents felt the internet would become more important and influential as a communication medium over the next several years. In China, 85% of internet users gave this opinion. Certainly, in all countries included in the research, consumers are already spending an average of 12–15 hours per week on the internet, about as much time as they spend watching television (except in China, where hours on the internet were twice as high as hours spent watching television). Excluding e-mail, a key study finding was that the internet has been growing as a recognized information source, rapidly catching up to off-line advice from friends, family, and colleagues. It also dramatically overshadowed information received through mass electronic and print media. For example:

- In the United States, 42% of those using the internet do not read magazines and 40% do not read a printed newspaper

- In Canada, 42% of those using the internet do not read magazines and 28% do not read a printed newspaper

- In the United Kingdom, 36% of those using the internet do not read magazines and 33% do not read a printed newspaper

France, Japan, and Germany reported similar results. In China, while few internet users do not read magazines or newspapers, they are much more active and advanced users, particularly in mobile communication.

One fact is becoming obvious: The internet will make protecting and managing reputations exponentially more challenging. As noted by TechCrunch's Michael Arrington in an early 2010 blog post:

> Trying to control, or even manage, your online reputation is becoming increasingly difficult. And much like the fight by big labels against the illegal sharing of music, it will soon become pointless to even try. The skeletons are coming out of the closet and onto the front porch. We'll look back on the good old days when your reputation was really only on the line with eBay via confirmed, actual transactions and LinkedIn, where you can simply reject anyone who leaves bad feedback on your professional life.
>
> Today we have quick fire and semi or completely anonymous attacks on people, brands, businesses and just about everything else. And it is becoming increasingly findable on the search engines. Twitter, Yelp,

Facebook, etc. are the new printing presses, and absolutely everyone, even the random wingnuts, have access.

Open access and freedom of speech on the internet have bred "reputation snipers," individuals who set up contra websites, post videos on YouTube, and give extremely negative ratings and reasons. The root causes of what leads them to act with powerful emotion-based messaging can typically be found in poor product or service experiences, or an undesirable outcome of a registered problem or complaint. Increasingly, companies have to proactively monitor and prepare for brand perception and image attacks that can create negative advocacy (alienation and sabotage) within the customer base and among potential customers and the general public as well.

Many industries and companies—specifically banks, retailers, hotels, restaurants, and public transportation services—have been affected by reputation attacks. On TripAdvisor, a site used by many business and tourism travelers, it has been found that customers will more frequently give feedback when they have had negative experiences. Eurostar, the rail service linking London and Paris via the Channel Tunnel, was bashed on TripAdvisor in late 2009 and early 2010 when successive snow-related issues caused hundreds of people to be stranded on the train, and in the tunnel, for hours (first at Christmastime and then at the beginning of January). This assault on the line's reliability had tremendous, and lasting, negative revenue impact for Eurostar. In another example, an Avis customer who booked a rental car online was told upon picking up the car that her actual rental price would be higher than the internet price quoted. The customer complained, and the furor caused Avis to send refunds to over 20,000 customers.

One particular example of a snowballing viral sniper attack is the song and video "United Breaks Guitars," written by a disgruntled airline passenger whose expensive Gibson guitar had been damaged by United Airlines baggage handlers. The video has had over 10 million views on YouTube and much exposure in print and electronic media. Had United made an early and appropriate response, this negative publicity would never have gotten out of hand. The second "United Breaks Guitars" video has had over a million YouTube views.

Another widely viewed example of online alienation and sabotage is the "Sleeping Comcast Technician" video, which has had close to 2 million YouTube views. This video was taken of a Comcast technician who was in a customer's home to fix a faulty modem and fell asleep while waiting for a service representative to tell him specifically what was wrong and needed fixing. Here again, a company was left exposed by a viral sniper.

An important element of negative online product and service communication is the "long tail," or the staying power of these blogs, podcasts, and ratings. The "United Breaks Guitars" and "Sleeping Comcast Technician" reputation grenades have been on YouTube for several years, and they continue to get publicity and views. A comment made February 7, 2008, on Canada.com spoke to this effect: "It's not the actual complaints, comments, or blog posts that hurt the most. It's the lingering Google search results that represent real death by a thousand cuts." Senior executives are, and must be, concerned about this. In its 2009 study, *Risky Business: Reputations Online*, a survey conducted among over 700 senior executives in 62 countries (mentioned earlier in this chapter), Weber Shandwick found that nearly 4 out of every 10 global executives surveyed fear that a dissatisfied customer or critic will launch a negative campaign against their company.

Two examples of this were covered in Chapter 2. Off-line and online criticism of R.J. Reynolds' "Joe Camel" campaign as being directed at adolescents and teens resulted in the character and the program being canceled. The negative site established to take on the pricing approaches of Bally Total Fitness gained much publicity, both on the internet and as a result of

Bally's losing suit in federal court against the site developer. As an article on the impact of online criticism noted:

> Armed with little more than a Web connection and a keyboard, these detractors can do everything from irritate, via a scathing review, to causing serious business problems by using message boards to reveal company secrets or spread rumors of unethical behavior. (Chura 2007)

A new breed of review sites has recently been developed, specifically to allow angry and unhappy customers (and employees) to vent with detracting, and even defaming, assessments of companies. One of these, a site called Honestly (which was originally called Unvarnished), was set up by founder and CEO Peter Kazanjy to provide an authoritative and anonymous alternative to the positive reviews often found on other social media, such as LinkedIn. What has made Honestly so controversial is that, while there are promises that truly "abusive" reviews will be identified and removed (because they may border on libel, which is a very specific, legally defined condition), no restraints are placed on what are identified as honest opinions. Essentially, the site has become a magnet for individuals with personal agendas (and they could be customers or employees) to submit negative posts. The concept of Honestly is not particularly new, as sites such as Ikarma and Jerk have been around for some time. Honestly, however, has gotten much more attention and has generated much more activity (and financial support).

With the rate of new consumer postings (one about every five seconds, according to Bob Crumpler [Boland 2008], CEO of BuzzLogic), companies must develop strategies to counter negative word-of-mouth and potentially leverage it to their advantage. One example of this is Starbucks, criticized through an online attack claiming that the company had denied a request for its coffee by US Marines in Iraq because Starbucks executives don't support the war. Starbucks acted quickly, posting on its website the number of pounds of coffee it gave to the

USO in Afghanistan, Kuwait, and Iraq, and using social media sites that have independent fact checkers and established credibility (like Snopes, Hoaxbusters, Truthorfiction, and Boycottwatch) to investigate and declare the rumor to be false.

There are also many examples of corporate overreaction, such as the federal court suit brought against the site developer of BallySucks.com, in which Bally lost its case on free speech rights guaranteed by the First Amendment of the US Constitution. Another instance, cited by Leslie Gaines-Ross (2010, 5), chief reputation strategist at Weber Shandwick, demonstrated how poorly prepared many corporations are to quickly and effectively deal with sabotaging online customers. This situation involved Horizon Group Management, a Chicago apartment leasing and management company, and is described as follows:

> In July, 2009, it [Horizon] sued Amanda Bonnen, a former tenant, for $50,000 because of the following rather modest tweet to her 20 or so followers: "Who said sleeping in a moldy apartment was bad for you. Horizon realty thinks it's okay." As the *Chicago Tribune* reported, the tweet came to light only after Bonnen's lawyers filed a class action suit against the firm for allegedly violating Chicago housing ordinances. Horizon, no doubt believing that turnabout was fair play, claimed that Bonnen had "maliciously and wrongfully published the false and defamatory tweet, thereby allowing the tweet to be spread throughout the world." To most minds, a $50,000 suit over a message read by two dozen people was an overwhelmingly disproportionate response. It instantly made headlines and soared to the top of news aggregator sites such as Google, News, Digg, and Techmeme. The judge threw out Horizon's claim; the only thing the company had accomplished was to create a public relations disaster.

EMPLOYEES AS SABOTEURS

A key source of alienation and sabotage can be a company's own employees. Like customers, employee attitudes and behaviors toward their employer can range from advocacy, which we will label as ambassadorship, to negativism and sabotage. Companies need to be alert and concerned, of course, about sabotage in the form of property destruction, security breaches such as hacking into salary and medical records (as has happened to companies like Yahoo, eBay, and Amazon), theft of proprietary information (such as trade secrets), and the like. Here, we are addressing negative employee communication to employees, customers, and others inside and outside the company, off-line and online.

Sabotage can be created by a single employee or by a group acting in concert. Domino's Pizza suffered a nightmare in 2009 when three restaurant employees made a video of themselves doing mischief with the ingredients that go on the company's pizzas and sandwiches. They posted the video on YouTube, and it received over 1 million views and was covered in print media such as *Advertising Age* and electronic media before Domino's succeeded in getting the site to take the video down. This incident took place a little more than a year after Taco Bell had to endure the negative fallout from an internet video posted by employees in one of its New York City restaurants showing rats in the kitchen. Both fast-food organizations engaged in online and off-line damage control, but this kind of sabotage affects the brand, sales, customers, noncustomers, and other employees. It underscores that in our transparent social media world, great damage can be done by a YouTube video, a Facebook update, or a Twitter tweet.

In research we have conducted to identify drivers of employee advocacy and sabotage, ambassadors were found to be both positive and vocal promoters and representatives of the company as a place to work, while most saboteurs never, or at least less frequently, said anything good about the company as an employer. Similar results were found for employees representing the company's products and services (i.e., its brand promise) to others both inside and outside the organization. The disparity between ambassadors and saboteurs in saying good things about the company's products and services was dramatic: Over 20 times more advocates always or almost always said positive things, compared to saboteurs (78.3% versus 3.7%). Saying negative things about the company's products or services was also significantly more prevalent among saboteurs. Over 45% of employee saboteurs said negative things about products or services at least some of the time, compared to only 2.6% of advocates. Again, companies need to focus on the multilayered consequences of such results, because they are both cultural and viral. This is covered in detail in Chapter 11.

Frontline employees, and those with clerical and mundane responsibilities, are frequently identified as the wellspring for corporate detraction and sabotage. They are portrayed as such in films such as *Office Space*, where fired employee Milton Waddams—who burns down the Initech building in retaliation for the company's moving his desk, taking his stapler, and firing him—goes on vacation to Mexico and famously says to the waiter serving him drinks on the beach: "Excuse me? Excuse me, señor? May I speak to you please? I asked for a mai tai, and they brought me a piña colada, and I said no salt, NO salt for the margarita, but it had salt on it, big grains of salt, floating in the glass . . . [as the waiter walks away] . . . And yes, I won't be leaving a tip, 'cause I could . . . I could shut this whole resort down. Sir? I'll take my traveler's checks to a competing resort. I could write a letter to your board of tourism and I could have this place condemned. I could put . . . I could put . . . strychnine in the guacamole. There was salt on the glass, BIG grains of salt. . . ." Now that's a saboteur!

Here are three notable recent instances of online and off-line employee sabotage, and what the victimized organizations did about them:

- At Lockheed Martin, a disgruntled employee was fired after sending a mass e-mail to 60,000 coworkers, crashing the company's system for almost a day. The e-mail asked for a receipt, doubling the congestion already created, and it took a team of IT experts and several hundred thousand dollars to recover the system.

- A former Intel employee sent mass e-mails to current and former Intel employees, criticizing the company. After Intel requested that the employee stop the e-mails and endeavored to block them, the company endeavored to sue him in the California Supreme Court. The court ruled that the employee's e-mails did not amount to trespass against Intel.

- A Walt Disney employee tampered with video release versions of the company's animated film *The Rescuers* by embedding obscene photos in several of the frames. Disney was forced to recall 3.4 million of these videos.

It should be recognized, however, that alienation can come from any level or function within an organization. In Weber Shandwick's 2009 *Risky Business* study, one of the key findings was that more than one-third of the executives interviewed reported knowing of a business colleague who had written something negative about his or her company online.

In that same study, online employee criticism was identified as a major concern of senior executives; it tied for first place with leaked confidential information (41%). Additionally, two-thirds of these executives either were not aware of or did not want to admit to the possibility that employees could be making negative statements about their employer online, which left one-third who knew of one or more employees who had posted something negative about the company online. Going forward, one of the study's key conclusions is that employees' online criticisms as reputation snipers will become a growing threat.

One result of employees' increased use of social media, both during and after working hours, is the need for policies and guidelines. Some companies, such as Zappos, recognize the value of blogs, communities, and forums, and they encourage active use of social media on the job. Others forbid it and make its discovery grounds for instant dismissal. Employees must be encouraged and trained to be ambassadors for the brand and to use social media in ways that will support their employer's reputation, not detract from it.

LESSONS AND PRESCRIPTIVES

In RightNow Technologies' 2010 customer experience impact report, the percentage of people who have told others about a poor experience had risen to 79%, its highest level ever. Of this group, 85% said that their motivation was to inform others, 66% wanted to discourage others from purchasing, and 55% just wanted to vent their anger. That's the bad news. The good news is that 92% of those who stopped doing business with a company because of poor service would go back if they received an apology or correction (63%) or were shown proof that the company had put processes or staff in place to enhance customer service (49%).

So the opportunity is there, but customers posting on social networking sites like Facebook and Twitter expect a response from the company—42% expect that response within a day. According to the study, only 22% of these customers actually get a response, so it is clear that companies have some way to go in monitoring negative online communication and providing feedback to alienated customers.

The negative word-of-mouth prescriptives, to the extent that alienation and potential sabotage can be managed off-line or online, are proaction when poor experiences occur, rapid apologies to the customer as warranted, and processes and training to prevent recurrence of these kinds of situations. Early in November 2010, a Carnival Cruise Line ship with nearly 3300 passengers and over 1000 crew members aboard was stranded without power off the coast of Mexico in the middle of a seven-day Mexican Riviera cruise. This was a result of an engine room fire. All key electrical systems were affected, including the air conditioning, hot-food service, and the telephones.

Carnival immediately dispatched tugboats to the location—about 200 miles south of San Diego—to tow the Carnival *Splendor* to Ensenada, Mexico (it actually ended up being towed to San Diego). At Carnival's request, the US Coast Guard station in San Diego and an American aircraft carrier from the Navy, the USS *Ronald Reagan*, provided assistance. Navy helicopters flew in food and other goods for the passengers and crew. Carnival offered magic shows (a convention of magicians was on board), blackjack tournaments, and trivia contests. The ship's bars offered free beer and wine during the Carnival *Splendor*'s last night before reaching San Diego.

Carnival quickly began sending announcements to the guests, keeping them updated on the situation. The ship's crew provided bottled water in addition to sandwiches and other cold food. Recognizing that the situation had been very trying for the guests, and in appreciation of their patience and for the inconvenience caused by the fire, Carnival's CEO advised passengers that they would receive a full refund and reimbursement for their transportation costs, along with a complimentary future cruise equal to the amount they paid for their Mexican Riviera voyage. In addition, they were offered the option of staying in San Diego an extra couple of days. Discounts were also issued for customers who had reserved passage on the Carnival *Splendor*'s next voyage. In cases such as this, especially where safety is an issue, the best defense against negative word-of-mouth is a good offense.

Leslie Gaines-Ross (2010) offers several techniques designed to help protect organizations from customer saboteurs and reputation snipers:

- *Avoid any show of force that could be perceived as grossly disproportionate* (such as the suits by Bally Fitness and Horizon Group Management). If history affords any lesson here, it is that the offended party, usually a large corporation, will come out on the wrong end of the reputation wormhole.

- *Respond at high speed with instincts honed by advance training.* Gaines-Ross notes that most companies are slow-moving and consensus-driven when working out a defense or response to an online (or off-line) reputation attack. Companies need to train themselves, or be trained, in how to utilize new media in a consistent manner for stabilization when saboteurs threaten them.

- *Empower frontline teams to meet sabotaging messages with positive messages.* Although we recommend that all employees be thought of as ambassadors and advocates for the company and its messages, it is particularly vital for frontline employees—sales and customer support— to perform this role.

- *Think "out of the box" in responding to threats, or as Gaines-Ross advises, "go rogue."* Earlier in this chapter, reference was made to a video made and posted by Domino's employees in North Carolina that cast Domino's in an unfavorable light. Domino's US president, Patrick Doyle, elected to use the same tactic his employees used in responding to the threat. He used YouTube because it was the same medium that the employees had used to sabotage Domino's. And, it had a sidebar benefit in that the use of YouTube by a corporate executive became a story in and of itself.

- *Recruit and deploy "force multipliers" who will echo your message.* Elsewhere in the book, reference was made to a quote by Professor Philip Kotler of Northwestern University, in which he advised corporations to recruit advocates to do their marketing for them. The same can be said of reducing or eliminating the threats posed by saboteurs. For example, Royal Caribbean International received negative press and blogs after docking at a private beach 60 miles from the site of the earthquake in Haiti, which had recently occurred. Unmentioned in this assault was the record of the cruise line's humanitarian aid to the country. Advocates used the blog site of Royal Caribbean's CEO, Adam Goldstein, to support the company's efforts to help victims of the devastation and rebuild the local economy. As a result of this positive counter-publicity, Royal Caribbean's election to continue cruises in the area, and also deliver relief supplies, was supported by two-thirds of respondents in an online survey by the site Cruise Critic.

- *Go into battle with credentials in place.* Reputations are a bit like bank accounts: subject to quick withdrawals and slow builds. Organizations like Baptist Health Care, the Container Store, Southwest Airlines, and Wegmans enhance their reputations by attaining such recognition as the Malcolm Baldrige National Quality Award and being included in *Fortune* magazine's "100 Best Companies to Work For." They can further polish their corporate apple by being known as supporting "green" initiatives and ethnic and gender diversity and by having immaculate ethics. All of these serve as forms of reputation armor and do much to protect companies from saboteurs and snipers.

As this chapter hopefully has demonstrated, sabotage is an outcome and consequence of B2B and B2C customers' ownership of greater control of the decision-making process, and even the

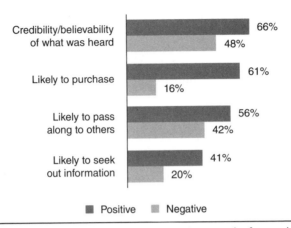

Credibility/believability
of what was heard — 66% / 48%

Likely to purchase — 61% / 16%

Likely to pass
along to others — 56% / 42%

Likely to seek
out information — 41% / 20%

■ Positive   ■ Negative

Figure 7.1   Effect of positive versus negative word-of-mouth according to internet users in the United States.

Source: Keller Fay Group, "Unleashing the Power of Word of Mouth," August 2010, http://kellerfay.com/consumers-believe-in-positive-word-of-mouth.

positioning of products, services, and companies. Organizations will need to adapt and prepare—and quickly—if they are to keep disaffected, angry, and even sabotaging customers and employees from undermining their ability to compete and survive. It's noteworthy that Weber Shandwick has gone so far as to create a social media crisis simulator, FireBell, for helping clients ready themselves for attacks from such individuals.

At the end of the day, according to studies by Keller Fay, though there is a pervasive belief that negative word-of-mouth has significantly more influence on customer decision making, the facts strongly suggest a different story. Positive informal communication not only dominates when brands are involved but also has more impact on attitudes and behaviors (see Figure 7.1).

There is considerably more credibility and believability associated with positive, brand-related word-of-mouth. As a result, this creates more of the trust that consumers need for decision making. Thus, the lesson of this chapter is that marketers should pay attention to the potential for negativism while they are focused on creating customer advocacy behavior.

8

Intersecting Inside-Out and Outside-In Customer Advocacy

Stakeholders are part of a complex network of interests that function in a matrix of interdependencies.

— Rajendra Sisodia, David Wolfe, and Jagdish Sheth,
Firms of Endearment

Marketers are—or should be—always concerned about what drives customer commitment and advocacy behavior. They tend to believe that customers gain experience with their enterprises—hopefully resulting in loyalty behavior—entirely through people, products, and services. This is largely true, as far as this thinking goes, but organizations often don't have enough awareness that what is said to customers—and how, when, and where it is said—has an equal, if not greater, behavioral impact. Communication is about *relevance, authenticity,* and *trust,* three essential elements in the way customers see suppliers. This is certainly created by employee interaction and other experiences, but it also comes from their own messages, plus customers' friends, relatives, and business colleagues.

In a time when customers have grown increasingly skeptical of supplier interest in their personal benefit—and also the traditional supplier "push" messages delivered from companies in any form or fashion—relevance, authenticity, and trust must be delivered at every touch point. This absolutely requires that the meld between messaging and experience be as seamless as possible. If companies want customers to advocate for them on the outside, the advocacy process needs to begin with the right messages, the right media, the right processes, and the right strategic experience creation. Banks, airlines, wireless telecoms, retailers, insurance companies, real estate agents, utilities, B2B companies, and even government agencies feel compelled to express the strength of their focus and allegiance, particularly in areas of service and relationship building, often as statements of commitment. Are the words companies use true differentiators of perceived benefit and value and of customer loyalty and engagement, or are they just reflections of expected basics of performance and often disbelieved?

When customers are considering alternative suppliers or making final purchase decisions, it is now becoming well understood that the principal, previously neglected choice criteria are the intangible, emotional relationship benefits, often with much of what is tangible, functional, and rational seen as one-dimensional and nondifferentiating. How well a company communicates and connects (i.e., bonds) with its prospects and customers—on both a transactional experience and strategic basis—is often the critical selection factor.

So, it's important for marketers to understand that customer commitment and advocacy behavior can happen in one of two ways. The first way, "inside-out" customer commitment and advocacy, is where companies endeavor to manage and influence attitudes and perceptions of customers (and prospects), as well as where, how, and when communication takes place. Note: "Outside-in" advocacy, the principal subject of this book, is brand impression/favorability and evidence of positive and negative informal peer-to-peer communication on behalf of the brand.

Many thought leaders offer insights into how organizations can create benefit for stakeholders through culture and value. Glen Urban, professor of marketing at MIT, initially outlined this very well in his book *Don't Just Relate—Advocate!* (2005). But another book, *Firms of Endearment* (2007), by marketing professors Rajendra Sisodia, David Wolfe, and Jagdish Sheth, does an even better job.

FIRMS OF ENDEARMENT: RECOGNIZING HOW THE NEW OUTSIDE-IN COMMUNICATION DYNAMICS ARE AFFECTED BY INSIDE-OUT ADVOCACY CREATION

In the book *Firms of Endearment*, Sisodia, Wolfe, and Sheth (2007) identify elements of a *stakeholder relationship management* (rather than a traditional stockholder and stock-price-focused) model for creating a strategic and emotional bond between the enterprise and its customers. Importantly, they recognize that the "invention" of the World Wide Web (by British software engineer Tim Berners-Lee) in 1991 fundamentally changed the balance of decision-influencing and informational power to the B2C and B2B consuming masses, along with changing the form and amount of interaction between peers. Most critically, it forced organizations to act with greater transparency.

Skepticism, information availability, and economic instability have combined to change the landscape of product and service decision making. As B2B and B2C consumers seek more meaning from everything—their work, their relationships, even the companies with which they do business—this means that organizations will be perceived as partners to the degree with which they can align their products, services, values, and culture with the needs of stakeholders. Very few companies have been able to do this, either at creation or through transformation; however, those that have succeeded are true performance exemplars.

Sisodia, Wolfe, and Sheth (2007) call such organizations "humanistic," as they seek to maximize their value to each group of stakeholders, not just to shareholders. These "firms of endearment" companies, which the authors refer to as "FoEs," have succeeded in aligning (not just balancing) the interests of all stakeholders. They are focused on employee hiring, training, and teamwork, and they empower employees to optimize and "humanize" customer experiences. They work in partnership with suppliers. The authors identify companies like Southwest Airlines—an organization with a 93-member Culture Committee, whose charter is to preserve Southwest's leadership position among airline companies and develop employee leaders on a local level who will live and share the culture with other employees, passengers, and the public—as unique.

For the authors, a truly great company is one that makes the world a better place because it exists. Simple as that. In the book, the authors identify about 30 companies from multiple industries that meet their criteria. They include, in addition to Southwest Airlines, CarMax, BMW, Costco, Harley-Davidson, IKEA, Jet-Blue, Johnson & Johnson, New Balance, Patagonia, Timberland, Trader Joe's, UPS, and Wegmans. Had the book been written a bit later, it's likely that Zappos would have made their list as well.

Sisodia, Wolfe, and Sheth (2007, 16) compare the financial performances of their selections with the 11 public companies identified by Jim Collins in *Good to Great* as superior in terms of investor return over an extended period of time. Here's what they learned:

- Over a 10-year horizon, their selected companies outperformed the *Good to Great* companies 1028% to 331% (a 3.1 to 1 ratio)

- Over five years, their selected companies outperformed the *Good to Great* companies 128% to 77% (a 1.7 to 1 ratio)

The public companies singled out by *Firms of Endearment* returned 1026% for investors over the 10 years ending June 30, 2006, compared to 122% for the S&P 500, more than an 8 to 1 ratio. Over 5 years, it was even higher—128% compared to 13%, about a 10 to 1 ratio.

How did they do it? By what magic did these companies achieve such stellar results? According to the authors, it begins with "emotionally intelligent" management—a concept from author Daniel Coleman, who wrote on this subject in the 1990s. This is the ability to be self-aware and self-regulating, emotionally and socially—a capability the authors recognize as being absent or ignored in most organizational cultures, even those that are otherwise fairly customer-centric. However, it is a necessary component of leadership development at all levels and in all functions of any company. Without it, the authors assert, the tone of the enterprise and its culture—how much people give and want to give, and how much they care about the enterprise and its stakeholders—will be blighted, yielding low morale and interpersonal consideration, and high levels of conflict and stress. The result is that business effectiveness, that is, bottom-line results, will suffer.

Also recognized is the power of communications, both inside and outside the organization. As the authors state, "Instead of business-controlled monologues, the marketplace is now dominated by conversations. People talk to each other as never before about the companies they work for, buy from and invest in. This is forcing companies to operate with greater transparency. But that is not a problem for companies with nothing to hide, as firms of endearment have discovered. Transparency helps customers, employees, and other stakeholders develop trust in a company. It has proven to be effective as a motivating force among employees" (57). The importance of *trust, authenticity,* and *transparency* in communication and advocacy creation was discussed in detail in Chapter 3.

Zappos is an example of such organizational faith in employees and their communication, with one another and with customers, that staff members are encouraged to interact with one another, and with customers and the general public, through high-participation Twitter accounts.

Much of the creation of trust, per the authors, has to do with the employees who create differentiated customer experiences. Though this will be discussed more fully in Chapter 11, the relevant points made by Sisodia, Wolfe, and Sheth are that, beginning with the hiring process, firms that create strong bonds with their customers select employees on the basis of both skill set fit and fit within the culture. L.L. Bean looks for employees who are dedicated outdoor types. Whole Foods and Trader Joe's look for people who like dealing with food as a key part of their lives. Harley-Davidson looks for new staffers who are into motorcycles.

Finally, the authors identify some unique operating traits among their chosen examples of cultural excellence (8–11):

- Decision making is decentralized, but in ways that actually increase the visibility and influence of key executives throughout the company

- Frontline staff (i.e., those dealing directly with customers) are paid higher rates compared to their peers at other companies

- These companies spend far less on marketing and advertising than their competitors, depending more on their inside-advocacy creation abilities to drive outside-in customer advocacy (a cornerstone of the book)

This last point, of course, is particularly important. Truly excellent companies rely on advocating customers, employees, and suppliers to spread the word, reducing the need for advertising to build awareness and public relations to build reputation. Google, for instance, became one of the world's most valuable brands without any advertising. The authors note that one of their example companies, Jordan's, spends only about 2% of gross revenue on marketing, compared to 7% for the average furniture retailing chain, yet generates square-foot sales that are five times that of most furniture stores (10).

To create an organizational culture that is loved and respected by all stakeholder groups, three primary elements are required: a strategic vision, a set of core values, and perceived energy and perseverance. This vision, a common theme to all companies studied in *Firms of Endearment*, is based on maximizing creation of value. The binding force for keeping these companies focused and centered is the set of values to which they commit. The energy, visible to customers as they interact with the company and to employees as they go about their work, is a reflection of the passion and commitment they generate.

DELIVERING HAPPINESS—THE ZAPPOS STORY

Zappos, the highly successful online footwear and clothing retailer, has been mentioned quite a lot in this chapter, so it's time to provide some additional details about the distinctive alchemy of the organization. Zappos has all the traits identified in *Firms of Endearment*.

First, serial entrepreneur Tony Hsieh, CEO of Zappos, is an evangelist for his company's culture and what makes the company successful. He has traveled the country (in a specially designed bus, no less) presenting the Zappos story—"Delivering Happiness" (see Figure 8.1)—to rapt marketing executives and students eager to learn what has taken the company from $0 to over $1 billion in sales in a few short years. Hsieh describes the culture as being built on a foundation of

Figure 8.1 The outside-in advocacy Zappos has created is pretty straightforward.

inside-out and outside-in stakeholder advocacy. Zappos has been one of *Fortune* magazine's "100 Best Companies to Work For" for the past two years. Amazon purchased the organization, with the critical proviso that the company would remain intact and independent within the Amazon empire.

DIFFERENCES BETWEEN INSIDE-OUT AND OUTSIDE-IN CUSTOMER COMMITMENT AND ADVOCACY

It's fair to summarize the differences between inside-out and outside-in customer advocacy simply by saying that outside-in advocacy can't exist without first having an enterprise single-mindedly focused on creating value for customers. There are no chicken-and-egg questions here, but there are love-and-marriage issues. Love, through experience, is where the advocacy relationship starts; marriage is where it sustains.

Here are several additional quick examples of inside-out customer advocacy, two of them from *Firms of Endearment*, where companies are successfully managing both message and experience:

- *American Express (Red)*—This is a UK program designed for high-net-worth "Conscience Consumers" (or "Cappuccino Liberals," as American Express defines them). This market segment was estimated at 1.5 million in 2008, growing to 3.5 million by 2009. The American Express (Red) program affiliation is through U2 front man Bono and Robert Shriver (chairman of AIDS/Africa group). When cardholders spend up to $10,000 per year using this credit card, 1% goes to the Global Fund for HIV/AIDS; the amount rises to 1.25% above $10,000 per year. Special events for (Red) program members are held on a regular basis, which represents millions of dollars in promotion for American Express and the program, with almost no advertising.

- *Harley-Davidson*—Harley-Davidson, which was almost bankrupt in 1985, is now the most successful motorcycle company in the world, with over $14 billion in capitalization ($2 billion higher than General Motors). The organization spends less than $1 million on advertising each year, instead depending on "mystique" and customer engagement, with direct customer input into company operations for new products. Harley-Davidson's recipe for profitable growth has been largely through Harley Owner's Group (H.O.G.) clubs, where new members enjoy their first year for free. Since its formation in 1983 with 50 original members, the club has grown to almost 1 million members in 25 countries, with 1200 local chapters. Half the H.O.G. members attend Harley-Davidson events and rallies at least once a year.

- *LEGO Group*—Based in Denmark, LEGO Group is one of the top five toy companies in the world. It produces over 15 billion "bricks" a year, covering 2400 products, with

90 colors. Word-of-mouth is essential for LEGO Group. It has, for example, created clubs for kids ages 6–12, which now have over 2 million members. It also has a magazine for children that is printed in four languages. In addition, LEGO Group has clubs and an active blogging and event program for adult LEGO enthusiasts. Its website has over 5 million visits per year. The company sponsors the FIRST LEGO League for kids ages 5–14, where teams of 10 build LEGO robots in tournaments. At the LEGO Learning Institute, educators study how children learn best.

- *Commerce Bank (now TD Bank, as of late 2008)*—Identified as "America's Most Convenient Bank," Commerce Bank is the nation's fastest-growing financial services company, with over 400 "stores" in eight states along the eastern seaboard. Commerce Bank has a unique retail concept, built on an advanced service model (including seven-day branch banking, extended weekday and weekend hours, and staff trained at WOW University). This is a highly proactive, customer-centric culture, with programs aimed at building family-based relationships (WOW Zone activities and financial training for kids, Penny Arcade for counting coins, etc.). Until recently, the company did almost no traditional media advertising, but now uses Regis Philbin and Kelly Ripa as spokespeople.

There are now brands such as Google, Harley-Davidson, Trader Joe's, Red Bull, and Apple, each having a dedicated and enthusiastic group of customers or users who are more than just loyal; they are customer advocates. Once these select companies built a corps of customer advocates, they began to enjoy benefits that most brands could only imagine. They get massive word-of-mouth exposure, they have lower customer acquisition costs, they have lower customer service and marketing costs (or none in the case of Google), they can readily enter new market areas, and so forth. The most remarkable example of customer advocacy may be Google, which not only doesn't do any marketing (in the traditional sense) but also doesn't have any customer service. And yet, Google still has a large cadre of users who are passionate about its value proposition.

"Outside-in" commitment and advocacy occurs when customers informally influence the behavior of others (customers and prospects) in behalf of selected (i.e., strongly, and often singularly, preferred) suppliers. This takes place through one-to-one or group communication, online and off-line, including positive communication and/or direct or indirect recommendation. The way we measure customer advocacy (identified as the active expression of commitment) enables companies to identify what drives both true advocacy behavior (leading to high wallet share) and indifferent, or even sabotage, behavior.

Figure 8.2 identifies the components of word-of-mouth communication, as well as each component's potential impact on brand/supplier perception and customer behavior.

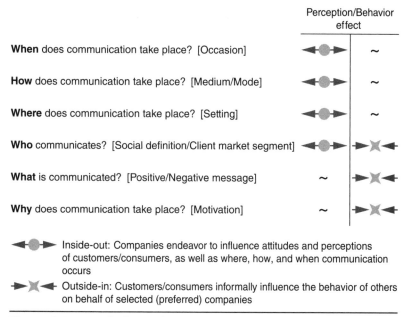

Figure 8.2 Word-of-mouth communication impact grid.

If companies manage to successfully drive either inside-out or outside-in customer commitment and advocacy, then the challenge is to create *both* inside and outside advocacy. As good an example as Harley-Davidson might be of achieving this, I'd suggest that there's a better one. It's IKEA. Of all the retail companies, IKEA's combination of a unique selling concept, low prices, and terrific customer service has yielded a level of customer commitment and advocacy unmatched around the world. At the same time, the company has balanced customer commitment with a peerless product sourcing, inventory management, and staff training program.

SUSTAINING THE EXECUTION: CUSTOMER-FIRST TEAMS AND GROUPS

In the late 1960s and early 1970s, Xerox Corporation's Palo Alto research and development labs in California created embryonic versions of what would become the personal computer. They even developed a working model of the internet.

However, Xerox didn't capitalize on the opportunity this represented. Its executives only saw Xerox as the leading copier company, and no amount of effort by the Palo Alto engineers and researchers could change their minds. Instead, young entrepreneurs like Steve Jobs and Bill Gates, who were exposed to what was going in Palo Alto, incorporated Xerox's leading-edge ideas into their own work. Today, Xerox is in a catch-up position within the computer industry, rather than leading it.

What are the key lessons here? We believe it's that the voice of the customer, a key component of the customer-centric organization, wasn't a focus within Xerox, and that the combined strength of staff beliefs and customer interest wasn't sufficient to move executives to support and encourage the development activity. Companies succeed in their markets—and succeed in keeping the customers they want and leveraging their behavior—by using mechanisms that enable them, at all times, to be as close to their customers as possible. Perhaps the best way to do this is through flatter organizational structures and formation of "customer first" teams throughout the company.

It's safe to say that most companies give little or no thought to creating a team-based culture that optimizes employees' efforts to create customer loyalty and advocacy and, at the same time, builds in team mechanisms to keep customers from defecting.

Creating a team-based customer culture requires an understanding of the customer, and then reflecting that understanding in the structure and systems that are designed. Two key questions should be asked:

1. How well and how often is teamwork directed at the goal of customer loyalty and advocacy behavior in the company?

2. What approaches can be taken to move from a traditional hierarchical structure to a customer-focused organization?

Although somewhat rare, there are companies that have been able to effectively create teams, and demonstrate teamwork, where the customer is intimately involved. Examples of this are Southwest Airlines, where customers are included in teams that make personnel hiring decisions, and Chrysler Corporation, whose Design Center has customers work with teams of technical company specialists to develop new vehicle concepts. In the car rental industry, one company created a cross-functional team that included customers to address a major customer headache—transaction time involved in the rental itself. One result of their work was the upgraded service that enables customers to be taken directly to their vehicles without having to stand in line or fill out paperwork.

THE VALUE OF CUSTOMER-FIRST TEAMS

IBM has refocused its business. The guiding vision of former CEO Louis Gerstner was to make IBM the information technology company for America's corporations. As he's said, "I came here with the view that you start the day with customers, that you start thinking about a company around its customers, and you organize around customers" (Griffin and Lowenstein 2001, 231–232). Much of IBM's new focus, commitment, and service orientation have been achieved through a more team-based architecture.

David Gee is an example of how IBM gradually turned itself inside out to get closer to customers. In the basement of IBM's Almaden Research Center in San Jose, Gee heads up a team of 12 staffers whose mission is to reinvent how the company does business. Their program, alphaWorks, is IBM's "online laboratory," which was created to change how the company commercializes products and communicates with customers. As Gee says, "And part of our job is to shake up the status quo. We want to get in trouble. We bend the rules" (Ramsdell 1998, 182).

AlphaWorks has not only introduced five new internet-based products but also achieved success in a manner that would have been a much greater challenge within the structure of the "old" IBM. Gee's team has assembled a network of over 60,000 users who demo and experiment with alphaWorks's new ideas. In other words, they've found a way to incorporate customers directly into the development and follow-up operational support aspects of their programs. That has made a significant impact on the rest of the company. As Gee concludes, "I'm not going to tell you that we've changed the world. But, we are making a difference. And in a company this size, even a small win is a huge victory" (182). If a large company like IBM can see the advantages of customer-first teams, any company can.

Tom Peters (1992, 12) has said that, in the future, "most work will be done by project teams. The 'average' team will consist of various people from various 'organizations' with various skills. Networks of bits and pieces of companies will come together to exploit a market opportunity." Such can certainly be the case with customer loyalty and customer recovery programs.

MathWorks in Natick, Massachusetts, is a matrix-run company where everyone in the entire organization is on multiple cross-functional teams. A leading developer of high-level math software, MathWorks has several hundred staff and over 100,000 customers. It has succeeded in weaving cross-functional teams and customers not only into its structure but into its culture and company values as well. Elizabeth Haight, MathWorks's vice president of operations, spearheaded the structural move to teams several years ago. In an April 2000 telephone interview with the author, Haight described what they've accomplished:

> We pretty much have a matrix-run organization. Title doesn't mean much here. Everything we do is through cross-functional teams, at every level. So, the goal here is to get the right people with the right knowledge in the room, not to get the people with the right title in the room.
>
> People come in to our company expecting to work cross-functionally. Another thing that has helped make us successful is that we've rolled out values that people live by. We went through a process of discovering what our values were, and we invited people throughout the organization in defining what they were. We've now folded values into everything we do, whether it's management training, people's vocabulary, how they act, and even what they're rated against.
>
> I think we've been successful with it mostly because it's from the president on down. The president lives these values, and I think that's where a lot of companies go wrong. They discover what they are, they roll the values out, and then the executive group goes off and behaves in any manner they want.

Jordan's, a New England furniture chain, is another example of a company that succeeds in part because of its J-team concept. All employees, as ambassadors of the organization, are empowered to do whatever it takes to serve customers. This team-oriented approach, as at other leading companies, gives employees a sense of both empowerment and purpose, as they help optimize customer experience.

INSIDE-OUT CUSTOMER-FIRST APPROACHES AT ROYAL BANK OF CANADA

Within banking, as in many other financial services markets, studies of customers often reveal strong commoditization, one-dimensional nondifferentiation where one bank seems much the same as another. Although there is a certain amount of inertia in this marketplace—difficulty in moving accounts and relationships between financial institutions—there is also very little true commitment, or customer advocacy, behavior in this business sector.

Royal Bank of Canada (RBC) is one of very few institutions that are bucking that trend. RBC studies have shown that the level of employee commitment accounts for 60%–80% of bank customer satisfaction, and 40% of the difference in how customers view RBC's services can be linked directly to their relationship with bank staff.

One key area of focus for RBC's Client First initiative has been the contact center. RBC has identified contact-based loyalty drivers and detractors for each line of business. For example, one detractor is long hold times in the contact center, and one driver is a bank employee offering someone financial advice. RBC calls such detractors value "irritants," and executives decided to eradicate those annoyances. Now, tracking and removing them is a declared strategy for every line of business.

Successful execution of the Client First strategy has turned the RBC culture into a service organization. The contact center, consisting of 5000 employees across five large centers and multiple smaller ones, has significantly elevated its service levels because of agent empowerment, an initiative to actually listen to customers and parlay agent-monitoring techniques. That's where the "I Make It Right" program comes in. RBC supports its agents by exposing all senior executives to bank customer contact center experience and having them periodically listen to calls.

The company also helps CSRs improve their first-call and problem resolution by investing in frontline resources like training and coaching and by monitoring processes and technologies. One of the contact center's main goals in supporting its agents is to try to make it easy for customers to conduct business with RBC. Uniquely, the bank calls itself a "relationship organization," emphasizing long-term, positive, and strategically differentiated customer value. RBC achieves this by having agents listen closely to customers to understand their needs and then connect to them in an emotional way that brings their experience to life.

Client First, in the contact center and throughout RBC, is considered a continuing journey. In the first 18 months of the program, the company saw service levels improve by 50%, along with consistent improvements on all key loyalty drivers, such as overall customer satisfaction, first-call resolution, the quality of financial advice, ease of conducting business, and the likelihood of recommending products or services to others. The Client First strategy has definitely changed the way customers perceive RBC, significantly improving both loyalty and bottom-line profitability.

TEAMS PUT PATIENT SERVICE ON THE ROAD TO RECOVERY

A fitting final example of how customer-first approaches, typically through employee teams, can affect customer loyalty and customer win-back as well as staff loyalty, comes from Baptist Hospital in Pensacola, Florida. Several years ago,

Baptist Hospital ranked close to the bottom of all hospitals in national surveys of patient service performance. This situation also contributed to both declining patient populations and low staff morale.

As part of its improvement journey (covered elsewhere in this book), Baptist Hospital formed 10 cross-functional employee teams to examine every aspect of value delivery to patients and their families. More than 150 hospital employees now participate as team members. Each team has membership as diverse as corporate vice presidents and cafeteria workers.

The product of the teams' work has been literally hundreds of recommended and applied initiatives that, viewed collectively, have significantly upgraded patient care. Among the changes they made were:

- Developing a series of scripts for staff to use when interacting with patients. For example, after cleaning a room, janitors are trained to offer their help to patients, such as closing a window shade, changing the volume on their television set, or opening or closing doors. Calls to nurses for such tasks have declined by 40%.

- Empowering employees to spend up to $250 to replace lost patient property or purchase flowers in response to patient complaints.

- Encouraging employees to be more proactive with patients. Accomplishments are featured in hospital newsletters and local newspapers. One example is a hospital cashier who voluntarily washes laundry for patients' out-of-town visitors.

Patients and their families have seen the tangible differences in patient service. As a family member of a Baptist Hospital patient remarked, "We got lost when my mother was a patient here, and a cleaning lady, instead of pointing, took us where we needed to go."

Today, Baptist Hospital's service performance ranks among the very best in national customer surveys, its market share has significantly improved, staff morale is higher, and staff loss—and the money previously spent for recruiting as a result of turnover—has declined. Hospital executives do their part to sustain the culture of commitment. They regularly e-mail patient comments to department heads and key team members. One recent e-mail described praise from a parent of a patient on the outstanding performance of Baptist's ER department and Heart Center, and it speaks directly to the positive impact of teams on patient recovery:

> Her son was a patient here recently, and she said the kindness, care and compassion exhibited by these people was incredible. In fact, she said she didn't like Baptist before this encounter, but that she would seek her future healthcare here.

A definite testament to the power of inside-out customer advocacy creation.

WHAT KINDS OF TEAMS WILL ENHANCE CUSTOMER LOYALTY— OR BRING BACK LOST CUSTOMERS?

As demonstrated by Baptist Hospital, companies have lots of options regarding the kinds of loyalty-enhancing project teams they can form or the tasks they can accomplish. There could be a team that examines products and services. Elements of the company's array of products and service offerings could be analyzed for potential negative impact on customer loyalty. Team members would evaluate trends in usage of the product or service by product group, setting up or drawing from a database of customer information on their usage, and perhaps conducting original qualitative or quantitative research or getting direct input from current or former customers during team meetings.

Another team might look at communication methods and contact processes. For instance, are there elements of the company's customer service techniques, such as the words or the tone that representatives use with customers, that can be improved? Are hiring and training practices optimal? Is it easy or difficult to reach the supplier to place an order or ask a question? Finding out where staff require training or which processes need to be improved can greatly increase the value created for customers, as can bringing in the most customer-oriented new staff. Do methods of communication convey value to customers? Do they strategically differentiate your company in a positive way? Does the company have listening posts for regularly hearing the customer's voice, and understanding how customers feel about the company and its competitors? These can certainly be a team focus.

One organization that has a customer relationship management team is Vistakon, the Johnson & Johnson company that produces and distributes disposable contact lenses. Vistakon actively believes in using multilevel, cross-functional teams for addressing key decisions. This team was formed to survey its customers' needs and expectations, measure the company's effectiveness in meeting those needs and expectations, and deliver useful, actionable information to its internal business partners.

Does the company take advantage of new technologies, such as online customer personalization and targeted messaging? Is the company's information system set up to aid in decision making regarding customer loyalty? Is the computer set up to use all of the material that cross-functional teams could evaluate about company's website for areas of greater potential customer value? A team could be assembled to analyze customer complaint data, both complaints that the customer communicates directly and complaints that the company uncovers through proactive means, such as loyalty research. Some complaints, obviously those most closely related to perceived customer value, have the power to cause defection. Team evaluation of complaint root causes could yield significant process or communication method improvement recommendations.

With regard to customer loyalty programs themselves, teams could be established to look at frequency marketing or customer reward programs, perhaps conducting original research. There is such an array of points-based approaches, added services, and volume purchase incentive techniques in use that this could be addressed by more than one team.

The array of cross-functional customer-first team possibilities is limited only by an organization's willingness to embrace the concept. Bottom-line: Customer-first teams enhance loyalty and advocacy behavior.

SEEKING CUSTOMER INPUT ON A DIRECT BASIS

Increasingly, companies in different industries are seeking customer guidance on everything from service evaluation to communication planning as a means of leveraging customer advocacy behavior and growing the enterprise. If other companies follow their examples, this could change the face of business in a positive way, for customers and for the businesses themselves.

Southwest Airlines

Today, there's very little argument that employee behavior directly and indirectly influences customer marketplace behavior, especially at critical engagement touch points. Few industries experience as many opportunities for relationship success or failure as airlines. Southwest Airlines, long known for having the highest perceived value and strongest levels of customer loyalty in the business, puts a great deal of emphasis on employee selection to make certain the company maintains its strong customer franchise. Southwest leaders consider organizational alignment with customer needs, particularly in positions with direct customer contact, so important that each year the company hires only 3% of the pool of applicants—those the company has identified as most closely reflecting and representing Southwest's unique culture and personality.

Selecting motivated and customer-oriented employees requires rigorous and creative interviewing and screening. Part of the multistage staff choice process at Southwest includes team interviewing of each applicant. Teams are made up of human resources staff from the field and from headquarters, but they also include loyal business and pleasure fliers. The teams quiz prospective employees on their most embarrassing moments and how they handled them, their greatest accomplishments, and how they would function in difficult situations, such as canceled flights.

John Deere

John Deere maintains a dealer advisory council for helping the company with merchandising, marketing, and channel decisions. For instance, when the company made the decision to sell entry-level products at the Home Depot, its retail advisory council helped John Deere address the resistance some dealers felt and helped capitalize on the increased exposure among consumers. And, as John Deere has increasingly moved into nonfarm products and simultaneously sought to make its retail experience more consumer-friendly, the advisory council has helped with both store layout and retail formatting.

An additional, and very specific, use of the advisory council's direct input to marketing decisions has been John Deere's focus on women. The company's research indicated that women influence or directly make 80% of lawn tractor purchases, leading the advisory council to help prepare clinics for women to learn about lawn care and the company's products. This has been essential in building relationships with dealers and customers in this marketing push.

John Deere is also proactive in having the customers themselves contribute directly to product and service development. A good example of this is the company's line of golf products. Each year, John Deere flies groundskeepers from around the country to its headquarters in Moline, Illinois, for the purpose of providing direct input to design and production staff on its golf course equipment development.

Dorothy Lane Markets

Known as "the store that accommodates," Dorothy Lane, a three-store high-end specialty supermarket chain in suburban Dayton, Ohio, prides itself on exceptional customer service. While it carries many products that are similar to the inventory of conventional supermarkets, the store is noted for its extensive selection of perishable and specialty items, artisan products, and natural and organic foods.

One of Dorothy Lane's approaches for generating customer insight, and optimizing each customer's shopping experience, is unique within the supermarket industry. Each of the three stores maintains a consumer advisory board, a cross section of Dorothy Lane Markets shoppers who offer suggestions for improvement. The advisory board, with members recruited to serve a two-year term, meets regularly at the store.

CONCLUDING THOUGHT

Our primary and secondary research into the underpinnings and drivers of customer loyalty behavior show that organizations can manage customer commitment and advocacy only to the extent that they can create and sustain strength of the brand or the company's value proposition franchise. This is inside-out advocacy creation.

In a study by the Chartered Institute of Marketing in the United Kingdom of 1,000 adults, only 8% believed that regular contact with suppliers was more beneficial to them than to the suppliers, while 50% thought that such an ongoing relationship benefited the suppliers. Worse, only 9% of the respondents said they wanted that contact to be driven by the supplier (Jackson 2001). These are alarming numbers, and they strongly suggest that consumers are rejecting common customer relationship practices.

To succeed at customer relationship and experience management, the cold reality is that frequency programs are not enough. Great product is not enough. Exceptional service and customer-sensitive staff, though incredibly important, are not enough. Use of new communication technologies and multiple channels is not enough. Tight, efficient operational processes are not enough. What truly leads to loyalty and advocacy is the company-wide commitment to customers—strategic customer centricity, if you like—along with the ongoing creation of customer-perceived value and barriers to exit.

Success is defined by three outcomes: the highest share of customer possible, optimal lifetime customer value generation, and the lowest voluntary churn. This requires both discipline and commitment. It's not easy, and nobody promises it will be. But it is elegantly simple.

9

How Do Companies Create Higher Levels of Customer Advocacy Using Informal Social Communication?

Word-of-mouth and evangelism are gifts that customers give you,
but you must first earn them, for money doesn't buy goodwill.

—BEN MCCONNELL AND JACKIE HUBA, *CREATING CUSTOMER*
EVANGELISTS: HOW LOYAL CUSTOMERS
BECOME A VOLUNTEER SALES FORCE

N ow that the marketing and monetary value of customer advocacy creation through voluntary, informal social communication has been established, this chapter will provide some strategies and tactics for effective, positive brand building and customer behavior leverage.

The roots of today's worldwide social networking growth, particularly online, have been well documented. Networking is the confluence of several factors, one of which is the rise in use of the internet and the mobile devices to access it. Another is societal. This book is entirely about what influences consumer behavior in today's world and how marketers can leverage these factors, but the sociological trends behind behavioral drivers also deserve mention. In books like Robert Putnam's *Bowling Alone: The Collapse and Revival of American Community* (2000), the isolation of individuals and the desire for community (through technological means) are thoroughly chronicled. Putnam identifies this as the decline of "social capital" found through community activities, and connections in general, and asks how it can be rebuilt. Shortly after Putnam's book was published, embryonic online communities such as iVillage began to gain recognition. In addition to these communities of interest, very progressive companies also paid attention to the networking phenomenon. Organizations like Amazon began building customer communities, and thus, what we know as the "network effect," better understood as viral communication or word-of-mouth, had begun.

Consumers could now give positive and negative voices to their feelings, attitudes, and opinions. For marketers, the challenge became how to harness and use these social networks and the mountains of available consumer information to best effect. Many books, such as Andy Sernovitz's *Word of Mouth Marketing* (2009b), do an excellent job of offering global how-to guidance on ideas, tools, and methods for creating more active word-of-mouth. Using Sernovitz's Five T's model (Talkers, Topics, Tools, Taking Part, and Tracking) as a general template, the initial and final parts of this chapter will focus on what companies should be doing to engage with, have dialogue among, and create customer advocates, both online and off-line. This includes:

- Online social platforms—blogs, chat rooms, instant messaging, message boards/forums, video-sharing websites, social networking websites (Facebook, MySpace, LinkedIn, Plaxo, Digg, and YouTube), and mini-blog sites (Twitter)

- Review sites

- Wikis

- Texting

- Promotional and demonstration events: dealerships, retailers, high-tech and telecom companies, and so forth

Increasingly, organizations have been applying online and off-line social communication to build business and customer relationships. For example, Lenovo leveraged its $120 million Olympic sponsorship in 2008 by recruiting 100 Olympic athletes, offering each a free technology solution and asking them to blog live from Beijing. The athletes recruited weren't "names" from major sports who would draw high media attention, so this was not a typical paid endorsement. The Lenovo campaign, offering an insider's view of the Olympics, was a tremendous clutter-breaking success. More recently, Disney developed an online viral campaign that invited people to apply for their "dream Disney character job," and this resulted in an overwhelming response that the company used to build overall and individual engagement with both current customers and the traveling public.

Major companies such as Procter & Gamble, Kraft, Walmart, Heinz, Texas Instruments, McDonald's, Pepsico, and Dell have actively invested in online social media in recent years. General Motors, for instance, has invested over $1.5 billion in social media, while maintaining a substantial (though somewhat reduced) budget for mainstream advertising. Moving away from traditional broadside, "boil the ocean" types of advertising and promotion doesn't mean that, going forward, advertising can't be an effective part of an overall marketing program. It does mean, however, that new, less controlled approaches need to be incorporated into any communication strategy. Generating more purchase-driven social word-of-mouth through informal off-line and online peer-to-peer communication will mean increased customer-related proaction on the part of companies: engaging in face-to-face and two-way dialogue (especially for B2B); creating positive, authentic, and engaging experiences; and leveraging/creating more efficiency from traditional awareness and discovery-type communication approaches such as brochures, demonstration events and conferences, and print/electronic advertising.

There are unfortunate examples, such as Borders, of major companies completely failing to recognize the power of changing communication and customer experience dynamics. At the time of this writing, Borders was preparing to file for Chapter 11 bankruptcy, in large part because its lack of foresight didn't include the need to build a meaningful brand and sales presence on the internet. As reported in the *Wall Street Journal*, over the past decade Borders' bricks-and-mortar book sales were significantly declining in favor of e-books and online marketing (see Figure 9.1), which for the company was a late, "me too" merchandising strategy behind Amazon.

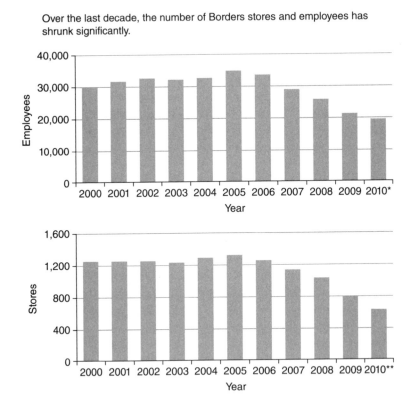

Over the last decade, the number of Borders stores and employees has shrunk significantly.

*Estimate.
**Quarterly report for period ended Oct. 30, 2010.

Figure 9.1 Book drop at Borders.

Sources: Jeffrey Trachtenberg and Mike Spector, "For Borders, a Scramble to Be Lean," *Wall Street Journal*, March 14, 2011; Mike Spector and Jeffrey Trachtenberg, "Chapter 11 for Borders, New Chapter for Books," *Wall Street Journal*, February 12, 2011.

Beginning in the early 1970s, Borders grew from a small family-run bookstore in Ann Arbor, Michigan, to a major national superstore chain by the 1990s. Though it had created a website along the way, the company didn't anticipate or comprehend the changing book purchasing and communication habits of consumers, principally the move to digital dialogue and greater convenience. In 2001, Borders sold its unprofitable internet site to Amazon. By the time Borders relaunched its own website seven years later, Amazon was very well entrenched, with a well-documented history of both online marketing and customer experience innovation and stable, mature customer relationships. The internet book retailing and communication ship had sailed, and Borders was not a passenger.

This movement to online media, marketing, and greater channel diversity is particularly challenging for small businesses, which often use traditional awareness-building techniques such as cable television commercials or newspaper and radio advertising. But these approaches rarely have the requisite targeting, reach, or staying power to either create and sustain unique perceived value or generate sales. When coupled with the growing lack of advertising credibility, and the acknowledged glut of B2B and B2C daily advertising messages seen by consumers, the necessity of cost-effectively breaking through the clutter and becoming top of mind has become a priority for all marketers.

Peer-to-peer informal, voluntary communication (or word-of-mouth) marketing means, simply, giving customers, potential customers, and other people value-based reasons to talk about a company's products and services. It also means utilizing methods to make it easier for those conversations to take place. Even in elements of value that are tangible and functional there are emotional drivers. Word-of-mouth is heavily driven by emotional connections, as described in earlier chapters, the soul of trust, objectivity, and authenticity that customers experience with a brand or supplier at each touch point.

The power of word-of-mouth as a key decision-making influence appears in virtually all markets. A study among 1721 adult women (who were either pregnant or had one or more children aged five or under) conducted in 2008 for BabyCenter by Keller Fay, for example, determined that new and expectant mothers have over 100 peer-to-peer conversations per week about products, services, and brands. On a day-to-day basis, this segment engages in more than one-third more conversations than either the total public or women in general. About two-thirds of the conversations include recommendations to consider, try, or buy the brands under discussion (with 69% actually expressing high purchase likelihood), and positive brand impressions outweigh negative impressions by a 10 to 1 ratio. In addition, the study found that pregnant women and new mothers actively converse (i.e., about half having at least one dialogue per day) about technology (about seven conversations per week, mentioning five brands), media, financial services, healthcare, packaged goods, and retail experiences (about eight per week, and mentioning eight brands).

In order for any online or off-line word-of-mouth marketing program to be successful—that is, to capitalize on some of these cultural conversation dynamics where people have a natural desire to share ideas and information with one another—companies must focus on and consistently deliver promises made and repeated to consumers in all forms of communication, realized in consistent and superior customer experiences. Earlier in the book we extensively covered what drives brand trust. According to studies by Nielsen, McKinsey, and other organizations, it is the credibility of information conveyed that drives reliance on informal communication. For instance, in a Nielsen Global Online Consumer Survey from July 2009, 90% reported that trust derived from positive statements and recommendations direct from consumers was the highest form of influence, followed by 70% who identified consumer opinions posted online. Other forms of media advertising were lower: brand sponsorships (63%), newspapers (61%), television (61%), magazines (59%), radio (55%), e-mails (55%), ads before movies (52%), search engine ads (41%), online banner ads (33%), and text ads on mobile phones (24%).

The next chapter contains a comprehensive evaluation of the role of advertising in creating advocacy behavior, especially relative to social online and off-line word-of-mouth. There is a strong argument for combining advertising with informal communication for greater net leveraging impact. According to statistics generated by Keller Fay (2008), 2.3 billion brand impressions are created each day in the United States through informal online and off-line consumer conversations. Further, 20% of these conversations are stimulated by advertising, representing 460 million brand-related conversations each day.

Loyalty programs, as a component of both advertising and marketing, are also examined in Chapter 10. For now, all that really needs to be said about loyalty programs and word-of-mouth is that, according to studies by Colloquy, program members are 27% more likely to be active, positive communicators about their program membership and the companies sponsoring them than the general population. And if the program sponsor can create more active engagement among members, there is a significant reward: Two-thirds of actively communicating members will recommend the program sponsor's brand within a year, and active participants will communicate, and positively behave, at a rate three times greater than nonactive members and seven times that of nonmembers. The challenge, however, is that only about one-third of members are active online or off-line communicators in behalf of the program. A key conclusion drawn by Colloquy is that in most instances, a company's loyalty program database is underutilized as a social network that marketers could leverage for more frequent and more positive word-of-mouth activity (Hlavinka 2010).

THINKING AND ACTING COLLABORATIVELY

Loyalty behavior is rapidly becoming more a function of engagement than of marketing. One of the new realities of sales, branding, customer experience management, and building long-term relationships is collaborative online and off-line communication, interaction, and real engagement between vendor and customer. When organizations think "media mix," the term must now be expanded to actively include nontraditional channels and techniques.

Though there are case studies of companies successfully utilizing such channels as Twitter (with 20 million people in the United States and 50 million worldwide) to foster such dialogue and collaboration, especially among smaller and start-up organizations, there is ample evidence that larger companies still have some way to go. A Weber Shandwick (2009a) study among the *Fortune* 100 showed that these companies were in the relatively early stages of use and application. For example, while 73% of the *Fortune* 100 companies had Twitter accounts (a total of 540 accounts), three-quarters rarely posted tweet mini-blog messages, and over half had little member engagement (measured by links, references, and retweets). Further, half the Twitter accounts had fewer than 500 followers, and another 15% were almost completely inactive. About 10% were identified as placeholder accounts, which Weber Shandwick indicated were a type of insurance to guard against "brandjacking," an unauthorized third party using a company's name.

Weber Shandwick concluded that although many leading companies recognized the importance of safeguarding their brands, they were not yet convinced of the value of collaboration and dialogue with customers and others. There was relatively little evidence of what Weber Shandwick identified as collaborative best practices.

Much of the adoption of effective online engagement, whether through communities, forums, or mini-blog sites like

Twitter, involves both active listening and active conversing, offering fresh content, updates on processes and programs, and value-based information. These approaches are fundamental changes from the "push" communication and advertising that the majority of companies, small and large, have been doing for decades. They are also an upgrade and the next iterative step from just observing or reacting to customer discourse.

Most of the *Fortune* 100 companies, according to the Weber Shandwick study, did little or none of this, failing to proactively leverage social media channels as engines or servants to increase brand awareness, generate new customers, or provide customer service:

- One-quarter of their Twitter accounts were one-way (i.e., outbound) information streams, offering no opportunity for customer-supplier interaction. While one-quarter of the Twitter accounts were used to create brand presence, they were simply signposts, or electronic billboards, with no community outreach or back-and-forth communication that would create trust among current or potential customers.

- Only 16% of the accounts were used principally as sales vehicles. Most *Fortune* 100 companies did not utilize Twitter to communicate special offers, provide coupons, or advertise sale prices. Further, the lack of two-way dialogue with consumers, identified in the first point, significantly limited the opportunity to build relationships through social media.

- Finally, only 9% utilized their Twitter accounts for customer service. Weber Shandwick concluded from this that, because leading companies utilizing collaborative sites like Twitter for service and reputation management respond quickly to questions or complaints by customers, there was a low level of commitment to online social media by these organizations.

It's clear that in order for social media to be effective as a set of marketing channels that interact with e-mail, direct mail, and mobile communication, these media can't remain a silo. Nor can they be one-way or generic. Weber Shandwick recommends an online social media strategy that is company-wide, demonstrates a consistent brand presence, builds a relationship-creating dialogue with both passive customers and advocates, and leverages loyalty behavior among the community of customers and prospects. Unfortunately, Weber Shandwick has concluded that the benefits of seeking opinions and encouraging discussions through such online dialogue and relationship-building are missed opportunities for the vast majority of major corporations.

THE ROLE OF EMPLOYEES— FRONTLINE TO CEO

An entire chapter (Chapter 11) is devoted to describing the multiple ways in which employees can drive positive or negative customer advocacy behavior. Much of that discussion is centered on frontline employees, particularly customer service, as ambassadors or envoys for the company's values and the values of its products or services, and how they can leverage this behavior both inside and outside the organization.

Here, we will focus on how corporate executives, especially CEOs, can help create or sustain (and also undermine) customer advocacy. According to a 2010 study conducted by Weber Shandwick, corporate CEOs in the United States are held in very low esteem by the general public. Given that the reputation of CEOs is directly linked to company image, this is extremely important. CEOs have a role as narrator and representative, and their words have an impact on investors, employees, customers, the media, and the public at large. Weber Shandwick's research showed conclusively that stakeholders greatly desire to hear from CEOs on a regular basis.

Weber Shandwick's analysis showed that CEOs are more actively taking responsibility for protecting their organizations' reputations through business press quotes, public speaking at conferences, and participation in events such as business school forums. Where they were found to not be so effective, however, was in their use of social media.

The study showed that social CEOs create a stronger reputation status for their companies. They use multiple channels, such as company websites, Facebook pages, Twitter, and YouTube (all of which have grown rapidly in recent years), but few CEOs actually had their own blogs. In the study, consulting organization Forrester's CEO is quoted as saying, "The Social CEO should not be chasing followers. He should be a Social Light—blogging six to eight times per year and posting on Twitter 12–24 times per year. This level of presence will reveal the broad thinking of the CEO, while matching up with the time demands of running a company" (8).

So, although many CEOs don't see a return on investment (ROI) on their limited time from new and unfamiliar media approaches, are uncomfortable and risk-averse with such efforts on general principles (and are concerned that, unlike with traditional marketing approaches, they would be less able to protect brand and/or corporate image), and may even have some concerns from a legal perspective about doing this, they are beginning to follow their competitors into the arena of online social communications and blogging. Scott Adams, ever the creative critic of all things corporate, has also weighed in on the authenticity and honesty of corporate blogs (see Figure 9.2).

Adams is not alone in his cynicism. Figure 9.3 illustrates the bandwagon, or "concept of the month," syndrome that corporations often fall into when benchmarking what other companies are doing in marketing and communications.

There are many sound reasons, all aimed at building corporate reputation and stakeholder trust, why CEOs and other senior executives should be actively using social media tools

Figure 9.2 Authentic CEO blogging.

Source: © Scott Adams, Inc./Dist. by UFS, Inc.

Figure 9.3 Why do I need a blog?

such as podcasts and blogging. Online publishing is easy, even for the technically challenged, and CEOs often use techniques such as blogs as opportunities for other senior executives to share authorship. Executive blogs get a lot of attention on search engines, and they can also be linked to other social media. CEOs who actively maintain blogs often become known as innovators or "thought leaders" for their company or industry, which positively rubs off on their organization. Finally, much of the value of executive blogs is that they create an opportunity for valuable stakeholder dialogue, gathering insight, proactively positioning the organization, and building authenticity and trust at the same time.

CEOs like Bill Marriott (*On the Move*); Mike Critelli, retired chairman of Pitney Bowes (*Open Mike*); David Neeleman, chairman of JetBlue Airways (*Flight Log*); Robert Lutz, GM vice chairman (*Fast Lane*); and senior executives from many tech and online companies have availed themselves of the voice represented by their company-sponsored blogs, and they have generated much interest in their observations and points of view. These, in the main, have been positively received and have reflected well on their respective organizations.

One of the more active, and voluminous, CEO blogs was that of Jonathan Schwartz, who was the CEO of Sun Microsystems until its takeover by Oracle in 2009. Aimed at the business and financial communities, his blogs (complete with graphics) were detailed and often creative short stories on Sun technical innovations and business results. Over a two-year period he wrote enough for a small book, and doubtless did much to enhance Sun's image.

Weber Shandwick, having learned through its study that 64% of CEOs are not engaged through company websites or social media, has encouraged senior executives and other business leaders to become more proactively vocal and visible in this new business climate, and to more creatively use these newer online social channels of communication. Among recommended approaches are repurposing internal videos, photos, and memos for use online; crafting a distinctive, positive narrative that is attention-getting; and developing a C-suite social media strategy. Above all, Weber Shandwick believes that an active social media initiative needs to be a core element in a corporation's reputation management program.

What is important here can be expressed by a Weber Shandwick conclusion: "As leaders come to fully realize that they must be content providers of the highest order, greater participation in the social media world seems inevitable" (8).

MAKING SOCIAL WORD-OF-MOUTH MONETIZE

In order for any off-line or online social word-of-mouth program to be effective, there must first be full realization of what it can and can't do, and what it is and isn't.

There are four general "rules" for accomplishing this:

1. Be authentic, transparent, and honest. Saying that today's consumers are "savvy" only scratches the surface of their awareness, sophistication, and levels of discrimination in identifying what is real and what is fake. Informal communication programs can work, if and because customers feel they are getting information and advice from individuals and entities they know and trust. Messaging and positioning statements provided by companies must be up front and credible, because if they are not (or are perceived as not), the backlash results of negative word-of-mouth can be significant.

2. Be both strategic and tactical. Use of online and off-line social communication media isn't a replacement for advertising, but it is an effective partner for succeeding with individual initiatives and long-term dialogue and inclusion. It must also be recognized that people and processes in a business model, representing inside-out advocacy creation in such areas as leading-edge products or service and support capabilities, are a priority before effective word-of-mouth initiatives can, or should, be launched. Much of the evidence of tacti-

cal and strategic success of informal communication programs has been because companies were passionate about customers in the first place and made them feel like members of the family. Such is the reason that companies like Starbuck's, Wegmans, Southwest Airlines, and Zappos are readily acknowledged as both customer-friendly and proactive.

3. Seek to leverage and influence, not control. Up until electronic interaction—the internet and wireless devices for accessing the web on a mobile basis—changed the character of communication and engagement forever, marketers frequently deluded themselves that they were in control of the awareness and selling processes. While multimedia, mega-budget ad and promotional programs were extolling wonderful products and services offered by corporations, product quality and service performance, individually and collectively, was often in decline in the real world. Now, if customer experiences don't at least match the brand and services promises made through these communication programs, consumers express their feelings and opinions to the world with a single mouse click. Companies must pay attention or suffer the lasting consequences of negative word-of-mouth. A prime example of this is what became known as "Dell Hell," in which the poor service and product quality deficiencies that customers were experiencing from this popular manufacturer from roughly 2005 through 2007 sent shock waves through the internet. This led the attorney general of New York to sue Dell for false advertising, poor product quality (based on stories of overheating laptops catching fire), failure to provide adequate or efficient support services, and deceptive business practices (such as useless warranties). It was not until

Dell publicly apologized, brought much of its offshore outsourced customer service back in house, and opened collaborative employee–customer community sites that this situation gradually began to improve. In sum, the negative customer perception took several years, and much effort and expense, to erase.

As B2B and B2C consumers become increasingly mobile, being able to deliver content and communicate at each phase of the customer's life cycle has gotten much attention. In the PC, laptop, or notebook world, doing this is fairly straightforward, because computers and browsers enable internet users to navigate, consume, and transmit large amounts of targeted content very rapidly. Whether reaching consumers at awareness, consideration, retention, or recovery phases of the life cycle, consulting organizations have forecast that, over the next decade, the mobile web will be a key conduit for building customer relationships.

One element of adjusting to consumer mobility is, or will be, "proximity marketing," where the combination of GPS location, Bluetooth signal technology, and a detailed customer lifestyle database will enable B2C marketers to make purchase suggestions that are delivered on mobile devices and built around known consumer preferences. But this is only one method of leveraging the mobile web. The whole notion of mobile web connectivity and interaction is both perpetual and dynamic. Consumers can be anywhere—attending a sporting event, sitting in a dentist's office, or shopping at a supermarket—and marketers can use the mobile web, in real time, to create brand awareness, enhance engagement, and drive relevant experiences. Proximity marketing is inexpensive, user friendly, and can be readily tracked by vendors, all powerful incentives for continued growth.

4. Emphasize people and core values over "corporate" positioning. As noted earlier, customers can sense when companies are being honest and authentic, and when they're not. It's about hiring the most customer-sensitive, proactive staff, training them to be customer focused, and making customer processes as friendly as possible. In other words, customer centricity must become a mantra, where optimum product value, provision of superior experiences at all touch points, off-line and online word-of-mouth, and brand perception are critical elements of every decision. The goal, as covered earlier in the book, is to have a brand strategy that is the operating strategy, and to make customers the de facto unpaid sales force for company products and services. It is, finally, a recognition that word-of-mouth is what people say about an organization, not what the organization believes and says about itself.

To summarize, customers now expect more from social media. They are using it more, and more effectively, than ever before. Organizations will need to move past the fear of change and experimentation that social media represents to many C-suite executives. The fear, it must be acknowledged, is not baseless. Most social communities are minimally monitored or controlled. Quantifiable measurement is often a challenge. While much of the online social interaction is positive, there is definitely a dark side, too. Customers can, and do, readily express their frustration over poor product and service performance. Channels such as Twitter, YouTube, and Facebook are open forums for disaffected, even angry, customers or groups with special interests. Previously recounted, for example, was the story of Canadian musician Dave Carroll, whose music video, "United Breaks Guitars," has been viewed close to 10 million times on YouTube. Getting past the concerns associated with lack of direct control is the first stage of adoption, and companies, at a minimum, should be actively monitoring the social communication environment to gauge the opportunities for marketing application.

Once past the listening and monitoring stages, companies should move to engagement, getting beyond looking at social media as a traditional mass marketing tool, and utilizing it as a set of approaches and opportunities to make messaging more meaningful.

One of the challenges here is coordinating social media selected with other communication channels. Flexibility, and maintaining an approach that responds to changing customer dynamics, is key. For instance, a 2009 social media use study by MarketingSherpa found that learning about special offers and sales was a prime motivator for consumers to connect with companies through social media. Another factor was consumer interest in learning about new products and services from companies they were engaged with, indicating a desire for deeper, more strategic, and personalized relationships.

Beyond the opportunity for engagement and relationship building, a challenge is identifying methods for collecting data produced through off-line and online interaction, and driving intelligent decision making and action. Studies indicate that many companies are now using social media in their marketing efforts; however, most lack a consistent mechanism to measure the effect of their programs. This is where advocacy measurement is a tremendous advancement in understanding customer behavior. Whether getting information online or off-line, or communicating online or off-line as a result of an experience, advocacy research identifies the impact of transactions and longitudinal experience on customer actions. This is true, of course, for both B2B and B2C products and services.

What is clear is that companies will need to develop new road maps in which the information they convey and the consumer sentiment they harvest and analyze is interwoven into the business as decision-making insight. Expressed in more model-specific terms, information going out and data coming in need to be mapped to the functions and processes that are affected. This, in turn, shines a light on the technologies that support the processes, and the proficiencies of the people who execute the processes.

As concluded in a 2010 white paper by marketing software company Neolane,

> With the right technology, skill sets, and C-level buy-in, social media provides an opportunity for marketers to take a more personalized and interactive approach to achieve true engagement with customers and prospects. Utilizing targeted, complementary content and offers that are coordinated across other channels like email, mobile, and direct mail, social media interactions can be used to drive sales, refine and enhance existing customer profiles, convert passive followers into active customers and upsell/cross-sell to those already committed to the brand. Intelligence gained through engaging social media communities can be used to power hyper-targeted campaigns that drive inbound and outbound communications that propel your brand into a whole new phase of evolved customer engagement. So, stop broadcasting, start engaging and put your social media intelligence to work.

10

Advertising versus Social Word-of-Mouth and Advocacy

Good advertising does not just circulate information. It penetrates the public mind with desires and belief.

—LEO BURNETT, ADVERTISING INDUSTRY PIONEER

T he entire concept and set of approaches for conveying ideas and themes that motivate consumers to buy—and keep spending, be willing to be upsold and cross-sold, be receptive to learning about new products and services, be emotionally bonded to a single brand or company within a category, and actively and positively speak in behalf of that favored brand or company—have changed to a remarkable degree over the past couple of decades. If Rip Van Winkle were a corporate, brand, or marketing executive and had just recently awoken from his 20-year sleep, he'd scarcely recognize the customer life cycle, loyalty behavior, and relationship landscapes.

Marketing is, essentially and arguably, the way customers, prospects, noncustomers, and other stakeholders become aware of, perceive, and find benefit in a continued relationship with a company's, product's, or service's value proposition. Many companies and ad agencies have viewed traditional paid advertising as the way to influence that awareness and

229

perception, and as the central method of motivating and stimulating customer behavior. Over the past two decades, the role and value of advertising have seen significant morphing. So has the pressure on advertising, as a discipline, to produce results. Even so, relatively few companies or marketers have been sufficiently proactive or responsive to what has amounted to advertising deconstruction.

This is a subject that gets relatively little treatment in articles and books, but given the sea change taking place between traditional advertising and promotion and consumer-generated communication, it definitely merits some discussion. As informal off-line and online consumer media have increased in use, the decision-making impact of traditional off-line advertising and promotion, via electronic and print media, has been declining for years. These forms of communication have, likewise, been in decline. In fact, the wireless telecom panel at a 2006 Word of Mouth Marketing Association (WOMMA) conference said that, in their industry, social word-of-mouth was the number 2 purchase indicator (i.e., driver), while advertising was number 19 (even though at the time, advertising was still getting most of the marketing budget and social word-of-mouth was receiving little of it).

Budgets for social media advertising and promotion, however, have been on the rise over the past several years. Evidence of this can be seen in social media expenditure and investment increases, while, overall, corporate marketing budget declines and refocusing are taking place. For example, Procter & Gamble cut its 2009 advertising budget to $7.6 billion, down from $8.6 billion the previous year. It has reported beginning to use more nontraditional approaches for advertising and promoting its household products, such as having pages on social media sites like Facebook and targeting influential bloggers with new product samples. Considerably more than electronic and print advertising, these approaches can be quickly tested and launched. They are, in addition, relatively simple and inexpensive to execute, especially when compared with the complexities and costs involved in generating, placing, and evaluating mainstream advertising.

As an overarching trend in marketing, companies such as Procter & Gamble, having become enamored with online social media tools and venues, have tended to reduce their budgets for traditional advertising, or not see its integrated value. For example, MarketingSherpa reported that for B2B companies, direct mail, trade shows, and especially print advertising were all forecasted to see substantial declines during 2010. At the same time, website design/optimization, social media, virtual events/webinars, search engine optimization (SEO), and e-mail marketing were projected to see significant increases. Figure 10.1 details the extent to which both increases and decreases in marketing component budgets were projected to take place.

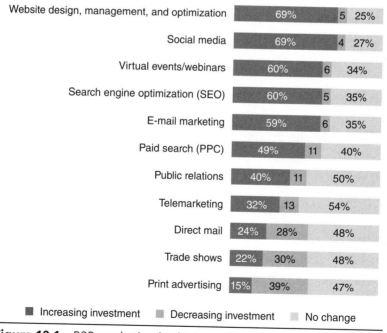

Figure 10.1 B2B marketing budget trends for 2010 (N = 935).
Source: MarketingSherpa, B2B Marketing Benchmark Survey, August 2010.

Online advertising such as web ads and e-mail ads did have some traction up until a few years ago (a DoubleClick study showed these as a "shopping aid"); however, as marketers have become somewhat more sophisticated in the use of social word-of-mouth, online advertising has tended to be sidelined.

As Mark Twain wrote in May 1897 on the widely circulated rumor of his demise, the "report of my death was an exaggeration" and premature. The same observation could be made for traditional advertising, especially with regard to its potential for melding with social word-of-mouth for greater blended impact. Some of our social word-of-mouth research has paralleled work by other organizations, such as the Keller Fay Group. We have found, for example, that 19% of consumers use advertising in traditional media as an information source for helping make purchase decisions, and this is even higher among 18- to 29-year-olds, while only 4% use social media (1%–2% by Keller Fay). Keller Fay's research, to be further detailed within this chapter, has shown that one in five word-of-mouth conversations about brands in the United States involves a reference to advertising. As found by Keller Fay, for those who influence the behavior of others, the role of advertising in generating social word-of-mouth is even greater.

This is significant because research by Keller Fay and others also shows that the level and effectiveness of social word-of-mouth are substantially increased when stimulated, encouraged, and supported by or conjoined with traditional advertising. In the automotive and financial services sectors, for example, Keller Fay's study results, when compared with companies in these sectors that the Nielsen Company identified as having made significant, moderate, and low budget cuts, showed that companies that maintained higher advertising levels during the high-pressure 2008–2010 time period generated much higher, and more positive, word-of-mouth. Further, in the financial services industry, where much of the news was negative during this period, maintenance of advertising budgets helped sustain a much more positive overall tone.

American Business Media (2003) has reported that in a recession, advertising is necessary to protect market position, maintain "share of mind," and protect brand perception. Coopers and Lybrand have stated that "during an economic downturn, a strong advertising/marketing effort enables a firm to solidify its customer base, take business away from less aggressive competitors, and position itself for future growth during the recovery" (in Johnson 2011). Nairman Dhalla has reported that, especially in times of economic instability, advertising should be regarded as a contributor to profits, not a drain. And as Keller Fay wisely concluded, "Silence, during times of crisis, is not golden."

THE EVOLUTION OF TRADITIONAL ADVERTISING AS A DISCIPLINE AND COMPONENT OF MARKETING

Many have come to believe that the classic print and electronic advertising of yesteryear is dying or, at best, on life support. As reported elsewhere in the book, much of this is a result of the decline in trust in corporate institutions and the media, the rise of consumer decision-making influence, and the sheer proliferation of B2B and B2C push messaging. In fact, there is a fairly pervasive belief, expressed by Andy Sernovitz (founder of WOMMA) in a graphic created for a 2010 conference on leveraging informal communication, that advertising is largely benign, boring messages embedded within costly creative packages (see Figure 10.2).

Columbia University professors Elihu Katz and Paul Lazarsfeld (2005) have concluded that advertising, in and of itself, has limited persuasive power because consumers tend to shield and protect their preexisting company, product, and service

Figure 10.2 A negative view of advertising value.

perceptions and beliefs. They have encouraged advertisers to better target consumer influencers, within society and for the product or service category, and the messages they would like to see conveyed by these individuals.

Today, what we're really addressing is 360° communications, represented by community participation, dialogue, and engagement—terms that can include advertising, sales promotion, event marketing, buzz or viral marketing, design, and off-line and online word-of-mouth (aka, social marketing, public relations, loyalty programs, SEO, and so on). Beginning in the late 1980s there was a term for all this—integrated communications. Customers and noncustomers now have the opportunity to engage in elective dialogues, with one another and with companies, that were not possible before. And, unlike in the past, even those who don't actively share opinions are listening, or "lurking," as others communicate. People participate in brand discussions as they have not done in the past, enabling potentially stronger brand engagement and engagement through multiple channels.

Rory Sutherland, vice chairman of Ogilvy Group UK, strongly believes in 360° communication (often writing and presenting on the subject), the perceptual and intangible value created by advertising, and the role of technology in making advertising a more vibrant and contemporary component of marketing. He believes that, to be most effective, branding must be created in contextual, timely, and immediate ways.

The stronger the bonding potential with the brand, and the more active and available the opportunity for engagement, the greater the likelihood for growth in positive customer self-image through the brand, with the result that advocacy can bud and flourish. This is the summation of melding together various disciplines to better answer the critical business issue of how to optimize customer behavior. It brings us back to the importance of customer promises made principally through outbound messaging and early impression relative to the actual long-term experience, delivered as the customer perceives it.

HOW ADVERTISING STIMULATES WORD-OF-MOUTH AND BRAND IMPRESSION (AND, POTENTIALLY, ADVOCACY)

Inevitably, there is a point of inflection where (imaginative, creative) advertising and word-of-mouth, leading to some elements of advocacy behavior, meet. Some corporations and media organizations have devoted part of their resources to focus on programs to reach "influencers," who, in turn, will stimulate marketplace buzz. In 2008, WOMMA published an influencer handbook, in which this type of individual was defined as "a person who has a greater than average reach or impact through word of mouth in a relevant marketplace" (Fay et al. 2008).

WOMMA has identified five types of influencers:

1. *Formal position of authority*—political/government leaders and business executives

2. *Institutional/recognized subject experts*—academics, scientists, industry analysts, and cause activists

3. *Media elite*—journalists, commentators, and talk show hosts (who influence through both traditional and new/social media)

4. *Cultural elite*—celebrities, designers, artists, and musicians (who influence through both traditional and new/social media)

5. *Socially connected*—neighborhood leaders, members of community groups, and social network activists

In this book, we are principally addressing the influence of the socially and electronically connected—the mavens, the starters, and the connectors identified by Malcolm Gladwell; lifestyle groups like soccer moms; and individuals and small groups who are known as spreaders, hubs, and alphas. While other types of influencers aren't unimportant, from a marketing perspective their effect is more difficult to study and leverage.

Again, an influencer isn't a customer advocate. An influencer, for example, may or may not have had personal experience with the product or service about which he or she is communicating. Credibility through actual use is certainly an element differentiating influencers from advocates. In national word-of-mouth studies conducted by Roper Reports, for instance, 93% of consumers interviewed said they would be likely to try a product or service if given positive information or a recommendation by someone who had used it themselves. This compared to 72% who had received information or a recommendation from someone who'd heard or read good things about the product or service (and 58% by someone given an incentive to introduce the product to them) (Chiarelli and Parker 2008).

That said, an influencer can have at least some of the same characteristics as an advocate and can do a certain amount of positive and negative advocacy table-setting. There has been a fair amount of study supporting this. Donald Lehmann, a professor at the Columbia University Business School, and colleagues found that online social hubs are earlier adopters of products and services and can be somewhat mobilized to influence market direction and size. Lehmann and his coauthors identified these hubs, and their networks, as targets for word-of-mouth campaigns (Goldenberg et al. 2009).

Barak Libai, management professor at Tel Aviv University, and colleagues have determined that social networks can influence both the adoption and the abandonment of products and services, especially on what they describe as "first-degree" direct contacts, also known as neighbors, in their social networks (2010). Like Lehmann, Libai has determined that influencers are profitable early adopters (and can increase profitability by 6%–14% when targeted for promotion via word-of-mouth, relative to targeting all customers); influencers can also significantly increase the likelihood of customer defection through their social interactions. In research, Libai has found that the "hazard" of defection can increase by 80% though direct connection with influencers in a social network.

Research by the Keller Fay Group has yielded several insights about the role of influencers in stimulating potential customer advocacy behavior (Keller Fay Group/Jack Morton

Worldwide 2007; Keller 2008; Keller and Fay 2009; Keller and Fay 2008):

- Social influencers have significantly higher word-of-mouth propensities. Compared to the average person, they have 60% more conversations each week about products and services, and they are 90% more likely to have brand-specific discussions. So, they generate reach, accelerate product and service adoption, and amplify advertising and promotional messages, all contributing to the building of advocacy behavior.

- As reported elsewhere in the book, Keller Fay Group studies reinforce the finding that, depending on the product or service category involved, up to 90% of peer-to-peer dialogue takes place off-line. It believes marketers should actively keep this in mind when designing programs to reach influencers.

- Word-of-mouth is, most typically, positive. Research conducted by Keller Fay, Weber Shandwick, and others shows that the vast majority of off-line and online product- or service-related word-of-mouth is neither neutral nor negative. Keller Fay has also found that positive word-of-mouth carries greater credibility, though negative word-of-mouth tends to get more attention.

- Connecting with influencers requires a blend of old and new techniques. Some organizations are targeting influencers and other early adopters for word-of-mouth programs, or product development initiatives, recognizing that these individuals, in parallel, are also seeking information in areas of interest to them and sharing it with peers. Nestle, for example, has done this with influencers in the fitness community for its Power Bar brand products, utilizing both off-line and online means. Other companies have recruited influencers to take leading roles in online communities, using them as hosts to solicit feedback. Couponing, public relations, and specialized events—all marketing tools that have been used for decades—can be applied with influencers to begin word-of-mouth communications.

- Traditional advertising and promotional programs can also help leverage word-of-mouth activity. In fact, Keller Fay studies have determined that, overall, one in five peer-to-peer conversations about brands makes reference to advertising; for influencers, this ratio is even higher. They have found television, print media, and the social and viral elements of the internet most effective at doing this.

This last insight is, we believe, perhaps the most important observation because it marks a point of inflection, or connection, among advertising and promotion, word-of-mouth influence, and customer advocacy behavior.

Influencers, like advertising and promotion, have a role in customer advocacy. They certainly help shape impressions. Moreover, influencers are considerably more active than the general public in creating word-of-mouth about products and services, whether they have personally used them or not. So, though some—such as Duncan Watts of Columbia Business School in *Small Worlds* (2003), and Dave Balter and John Butman in *Grapevine: The New Art of Word-of-Mouth Marketing* (2005)—may pooh-pooh the role of influencers, their impact, and potential impact, should not be dismissed.

Usually, word-of-mouth happens independent of advertising, which we identify as a potential component of outside-in advocacy. However, on occasion an advertisement or campaign is so refreshing and compelling that it can, by itself, stimulate word-of-mouth, though not necessarily advocacy. Examples include Budweiser's "Wazzup" television ad campaign and, going back some years, the Wendy's "Where's the Beef?" ad campaign. More recently, Old Spice ran a Super Bowl ad featuring a man offering men (and, by inference, women) a rich, fantasy lifestyle if only they would use this brand of aftershave. The ad was picked up by electronic media and ran on YouTube, where it has had several million hits.

This kind of result shows both the attraction and the weakness of traditional advertising: Although a breakout advertisement resulting in a word-of-mouth grand slam in terms of longevity and behavioral impact is possible, the normal result is pedestrian messaging that is caught in the clutter, has little or no impact, and is quickly forgotten.

LOYALTY PROGRAMS AS MARKETING, ADVERTISING, AND ADVOCACY DEVICES

One of the perennial challenges associated with traditional advertising is measuring, beyond awareness and purchase intent, its real impact on business outcomes. By contrast, loyalty programs, which are historically acknowledged to have at least some customer behavior effect, are—or should be—easier to measure in terms of real ROI. The hard results of loyalty programs include sales and revenue generated by increased member purchase frequency, which includes larger volume expenditures, upsell and cross-sell, and reducing the defection rate. Soft results include communication continuity and the opportunity to create a perception of extended product and service value.

Loyalty and reward programs classically have two basic intentions: (1) to generate important customer profile data that can be used for targeted—even micro-segmented—marketing, promotion, and communication initiatives, and (2) to leverage loyal behavior among the customer base and reduce the use of or consideration of competitive products and services. To meet both of these objectives, the program, its array of components, and the perception of personal value need to be optimal. Are they?

In the CMO Council (2010) study *The Leaders in Loyalty: Feeling the Love from the Loyalty Clubs*, the key findings revealed that neither of these objectives was being met. The study concluded that companies sponsoring loyalty programs were just using them to deliver general discounts and perks to the mass of members, ignoring customer profiles within the database that would help provide more targeted and relevant communication and stronger value perception among program members. Only 13% of marketers in the study felt that loyalty clubs have been highly effective in leveraging loyalty and brand preference among club members, and nearly 20% have no strategy in place to do this. Almost 30% of marketers reported that customers see little or no added value in becoming a loyalty program member, though marketers admitted that most of their program components were discounts, free products, or premiums rather than better service or improved customer handling.

Very significantly, more than half (54%) of loyalty program members surveyed in the study were considering leaving the programs or defecting from the brands and companies sponsoring them, principally due to:

1. The onslaught of irrelevant and off-target messages, and low or nonmeaningful program benefits

2. The impersonal treatment they received as members

At the same time, it has been well established in multiple studies, such as those by loyalty program development consulting company Colloquy, that customers who participate in loyalty or reward programs are much more likely than the remainder of the customer base to positively communicate their experiences and recommend the product or service of the sponsoring organization (Hlavinka 2010).

Colloquy has reported that retailers, especially, were leveraging loyalty programs as part of their advertising efforts in a more aggressive manner, even in the face of economic challenges. Many buyers, Colloquy has found, are utilizing loyalty program rewards and points as a way to stretch their incomes and purchase more basic products and services. This is particularly true among young adults aged 18–25 (who represent 27% of loyalty program members) and women aged 25–49 (who represent 22%). Next, and somewhat surprisingly, are households with over $125,000 in household income (also 22%) (Hlavinka 2010).

For instance, Colloquy found that loyalty program members are 70% more likely to be engaged in advocacy-type activities such as positive word-of-mouth and referral compared to the general population. More than two-thirds of a program's strongest advocates will recommend the program's brand within a year, and those who are most active (i.e., using benefits on a regular basis) are more than three times more likely than other members to engage in recommendation and word-of-mouth communication. Finally, those program members who have redeemed for experiential rewards, and thus deepened the relationship between them and the sponsor, are 30% more likely to be advocates than those members who used the program for discounts and bounce-back offers.

What is true of some of the more assertive companies in how they use loyalty programs as a form of both advertising and perceived value enhancement, however, is not true of most. Colloquy's studies determined that the same lack of perceived program relevance and value identified by the CMO Council carried over to the inability of marketers to identify within the program database those members most likely to be advocates for the program. Nor was there much evidence of building relationships or encouraging positive word-of-mouth. In the CMO Council study, key actions for improving club ROI included personalizing interactions and target messages (51%), increasing relevance of communications (39%), gathering more insights and intelligence (38%), and adding unique new benefits and incentives (36%).

Not every company is like leading worldwide supermarket chain Tesco, with DunnHumby as its customer loyalty program data analyst to conduct detailed evaluation of loyalty program member profiles that can be converted into more effective program components, targeted messages, and promotions. However, every company with a loyalty program can get smarter about:

1. Using loyalty program member data to best effect

2. Designing or redesigning its loyalty program to encourage participation and leverage positive word-of-mouth and purchasing behavior

THE POSITIVES, NEGATIVES, AND OPPORTUNITIES REPRESENTED BY LOYALTY PROGRAMS

Many consider loyalty programs to be inexpensive methods of attracting customers and getting them to come back and buy more. But although they are inexpensive, they may also be ineffective and even damaging. There is a potential for customer annoyance and disconnect, at least in terms of loyalty program design or redesign, especially if some desired benefits are eliminated. Loyalty program members can, and ideally should, actively represent the impressions of its host. But impressions, the tone of social word-of-mouth, and downstream behavior can quickly deteriorate—as many airline loyalty programs discovered to their dismay, when the number of points required for free trip qualification was increased. As studies by Colloquy have proved, customers are often far more likely to communicate with others about their experiences with the programs—the more active their program participation, the more likely they are to spread the word. But if they are disengaged with the loyalty program, or do not see the value represented by membership, these customers will become passive about both the program and the products and services it represents. Worse, they may become negative communicators or defect.

Too many companies belong to the *Field of Dreams* "if you build it, they will come" school of loyalty program development. They subscribe to the conventional wisdom that if they create what they believe, or what they are told, is a compelling program with attractive customer benefits, the company will be rewarded with both more customers and more sales as evidence of loyalty behavior. Once the program is built, customers may come, or they may not. They may spend more and make more referrals, or they may not. Recent research by the Hartman Group (2010), a marketing consultancy, determined that 74% of consumers agree that companies need new and better ways of rewarding loyal customers. Clearly, many loyalty programs are suboptimal in effectiveness.

For marketers who hope to build profitable word-of-mouth behavior from loyalty program members, the tools for doing so exist within the program database. They should identify the advocates embedded within their membership bases. Then, they should build relationships that reward these members for their positive word-of-mouth activity. To revisit a quote by noted marketing professor Philip Kotler of Northwestern University, who believes that standout organizations are those that can most effectively leverage these customers, "They use the word-of-mouth effect of unpaid advocates—truly loyal customers—to boost their reputation. Advocates will do your marketing for you if you mobilize them, listen to them and engage them." Loyalty programs, used effectively, can be an excellent vehicle for creating and extending customer advocacy behavior.

DEFINING CUSTOMER ADVOCACY AND ADVOCACY MEASUREMENT FOR LOYALTY PROGRAMS

Beginning around the year 2000, major consulting organizations began to recognize that critical changes in the marketplace were likely to have a profound impact on businesses, especially the shift from push marketing to dialogue marketing. The emphasis was moving toward optimization of customer engagement and perceived value. Instead of relying solely on such historical measures as satisfaction, loyalty, commitment, and recommendation, companies would need to identify and focus on something more contemporary, more actionable, and more predictive of key monetizing business outcomes, such as share of wallet. That "something" was ultimately defined as *customer advocacy* by consulting companies, academics, and business executives (i.e., behavior driven by a strong bond with the preferred brand and active, voluntary online and off-line word-of-mouth in behalf of that brand).

Customer advocacy could now provide organizations with many valuable business outcome benefits. This new consumer influence also meant that market research companies would need to evolve beyond historical methods of interpreting customer attitudes and determining how those attitudes could influence behavior, in order to incorporate drivers of customer advocacy. Some new models were created principally to evaluate emotional connection; however, in general, the market research industry has not embraced the new realities of customer decision making represented by customer advocacy. Having identified the power of customer advocacy to influence the customer's own behavior and the behavior of others, the next challenge was to create and prove the effectiveness of a state-of-the-art research metric or framework for measuring and leveraging the power of customer advocacy.

Advertising pioneer David Ogilvy is famously quoted as saying, "Advertising people who ignore research are as dangerous as generals who ignore decodes of enemy signals." We agree and would add that this applies to any and all communications that create awareness, build brand equity, or help sustain customer relationships. The research, however, must be closely correlated to likely business outcomes. We will examine how a customer advocacy framework can be applied to help optimize loyalty and reward program performance.

CASE STUDY USING ADVOCACY RESEARCH TO DESIGN OR REDESIGN A CUSTOMER LOYALTY PROGRAM

Advocacy occurs when:

1. Customers select a single supplier from among all those they might consider, giving that supplier the highest share of spend possible

2. Customers informally, voluntarily, and often frequently tell others about how positive their relationship is with the supplier and how much value and benefit they derive from it, without any form of compensation

It is principally based on positive, voluntary, and active customer word-of-mouth and impression of the brand or vendor. However, word-of-mouth is a double-edged sword: Customers' negative communication can have a damaging effect on other customers and noncustomers, as well as on the communicating customer.

Marketers have recognized that their number-one program priority must be to acquire and retain motivated and engaged participants. In the CMO Council study, 46% of marketing executives identified this as their principal challenge. Other performance obstacles included measuring marketing value and effectiveness (42%), deriving valuable insight and intelligence (38%), delivering more personalized offers and inducements (34%), and creating more customized communications (33%). All these key issues can be effectively addressed through targeted loyalty program advocacy research.

For our case study, we will use a wine buyers' customer loyalty program and call it the Wine Lovers Club. There are many of these programs around. They are offered by wine retailers and individual wineries, as add-ons to other loyalty programs, and as coalition or aggregated programs of multiple retailers, or retailers and other product and service providers.

This particular Wine Lovers Club program was introduced in 1999. As of this writing, it has 50,000 members. Cost of membership is $100 per year with a membership fee rebate beginning in the second year that is based on the amount of wine ordered in the previous year. The program has been built incrementally over time, with management adding elements borrowed from other loyalty programs that they felt would make theirs more successful. It now has nearly 20 program components:

- Personalized winery visit (United States, Australia, South America, Africa, and Europe) availability
- Points earned for every purchase
- Special events at wineries and locations around the United States with wine enthusiasts
- Free shipping on wine purchased by the case
- Instant discounts or rebate offers
- Access to pre-release, specialty, and limited-production wines

- A members-only catalog with program logo items and reasonably priced wine accessories
- Catalog accessories, food, hampers, and gift baskets are available for points earned through purchase
- Discounted wine storage rates
- Free personalization of wine labels for gift giving
- Referral benefits (discounts, points earned whenever a referred friend buys wine or puts it into storage)
- Tier levels, with higher points per purchase as purchases increase
- Discounts on wine purchases increase as tier levels increase
- Points, tier levels, and credits (usage of points) accounted for automatically
- Benefits earned never expire
- Priority ordering and exclusive wine selections
- Online Wine Lovers Club community
- Exclusive "ask the expert" online and telephone availability

Club membership has remained relatively static for several years, with about as many members defecting as joining. The program was rarely mined for customer profile data and is minimally profitable. It generates add-on sales, but principally rewards through discounts those members who are already active buyers. Apart from management opinions, there is no real evidence as to what elements of the program will most effectively drive member advocacy, or dampen it. Market Probe's advocacy framework was applied to help the Wine Lovers Club reframe and optimize its rewards program.

WINE LOVERS CLUB ADVOCACY RESEARCH RESULTS

We applied a unique research framework to evaluate the Wine Lovers Club's array of benefits, overall perception, and loyalty level relative to competitive wine clubs where Wine Lovers Club members belonged to multiple programs, on degree of advocacy. Club members were classified into four groups based on their answers to four questions regarding their experience with the Wine Lovers Club (future purchase intent, recommendation likelihood, brand favorability/impression, and evidence of positive or negative word-of-mouth):

> *Advocates*—Frequent buyers of multiple types of wine, significant use of club benefits, strong club brand recognition and favorability, active and positive word-of-mouth in behalf of the club

> *Allegiants*—Regular wine purchasers, moderate use of club benefits, generally positive club brand favorability, infrequent (though positive) word-of-mouth in behalf of the club

> *Ambivalents*—Moderate-volume wine buyers, occasional use of club benefits, neutral club brand favorability, little evidence of word-of-mouth in behalf of the club (but more negative than positive)

> *Alienateds*—Infrequent wine buyers, very little use of club benefits, low to moderate club brand favorability, generally negative word-of-mouth about the club

By our definitions, the Wine Lovers Club has about 12% advocates, better than some competitors but poorer than others. It also has 38% allegiant members, an attractive segment capable of stronger sales, deeper relationship, higher brand affinity and engagement, and more active and positive word-of-mouth.

	Wine Lovers Club	Lowest	Highest
Advocate	12%	5%	20%
Allegiant	38%	29%	51%
Ambivalent	21%	7%	29%
Alienated	30%	26%	39%

Figure 10.3   Wine Lovers Club advocacy segmentation.
Source: Market Probe, 2010.

Similar to findings of the CMO Council's study, the loyalty program also has a total of 51% ambivalent and alienated members who are minimally engaged and have the potential for negative communication and defection (see Figure 10.3).

Once the advocacy groupings were established, swing voter analysis was applied (see Figure 10.4). Some of the Wine Lovers Club program components, such as benefits that never expire, discounts, free shipping, and discounted storage rates, were found to be one-dimensional, that is, expected and nonleveraging, relative to other loyalty program elements. These features did little to drive loyalty perceptions and continued member patronage, and may even have caused some damage. Other components, such as referral benefits, points increases and increased discounts as tier levels rise, and a catalog with club logo items, might be described as driving negativism because they were compromising the concepts of exclusivity and lifestyle extension that are core to the club's concept and value proposition.

The most favorably perceived and leveraging program elements were those seen to have real meaning and enriching, personal significance for members. These included the winery visits, special events, access to pre-release and limited-production

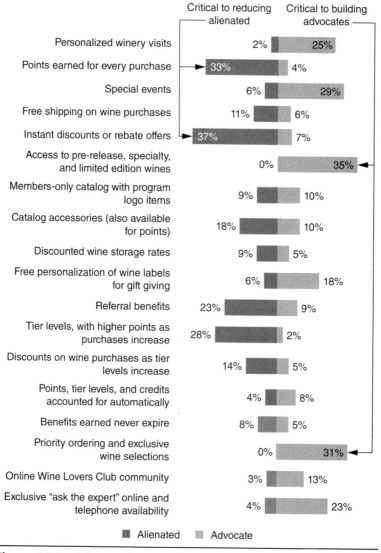

Figure 10.4 Advocacy impact of loyalty program components.
Source: Market Probe, 2010.

wines, priority ordering and exclusive wine selections, and the "ask the expert" online and telephone availability feature. These club program components were synched with members' lifestyles and self-perceptions, and advocacy research found them to be both attractive and differentiated.

THE WINE LOVERS CLUB OF THE FUTURE, AND THE FUTURE OF LOYALTY PROGRAMS AS ADVOCACY-BUILDING INSTRUMENTS

From 1987 to 1996, American Express' cardholder recruitment tagline was "Membership Has Its Privileges," promising exclusive elements of differentiated, personalized value to anyone who held an Amex card. This was an award-winning campaign and a high-water mark for American Express' growth. This has direct application to what the Wine Lovers Club could be in the future, and, indeed, it has ramifications for all loyalty programs as advocacy behavior builders.

Wine is a high-end consumable, and those who have strong involvement in wine see it as an extension of their lifestyle. The Wine Lovers Club's promises and components needed to reflect benefits with differentiated and personalized value to members. As a result of using member advocacy research and swing voter analysis to optimize its components, the Wine Lovers Club was able to emphasize those five elements that had the greatest personal interest to current members and that would best attract financially attractive new members. At the same time, the club was able to eliminate six costly and confusing components. The net result was a program that was more streamlined, more engaging, and considerably more profitable.

The Wine Lovers Club example is rather emblematic of challenges faced by customer loyalty programs as advocacy builders and sustainers. In many ways, these challenges are almost identical to those that must be overcome by traditional advertising. Namely, any change in message, positioning, or content is often viewed with suspicion rather than acceptance or positive anticipation. Loyalty programs, already seen by many as minimally valuable, must be especially careful with this. For example, Southwest Airlines, which for years had a very simple, trips-based frequent-flier program, recently went to a more classic points program based on miles in an effort to generate more revenue from business travelers. Though the jury is still out, substituting complex for straightforward has rarely created more loyalty behavior.

ADVERTISING'S EMERGING MARKETING ROLE IN DRIVING BUSINESS OUTCOMES

At the end of the day, we support the concepts articulated by Rory Sutherland of Ogilvy Group and word-of-mouth marketing consultant Andy Sernovitz. Namely, advertising, as both a craft and a component of marketing, can't afford to separate itself from the need to contribute to brand or product positive downstream customer behavior. If the advertising is passive, intellectually unstimulating and boring, undifferentiated, or, even worse, focused on being interruptive and doesn't contribute to generating customers and building advocacy, then its value is indeed limited. If it's energized and engaging, effectively cuts through the message clutter evident in both B2B and B2C advertising, and creates or reinforces a positive impression, then advertising can work effectively with, or dovetail into, the word-of-mouth desired from targeted customers.

What needs to be more openly and actively recognized by all parties involved in sales, marketing, branding, customer experience, and advertising is that online and off-line social word-of-mouth is now, and will continue to be, a fact of life:

- Consumer reviews are significantly more trusted—nearly 12 times more—than descriptions from manufacturers (*eMarketer*, February 2010)

- The average consumer mentions specific brands over 90 times per week in conversations with friends, family, and coworkers (Keller Fay, WOMMA, 2010)

- 74% of online shoppers are influenced by the opinions of others in their decisions to buy products or services (*Manage Smarter*, September 2009)

- 90% of consumers trust opinions from people they know; 70% trust opinions of unknown users (*Econsultancy*, July 2009)

- Social networks are growing in importance as a source of decision-making input. In a study by My Yearbook, 81% of respondents said they'd received advice through a social site from friends and followers relating to a product or service purchase, and close to three-quarters of those who received such advice found it to be influential in their decisions (ClickZ, January 2010)

This is, indeed, irrefutably strong evidence of the new realities for advertising.

11

Employee Advocacy (Ambassadorship) and Linkage to Customer Attitudes and Behavior

A part from customer loyalty, which is on the radar of every company, no other topic concerns organizations more than staff loyalty, commitment, and productivity.

Even with the economic softness felt throughout the country, staff turnover is near 20-year highs for many companies. Two research firms, Walker Information and Hudson Institute, recently joined forces to conduct a nationwide employee loyalty study. Their results confirmed that staff loyalty is in short supply (Freiberg and Freiberg 2010):

- Only 24% of employees consider themselves truly loyal, are committed to their organization and its goals, and plan to stay at least two years.

- Thirty-three percent of employees were high risk, not committed, and not planning to stay.

- Thirty-nine percent were classified as trapped. They plan to stay but are not committed to their organization.

- Among those who felt they worked for an ethical organization, 55% were truly loyal. For those who didn't feel they worked for an ethical organization, the loyalty figure was 9%.

The 72% of employees at risk or trapped represents another key, yet less explored, concern for companies. The lack of employee commitment frequently translates to being out of alignment with one another and with customers in executing the company's mission, goals, and strategic objectives and in appropriately representing the product or service value proposition. In other words, what they are doing on the job can be counterproductive and damaging. Since the issues influencing customer loyalty and commitment to a supplier are often highly correlated with staff productivity and proaction, optimizing employee loyalty and ambassadorship becomes doubly important.

Many companies don't even realize the depth of their staff retention, continuity, and alignment problems. While at the senior level, turnover may be only 4% or 5%, the real drain of talent is typically among employees aged 25–35 who have been at the same firm for 3–10 years. These staff members are often among the most productive and represent the highest long-term contribution potential for any company. They can also be among the most nonaligned with company vision and strategy, and in their commitment to customers. Yet, the vast majority of organizations don't track defections, threats of defection, or misalignment among this important group.

This "silent" defection and misalignment is particularly prevalent in large, decentralized companies with 20–100 divisions. On a single division basis, the defection and misalignment numbers among staff aged 25–35 may not seem problematic. But when viewed across all divisions of a company, the defection, potential defection, and misalignment numbers in this age group are often alarmingly high.

Firms pay a hefty price for staff defection, or *shadow* defection, where performance and commitment levels are very low. For starters, when employees defect, it has been found that customers are soon to follow. One customer defection study showed that roughly 70% of the reasons customers leave can be traced back to issues related to lack of staff commitment and staff turnover (Scheider, Parkington, and Buston 1980). And staff turnover often leads to more staff turnover. The departure of a valuable employee can send shock waves through a company culture, leaving remaining staff demoralized and disillusioned. If there is a trend toward misalignment, high staff turnover and low morale and disaffection will only cause it to increase.

Replacing the departed employee is expensive. Human resource executives estimate that when all factors are considered—the recruitment fees, discontinuity from defector's lost leads and contacts, the new employee's reduced productivity while learning the new job, and the time and energy coworkers spend guiding the newbie—replacement costs are estimated at approximately 150% of the departing person's salary.

Misalignment, too, carries a high price tag, though it's more challenging to isolate and estimate than the loss of an employee. A lack of alignment can be seen in places like the organization's style and culture, staff communication, teamwork, information flow, service to/focus on customers, level of training offered, productivity and efficiency, and management effectiveness.

When there is strong misalignment between employees and customers and/or between internal groups, the employees can suffer from both psychological and physical impairment. According to major employee research companies, positively engaged and focused employees feel they have better work–life balance, feel less stress, have greater optimism, and are more innovative and connected to the company. A Gallup Organization (2006) study, conversely, found that actively disengaged employees (about 15% of the workforce) cost the US economy about $300 billion each year in lower productivity and performance.

RESPONSIBILITIES AND OPPORTUNITIES IN CUSTOMER SERVICE: CUSTOMER LOYALTY ALIGNMENT

As discussed in Chapter 4, research studies in multiple industries indicate that customer service representatives (CSRs) across the United States handle an average of 2000 customer interactions each week. Training in proaction and relationship-focused processes can drive loyalty behavior. The reality, however, is that few organizations do this. Instead, they set unrealistic customer service productivity requirements, or they establish performance metrics and levels that are not based on customer input or need. Further, because customer service centers (also known as customer contact centers, call centers, or interaction centers) only recently have begun to be seen as profit generation centers, their vision and mission, as well as their operational construct, were seen in fairly myopic terms. Getting the most out of customer contact centers—indeed, from employees in all customer-facing and non-customer-facing functions—will require change; in many companies, this means significant change.

In order for commitment and ambassadorship to be optimized, companies will have to start focusing on people. Hal Rosenbluth, former CEO of the highly successful, multibillion dollar travel management company Rosenbluth International (now part of American Express Travel Related Services), said in his book *The Customer Comes Second* (2002, 24–25):

> We're talking about a change that puts the people in organizations above everything else. They are cared for, valued, empowered, and motivated to care for their clients. When a company puts its people first, the results are spectacular. Their people are inspired to provide a level of service that truly comes from the heart. It can't be faked.

Companies are only fooling themselves when they believe that "The Customer Comes First." People do not inherently put the customer first, and they certainly don't do it because their employer expects it. We're not saying choose your people over your customers. We're saying focus on your people because of your customers. That way, everybody wins.

Tremendous investments have been made in technological innovations—IVR systems, call routing, multimedia integration, and the like—yet investment in people and the processes to support them has been stagnant, lagging behind other efforts. To deliver on the promise technology offers in customer relationships, staff performance has to be prioritized. People have to be shown what to do, be given feedback about how they're doing, and be rewarded if they are doing well.

Meeting the objectives of a customer loyalty strategy means, for one thing, that targets and metrics set for CSRs must be balanced to incorporate productivity, quality of service delivered, and effectiveness of performance in behalf of customers. One of the most effective ways for accomplishing this, we have found, is through customer-first teams in customer service. There are several advantages to networked, team-based structures—as opposed to traditional hierarchies—as they strive to create value and higher trust levels for customers. They include better, more quickly shared information; greater decision agility; faster response time; and greater, more proactive, and relationship-building customer contact, as well as:

- Flattened, more matrix-based organizational structures for greater efficiency

- Minimizing non-value-added functional activities, better use of staff time and talent

- Assigning ownership of performance

- Greater opportunity for self-management and a wider scope of work in each job, with more (rotated) exposure to customers

- Linking performance objectives and individual and team performance to customer loyalty behavior

- More targeted employee training and skill development

Zappos, always ahead of the curve in these areas, labeled its call center the "Customer Loyalty Team." CSRs have no scripts. There are no call time metrics. There is no upselling or cross-selling. Instead, Zappos sees this group as integral to executing processes like its 365-day, no-questions-asked return policy.

Another organization whose belief in team-based customer service is legendary, and part of its DNA, is Southwest Airlines, perennially a leader in its industry. From the time the organization was founded, and with CEO Herb Kelleher at the helm, the company has made customer service a mantra. It has been a core philosophy, set down as part of the mission statement, repeated at meetings and celebrations, and extending to its "hire for attitude, train for skill" approach to bringing in only the most customer-focused new employees. Southwest also readily understands that it is impossible to create customer loyalty behavior without dedicated, empowered, trusted, and passionate employees. At the top of the organization, Southwest believes in "servant leadership," where egos are checked at the door and the emphasis is on helping employees develop and perform at their best in behalf of customers.

A fitting example of how customer-first teams can affect customer loyalty and customer win-back, as well as staff loyalty and performance, comes from Baptist Health Care in Pensacola, Florida (whose story is told in the following section). Several years ago, Baptist Health Care's patient service performance ranked close to the bottom of all hospitals in national surveys. This situation also contributed to both declining patient populations and low staff morale.

Baptist Health Care executives were determined to turn this around. Quint Studer, then the hospital's president, said, "We had to create the type of environment where people drive by two other hospitals to get here" (Lowenstein 2006). Baptist Health Care initially formed 10 cross-functional employee teams to examine every aspect of value delivery to patients and their families. More than 150 hospital employees now participate as members on these original teams. Each team has membership as diverse as corporate vice presidents and cafeteria workers. Additionally, Baptist has created ad hoc and ongoing teams to address areas such as customer win-back. Up to 30% of Baptist Health Care employees serve on teams at any given time.

Today, Baptist Health Care's service performance ranks among the very best in national customer surveys, its market share has significantly improved, staff morale is higher, and staff loss—and the money previously spent for recruiting as a result of turnover—has dramatically declined.

THE BAPTIST HEALTH CARE CUSTOMER-FOCUSED ORGANIZATIONAL CULTURE

Though a moderate-sized metropolitan area, Pensacola, located in northwest Florida, is among the 10 most competitive healthcare markets in the country. There are three healthcare systems in the marketplace; however, only one of them—Baptist Health Care (BHC)—is recognized as one of the nation's truly outstanding healthcare organizations, for both staff and patients.

In its advertisements, BHC leads with the headline "Happy Employees. Happy Patients" and states, "In health care, happy employees lead to happy patients." This only begins to inform its patients, employees, and the community at large about how well BHC understands the linkage between staff loyalty and patient loyalty.

For 10 straight years (2001–2010), BHC has been ranked among the best companies to work for in the United States, according to *Fortune* magazine's annual "100 Best Companies to Work For" list. The companies on this list are selected from a large national pool of candidate organizations, and ranking is principally based on how a random selection of employees responds to a survey measuring the quality of their workplace culture. Completing the patient–employee connection, BHC has been in the top 1% in perceived patient satisfaction for the past five years, according to research conducted among hospitals nationwide.

In addition, BHC has earned the following awards and notable distinctions:

- The USA Today/RIT Quality Cup for extraordinary results in employee and patient satisfaction

- The highest hospital employee morale in the country, as reported by a nationally syndicated employee attitude study

- The National Leadership Award for Excellence in Patient Care from Voluntary Hospitals of America

- Finalist visits for the Malcolm Baldrige National Quality Program in 2000, 2001, and 2002, and award recipient in 2003

As part of its routine training and job enrichment program, every quarter more than 500 BHC management and supervisory staffers attend what the organization calls "Baptist University" to learn about such topics as employee reward and recognition, change management, and customer loyalty. Prominent outside speakers and consultants are brought in to lead workshops. (I was pleased to conduct a daylong Baptist University workshop early in 2002 on customer risk, loss, and the customer life cycle, and the role of staff loyalty.)

BHC's culture is so advanced and unique that, during the past several years, over 1200 healthcare groups and 5700 healthcare professionals from 47 states have come to Pensacola to learn about the strategies and guiding philosophies that have yielded its best-practice results. In fact, BHC has set up a Leadership Institute to help others learn how to achieve similar success, which is itself an attractive profit center for the organization. For two days each month, key BHC department leaders hold seminars in Pensacola in which the curriculum includes presentations on the operational and service initiatives that continue to drive such impressive results for the healthcare system.

BAPTIST'S "JOURNEY TO EXCELLENCE"

As any employee of BHC will attest, these results, and this type of national reputation, cannot be achieved or sustained without vision, planning, organization, dedication, and pure hard work. Baptist has applied liberal doses of each to reach its goals.

Baptist's cultural transformation began in 1995 when senior staff took a long look at the organization. They weren't happy with what they saw. As Al Stubblefield, president and CEO of BHC, has said, "We felt like we had lost some of our focus on why we're here. We were caught up in the business side of things and lost touch with our true purpose—the patients."

By 1996, Baptist had determined that it wanted to be the best healthcare system in America. Continued Stubblefield, "We believed that we could build a competitive advantage if we could provide a level of service excellence not typically seen in health care." He also knew the level of commitment this would require of himself and everyone at BHC (Lowenstein 2006).

Baptist rapidly determined that employee involvement and commitment were the most effective foundation for the kind of service excellence it was seeking. All 5300 employees have been, and continue to be, central to its cultural and service transformation.

Senior management has been both supportive and active in what BHC calls its "Journey to Excellence." As noted by Pam Bilbrey, Baptist's former senior vice president for corporate development, "We're a service industry, so we don't have a tangible product—our product is our staff. You have to get your employees involved so that they feel a sense of ownership in the organization. Every employee is a stakeholder with responsibility for our overall success" (Lowenstein 2006).

BHC's cross-functional employee teams were formed to develop and establish methods and practices to reach its service excellence goals. The teams looked for improvement opportunities in key performance areas, and they also developed standards of performance for the organization. These now-formalized standards of performance include commitment to coworkers, limited waiting time for customers, privacy, safety awareness, and appearance—all elements that make a difference when dealing with patients and their families.

Within Baptist, a different behavior is highlighted every month, with contests and examples. So important have the standards of performance become that every job applicant at BHC is now required to read and sign a booklet explaining the standards.

By 1999, BHC had reduced its employee turnover from 27% to just over 19% and also substantially increased morale levels; however, it knew that setting standards of performance was only the beginning. The organization was challenged to build improvement into its program, as well as continuity. As explained by Bilbrey, "Now it's all about sustaining our efforts. You've got to sustain what you've already done and you've got to continuously improve. That's why we call this our 'Journey to Excellence,' because we believe that it's a journey without an end. We will never be perfect. We can always improve" (Lowenstein 2006).

Baptist's teams, established in 1996, are intact, continuing to find methods of enhancing the organization's performance. Employees are considered equals, having both empowerment and responsibility to act in behalf of patients, with everyone taking ownership and willing to share ideas and information. BHC has, over the past several years, also put in place a number of innovative approaches to involve, recognize, and reward employees for initiative. Here is a sampling:

- The *BHC Daily*, a written reminder of what's being done organization-wide around a particular performance standard, which is distributed to everyone.

- Open communication, including communication boards, employee forums, access to financial reports, employee lunches with administrators, an intranet site, and gathering/ sharing of patient–staff interaction anecdotes.

- Peer interviewing, where every job is peer interviewed and supervisors are interviewed by staff, enabling hard-wiring of accountability by using the selection form completed by the interview team.

- WOW certificates, an opportunity for staff to recognize one another, which helps reinforce standards of performance behaviors. Five WOW certificates are redeemable for $20 in the gift shop or a $15 gift certificate to a local merchant.

- Certificates of appreciation for employment tenure milestones; handwritten thank-you notes from the hospital president are sent to employees' homes, recognizing an outstanding contribution (supervisors receive e-mail confirmation of notes); "Champion" recognition for exemplary contribution, with posting of staff member's picture on a special hospital board and awarding of a plaque.

- "Legends of Baptist Health Care," recognition for going far beyond basic responsibilities in behalf of coworkers, patients, or the community. Those recognized receive limo transportation to the resort where board retreats are held. Their stories are showcased to the board in a video presentation. They receive a Legend pin and framed award, and their stories are presented to the rest of BHC staff in a booklet available at each facility.

Today, BHC has one of the lowest annual staff turnover rates for hospitals in the nation (just over 14%) and one of the highest levels of employee morale for *any* company in *any* industry. As reported by Celeste Norris, BHC's former director of human resources, the nursing vacancy rates within the organization are far below the national average, and there is little to no use of expensive agency or travel nurses.

Desperation Tactic versus Strategic Staff Loyalty Management: The Attempted Poaching of Baptist Hospital RNs, Baptist's Response, and the Outcome

As mentioned earlier, Pensacola is an extraordinarily competitive healthcare market. Of the three healthcare systems there, BHC and its principal rival account for close to 80% of patient admissions, with Baptist having a slight share advantage. Baptist Hospital, the system's 492-bed flagship facility, has low RN turnover; however, its major competitor cannot make the same claim. Consequently, the competitor was using costly part-time and agency-supplied RNs and seeking a quick, efficient solution to that problem.

Following RN raid concepts used in other markets, the competitor ran newspaper ads the weekend just prior to July 4, 2002, offering an aggressive signing bonus inducement to RNs in the community: an extra $500 per month over a 24-month employment period. Further, if one of the competitor's employees made a referral that resulted in the hiring of an RN, that staff member would also receive $12,000. Thus, the competitor could have paid out a maximum of $24,000 per RN hire. This, in sum, was an attempt to "buy" RNs.

The Monday after the ads ran, Baptist Hospital was abuzz with activity. Nurses at the competitive healthcare system were calling BHC nurses, because there was an attractive immediate payoff for them if they could get Baptist nurses to jump ship. Many rumors and much gossip traveled throughout Baptist Hospital, with calls to the Human Resources Department from nursing supervisors. With 377 nurses on Baptist Hospital's staff, representing almost one-fifth of all hospital employees, there was a great deal at stake.

Senior staff quickly began meeting with nurse leaders to get their direct reactions. Norris, who was Baptist's human resources director at the time, did an assessment of staffing, turnover and vacancy rates, employee morale, and customer loyalty levels. Her conclusion was that, overall, staffing, morale, and customer service levels were at the high levels BHC had come to expect. She also did a direct comparison of what Baptist Hospital and the competitor were offering nurses in terms of pay (including weekend, overtime, and holiday compensation), benefits, and retirement.

Addressing the issue head-on, the execs looked at what they could do, financially and otherwise, to counter the competitive offer. They did what-if scenario projections regarding raising salaries and/or weekend or holiday pay. They also checked with hospitals in south Florida, which had experienced a similar financial incentive battle situation between two healthcare facilities. In that situation, rival hospitals across town both advertised $15,000 incentives for RNs. Baptist wanted to learn exactly how it worked and whether either hospital had made any substantial nursing employment gains (or losses) as a result. Baptist discovered that the two hospitals ended up just swapping a few nurses—a lot of turmoil and expense with little positive result on either side.

After much consideration, Baptist Hospital decided to offer RNs modest pay raises, in addition to regular merit increases, based on years of service, called "Loyalty Pays." Weekend pay rates were also increased, and some limited referral and sign-on bonuses to match the competitor were announced.

E-mails were sent to everyone, explaining what management had heard from nurses and what it had elected regarding a response, and reinforcing their belief in the Baptist culture. Then a department head meeting was called. Although RNs represented the largest single staff group, other key support departments—pharmacy, ultrasound, radiology, physical therapy, and so forth—naturally wanted to know, "How come them and not me?" Some felt that they weren't valued as much as the nurses, and the reasons for management's decisions and actions were carefully explained and discussed. Department heads were then instructed to carry the message to their staffs. Calm and efficiency were quickly restored.

Every Battle Has a Conclusion . . . and Lessons for the Combatants

Forty-five days after the competitor placed its ad, the result of its having spent all that money on the attempted raid was that only nine RNs left Baptist Hospital to take full-time employment with the rival hospital. Another seven took employment with the competitor but stayed on as relief nurses at Baptist, working weekends. They wanted to maintain ties with friends and coworkers. In the same time period, by the way, Baptist hired over 20 new full-time RNs.

One of the defecting nurses came back to Baptist Hospital almost immediately, and several others came back somewhat later, because of the competitor's work environment. When the dust had finally settled, the net effect was that only a couple of Baptist RNs actually left the hospital and stayed with the competitor.

The reality is, of course, that at BHC very few employees *want* to leave, and very few did, even with an extremely attractive monetary offer dangled in front of them. There's a culture of patient focus, inclusion, and participation at BHC that employees desire and appreciate. Money is always part of the value employees see in their jobs, to be sure; but it's the environment, the training, and the daily and long-term experience that are so much more important to them.

At Baptist, employees respect one another's professions. It's well understood, for instance, that nurses are the direct link to patients. They're at the patient's bedside, the first line of patient–employee contact, just like CSRs. In a shared corporate value and climate of "patients come first," everyone pulls together. That's a central reason why BHC's rate of staff turnover continues to go down.

Just as lower pricing alone is both a one-dimensional strategy and a historically poor ploy for marketers, employers have to realize that salary and benefits alone are only a small part of the employee's value equation. Employees want enrichment. They want inclusion. They want communication and participation. They want training. They want recognition. They want to have pride in where they work. They want management to lead by example.

BHC is now using its superior performance in patient care and services as a springboard for moving to an even higher plateau. As described by Bilbrey, "We're pushing ourselves to move past the passion of service excellence to the next stage: customer loyalty" (Lowenstein 2006).

The array of cross-functional customer-first team possibilities is limited only by an organization's willingness to embrace the concept. Bottom line: Customer-first teams enhance loyalty and staff productivity. BHC is an excellent example of the success of customer-first teams. Every company should want to emulate BHC's achievements.

Companies are also going to have to do a better job of determining just how effective service groups are at creating perceived customer value and, ultimately, optimizing customer loyalty behavior. Traditional employee satisfaction studies, just like customer satisfaction studies, are much more about measuring superficial attitudes and past events—keying largely on salaries and benefits and the working environment—than they are about understanding how aligned staff are with customers, how productive staff are in behalf of customers, and how well supported and directed they are in providing value.

For customer-facing groups like those in customer service to have the same type of contribution, alignment with goals, and leadership seen in organizations like Rosenbluth International and BHC, and for these groups to help realize the promise of customer centricity, the three words that need to be emphasized are training, involvement, and measurement.

A QUICK HOW-TO PRIMER FOR STAFF LOYALTY, ALIGNMENT, AND ADVOCACY RESEARCH

Having reviewed hundreds of traditional employee satisfaction surveys over the years, and carefully studying how the results have been applied by companies, it's clear that the vast majority of them are about as superficial and challenged to provide real direction to corporate and HR management as their customer satisfaction survey cousins.

Employee loyalty and commitment study results are, as noted, often mirror images of what's going on with customers. For example, one of our clients was known to have a highly ineffectual regional director. In that director's region, both customer and staff defection were quite high. On the staff loyalty and alignment study, employees in that region rated teamwork and staff communication dramatically lower than employees in other regions. Likewise, the customer loyalty scores for that same region were also low, with particularly poor performance on customer communication and responsiveness. Bottom line: Staff loyalty, focus, and alignment problems ultimately become customer problems.

Compared with traditional employee satisfaction and engagement research, there's a lot to know about identifying the drivers of ambassadorship. Here are some guidelines to keep you on track:

- *Avoid measuring employee satisfaction.* Satisfaction has a strong tendency to deal with attitudes and not behaviors. Also, satisfaction has proved to be poorly correlated with actual loyalty and productive behavior. For example, a recent employee study showed that only 10% said they were dissatisfied with their employers and their jobs, but 25% said they would search for a new job within a year. Instead, ask questions that measure your company's performance as an employer (e.g., "On a scale of 1–5, rate our performance as your employer").

- *Measure employees' likelihood to remain with you.* Likewise, measure your employees' likelihood to recommend the company or otherwise communicate in positive ways to other potential employees (e.g., "On a scale of 1–5, how likely are you to recommend the company to other potential employees?").

- *Develop specific statements*—on a custom basis (through qualitative research)—about key aspects of employees' working life, relationships, how they are guided and supported, and so on, to be presented to all employees for performance and importance evaluation. These are known as attributes. I recommend that attributes be customized, rather than be identical to those applied at other companies, because the culture and operating processes of each company are unique. In your staff loyalty study, include attribute statements that address each of the following six themes:

— *Cohesion*—These attributes address teamwork and communication between and within groups, plus work quality, effectiveness, and staff/management interaction

— *Morale/Culture*—These attributes address the "fabric" of the organization, consideration of staff needs, and place of employment

— *Career security/Growth*—These attributes address the employees' sense of "shared destiny," or the belief that the company will support their security, growth, and career development

— *Business confluence*—These attributes address the extent to which employees partner and participate in the company's vision, mission, and strategic objectives

— *Customer focus*—These attributes address the employees' opinions of the company's proaction and responsiveness with customers, and how the tools they are provided help with that goal

— *Management effectiveness*—These attributes address employees' views of how well people and processes are managed

- *Ask staff members to rank elements of their jobs*—and to explain their reasons for those rankings. Employees are also asked to state reasons for low attribute and overall performance ratings, providing quantified anecdotal depth to the ratings data.

- *Identify areas of expressed and unexpressed staff complaints.* When complaints are unexpressed, determine the reasons; when they are expressed, ask about the outcomes. Look at—in other words, model—the impact of complaints, especially those frequently stated, on staff loyalty.

- *Model the impact of attribute performance and importance on staff loyalty and commitment to customers.* Report key findings and modeled results. Within the report, draw conclusions and make recommendations. Take action, including reporting findings back to staff.

- *Ask staff for their feedback*—it implies a commitment by management for action based on findings. Report findings in a timely manner to staff, along with an action plan for addressing key concerns. Do this, and you'll help grow employee trust and strengthen loyalty and alignment. Don't do it, and employees will likely blow off your next staff survey. Our quantitative methods are built around self-completion interviews and include online staff loyalty data collection, which enables almost real-time analysis and reporting of findings, conclusions, and recommendations to staff and management.

In our book *Customer WinBack* (2001, 251–280), coauthor Jill Griffin and I identify nine best practices for building staff commitment and ambassadorship. The following is distilled and summarized from about 30 pages in the book:

- *Build a climate of trust and authenticity that works both ways*—Employees appreciate and respond to empowerment and opportunities to learn and contribute. For most employees, trust is shown in one important way when they can manage their own time and resources. Trust needs to be woven into the company's mission and vision statement, and there should be a certain amount of transparency and a free flow of information between management and staff. This will also help mitigate negative communication and gossip.

As discussed earlier in the book, Southwest Airlines has a standing customer culture committee tasked with maintaining the company's values. Annually, Zappos produces a culture book for all employees. Half of an employee's review is based on his or her fit within the culture.

- *Train, train, train, and cross-train*—Task-related and non-task-related training is seen by many employees as the company's faith and investment in them. Training is the most productive and effective form of employee recognition and development; however, it is often the most vulnerable to budget cutbacks. Cross-training helps foster cohesiveness, involvement, and leadership. Training should be considered beyond the employee's immediate functional area to create more well-rounded, knowledgeable, and contributory employees.

  Over 80% of Southwest Airlines employees are cross-trained in at least one other function every year as one method of building leadership. Zappos gives new employees five weeks of training when hired, including two weeks on the phone with customers and time in the warehouse picking and packing orders. After that five weeks, new employees are offered $3,000 to quit (and only 2% of them take the offer). This helps ensure that the new employees are dedicated and motivated to support the Zappos customer value culture.

- *Make sure each employee has a career path*—Provide tools so employees can inventory talents and elements of experience, and encourage movement within the company. Many leading-edge companies find they can build leadership and loyalty by enabling employees to move freely into different groups.

- *Provide frequent evaluations and reviews*—Effective feedback systems play a big role in keeping employees productive and committed to their jobs and to the company. Research studies consistently find that employees are emphatic in their desire for as much feedback from management and peers as they can get. Don't wait to do this on an annual or semiannual basis. Do it as frequently as possible (e.g., "just-in-time," if this is workable), as it will help the employee grow and develop. Also, bottom-up feedback, where employees provide insight as to what management can do to make them more effective and productive, should be built into the review model.

- *Seek to inform, seek to debrief*—Employees often complain that even though they are working harder than ever, their thoughts about anything beyond their immediate jobs are rarely sought. Schedule frequent update meetings featuring employee input and contributions. Some companies have "radical inclusion" approaches: Arranging for people to hear news at exactly the same time sends a signal that everyone is valued and everyone is "in the know." Other organizations have novel ways of communicating with staff—from panel discussions to town meetings.

- *Recognize and reward initiative*—Best-in-class companies don't just do the expected for customers. They create top-end experiences, in part through proactive and committed employees. One of the key ways this happens is by fostering a culture that recognizes and rewards initiative. Employees should be both recognized and rewarded for building customer value (i.e., relationship building, creative solutions, empowered achievements, cross-functional involvement). When designing such programs, it should be kept in mind that these initiatives are rarely expensive, so the "we can't afford it" trap should be avoided. Also, companies should make clear distinctions between recognition and reward. The recognition should be special, a real token of appreciation that singles out the employee for his or her contribution.

- *Ask employees what they want (and give it to them)*—Conduct ambassadorship, linkage, and alignment research to find out how productive and loyal employees are and how well they are supported and guided in building value and equity for customers. Avoid measuring employee satisfaction, because, like measures of customer satisfaction, traditional employee studies provide relatively little useful direction. Also, survey results (and plans being developed as a product of survey findings) should be shared with staff in an expeditious manner.

- *By all means, have fun!*—Use creative means to give a lighter, more family-oriented "feel" to company culture. Ideas can include events around holidays, an open house for family members, special recognition prizes, and so forth. Some companies, recognizing that "playing together means staying together," have initiated novel approaches to lighten daily grinds. Ben & Jerry's, for instance, has a "Grand Poobah of Joy," who gives entertaining messages over the office intercom, accompanied by harmonica music (and employees also get two free pints of ice cream per day). Recognizing that happy employees do not necessarily equal happy customers, they also blend in more practical approaches for culture building.

- *Hire the right employees in the first place*—Profile top performers to identify success factors, and make recruiting top talent a key corporate value. Zappos, for example, is very careful to "hire for the culture" even more than for capability and experience. Some companies, such as Southwest Airlines, even make customers part of the employee recruiting process. Other organizations keep detailed records on their recruiting efforts, including debriefing both successful and unsuccessful candidates.

Creating a culture within the organization that nurtures loyalty, commitment, and productivity from the moment the new hire walks through the door and throughout the life cycle of the employee will go a long way to sustaining customer loyalty. The good news is that employees, particularly those in customer service, will want to be active contributors to that effort. As *Fortune* magazine columnist Thomas Stewart (1996, 146) said, "Human beings want to pledge allegiance to something. The desire to belong is a foundation value, underlying all others." When that "something" is the optimization of customer loyalty behavior, everybody wins, to repeat the guiding conclusion of Hal Rosenbluth.

LINKAGES BETWEEN EMPLOYEE ATTITUDES AND ACTIONS AND CUSTOMER BEHAVIOR

There is an amply proven, powerful relationship between employee commitment to the company/brand value proposition/customer and the employer's actual business and marketplace outcomes in financial terms. Yet, when considering and measuring the pivotal elements of staff performance and productivity, most companies are focused principally on employee attitudes around satisfaction, company loyalty, alignment with goals and objectives (such as corporate citizenship), and levels of engagement. These are important, to be sure, but historically they only superficially and weakly correlate what employees think and do with actual customer behavior.

Employees can significantly influence customer loyalty behavior toward their employer through a range of attitudes and actions in behalf of the brand, company, and customer. These attitudes and actions, as with customers, range from highly positive to highly negative.

We most typically concentrate on what drives active, positive, and vocal commitment (i.e., ambassadorship or advocacy);

however, it is equally important to identify where employee indifference and negativism (potentially leading to alienation attitudes and actions) exist, why they exist, and how they can be mitigated or eliminated. If employee advocacy is the North Pole, then alienation is the South Pole. In this part of the chapter, we will identify what starts an employee on the journey to the South Pole.

THE ROOTS OF EMPLOYEE NEGATIVISM

I developed a set of questions for full-time employees and conducted original research on employee negativism through a national polling service. A total of 1165 individuals completed the online questionnaire in September 2007.

One of the first objectives of the questionnaire was to identify employees' overall commitment level, loyalty, and impression about the company and its perceived ability to earn customers' trust and loyalty. This was accomplished through a series of four simple agree-disagree statements, shown in Table 11.1. Two of the questions—commitment to the organization's success and ability to earn customer trust and loyalty—had fairly high positivism. The two statements

Table 11.1 Key employee advocacy question results.

	Yes	No	Not sure
I am very committed to the success of my employer organization	78%	12%	9%
We consistently earn our customers' trust and loyalty	76%	12%	12%
I feel very loyal to the organization I currently work for	70%	20%	10%
I have a very positive impression about the organization I work for	68%	22%	10%

that addressed overall impression and loyalty—loyalty to the organization and positive impression about the organization—however, showed significantly greater negativity.

There were definite age-related differences on all these elements, with younger (18- to 24-year-old) respondents giving lower percentages of "Yes" scores on all measures. For example, on "I am very committed to the success of my employer organization," 63% of 18- to 24-year-olds answered yes, compared to 83% of respondents aged 50–64 and 86% of respondents aged 65 or older. Also, there was higher positivism among African Americans and Republicans. There also tended to be some polarizing on these statements based on income: On all measures, those with an annual income of $34,900 or less gave lower scores. On a geographic basis, respondents in the South more frequently answered yes on all statements. Finally, female respondents were more loyal to their organizations, had more positive impressions about their organizations, and more frequently answered yes to earning customers' trust and loyalty (81% females vs. 72% males).

Just as with consumer opinions and decision-making dynamics, informal communication from employees has a great deal to do with impressions of an organization, both inside by other employees and outside by customers, vendors, and the general public. Employees were asked whether they tell others how bad their company is as a place to work. A total of 43% said they do (7% frequently, and 36% sometimes).

Here again, there were differences by age, with a greater frequency of echo boomers (49%) saying negative things about their employer, and significantly lower percentages among respondents aged 62 or older (25%). Also, negativism was higher among males than females and lower among African Americans. It was also higher among respondents with low incomes (48%) and lower among respondents with high incomes (37%). Finally, negativism was very high among respondents with disabilities (52%), compared to those with no disabilities (40%).

THE POTENTIAL IMPACTS OF NEGATIVISM

In this research, my colleagues and I also wanted to understand the potential effects, inside and outside the organization, of negatives expressed by employees. We asked respondents if they ever tell others about how bad the products and/or services of their employer are. Over one-third said they do, either frequently (3%) or sometimes (32%).

Demographically, this is higher in the East, and among African American respondents (41%); it is also consistent with feelings about their employer—lower among respondents aged 50–64 (28%) and those over 65 (25%), but higher among 18- to 24-year-olds (42%). Males are also more negative about their company's products and services than are females (39% versus 30%). Those who identified their sexual orientation as GLBT also were significantly more negative (60%). There was marked impact of polarity by income level: 44% of respondents with an annual income of $34,900 or less, compared to 31% with an annual income of $75,000 or higher. Finally, there was greater tendency to tell consumers negative things (compared to businesses) and to speak negatively about products compared to services.

To better identify what was behind neutral to negative perceptions of their employer's products and services, we asked respondents why they believed their company does not earn customers' trust and loyalty. The array of key reasons included poor customer interaction and unfair treatment of both customers and employees, along with the following:

- *Profit is the only motivation for the company* (11%)— Told more to consumers (than to businesses)

- *Poor customer service* (11%)—Told more to consumers (than to businesses)

- *Lies to customers* (10%)—Almost entirely by baby boomers; more frequently from those with a high school education or less; told more about products than services

- *Inconsistent policies/treat different customers differently* (9%)—Strongly from baby boomers; more frequently from those with a high school education or less; told more about products than services

- *Does not treat employees fairly* (9%)—Strongly from baby boomers; more frequently from those with a high school education or less; told more about products than services

There have been extensive studies on negative employees, teams, and groups: how, when, and why "bad apples" spoil the barrel. Negative behaviors breed their own viral contagion and include withholding effort, withdrawal and lack of enthusiasm, defensiveness, "reputation sniping" communication, purposely violating interpersonal standards, and general lack of cooperation and proaction.

These behaviors can create localized or broader dysfunction, of course, and the results of any of them will create an equally unsettled response among customers when encountered. And just as important, they affect business outcomes such as customer and brand loyalty and "hard numbers" such as profitability, revenues, return on capital, and cash flow. Lack of employee engagement and advocacy also affects productivity and contributes to turnover.

LEVERAGING EMPLOYEE POSITIVISM

Employee positivism, the essence of advocacy, is absolutely critical for companies striving to be optimally customer centric. Even though customer experience management processes may be tightly managed, executing and sustaining them is virtually impossible without the enthusiastic and real support of employees. These experiences, and resulting levels of customer loyalty behavior, are greatly influenced by employee interactions.

For example, many studies have determined that customers who complain to an organization and have their complaints satisfactorily resolved tell an average of 5 other people about the good treatment they received, and they tell at least 20 people if they receive poor treatment. Many of these studies were conducted pre-internet, so the potential for negative informal communication (blogs, forums, chat rooms, online communities, rating sites, etc.) is much stronger in today's world (Tice 2009).

Service studies have also shown that of the customers who register a complaint, between 54% and 70% will do business with the organization again if their complaints are resolved. This figure goes up to 95% if the customers feel the complaints are resolved professionally, quickly, and proactively, depending on both systems and positive employee attitudes and actions.

So, it is both culturally desirable and financially rewarding for organizations to foster employee positivism. Compared with negative word-of-mouth about their employer as a place to work, our respondents tended to express positives more frequently, which is a very good outcome (for employers and customers) to this research. Overall, 34% of the respondents said they frequently tell others how good their company is, and 48% sometimes communicated positive messages. Within this positivism, however, it should be noted that the lowest frequent personal positive communication was by 18- to 24-year-olds (24%), and the highest was among those aged 65 or older (43%)—consistent, but in reverse, with age-related expressions of negativism.

Finally, we asked respondents whether they tell others how good the products or services of the company they work for are. Encouragingly, 88% said they do (38% frequently and 50% sometimes). Employers should be gratified by the marked proclivity of employees to be positive *and* vocal about their employer's products and/or services, compared to the likelihood of being negative *and* vocal. Nevertheless, the impact on customer behavior of both needs to be understood and consistently monitored.

THE CASE FOR EMPLOYEE ADVOCACY

How can companies keep a consistent customer focus and optimize business performance, which, after all, is the goal of customer centricity? Is it done with great products and product co-creation with customers? Is it through customer segmentation based on detailed profiling and interpretation? Or is it through outstanding service and original, effective marketing? Few would dispute that all these are important. At the vast majority of companies, sales, service, and marketing functions and activities tend to be discrete. And, discrete, siloed execution equals suboptimized results.

There are many ways to bring all these individual, rarely conjoined functions and capabilities into unison so that they are more effective in behalf of both the customer and the employee. Perhaps the simplest, and arguably the most sustainable and strategically differentiated, is to have employees directly and actively involved in making this happen. This—what we call *employee advocacy*—is clearly a worthwhile goal, with two key and immediate questions: (1) how do you make this a reality, and (2) how do you measure the effectiveness of what you're doing? I'll address the second question first, and then offer examples of what companies like Virgin, Eastman Kodak, Honeywell, Ford, NCR, ING, and Hewlett-Packard are doing to create and sustain a culture of employee ambassadorship.

A culture of customer "wow" begins with employee job satisfaction . . .

The history of companies measuring employee job satisfaction, and endeavoring to link employee perceptions with customer behavior, goes back almost 100 years. Organizational surveys began during the 1920s and 1930s, a result of emphasis on industrial engineering and time-and-motion studies, which began at the dawn of the twentieth century.

By the 1960s and 1970s, many companies were conducting *employee attitude and satisfaction* studies. These studies were further refined during the 1980s and early 1990s, and they focused as much on achieving quality as on creating satisfied employees.

. . . is enhanced through employee alignment with the company's mission and brand promise . . .

In the mid-1990s, more-progressive companies moved on to *employee engagement* research. This was a significant step for human resources professionals. Companies recognized that they needed to view employees not only as a resource but as partners in helping reach overall business goals. The principal intentions of employee engagement, then, are to identify:

- What originally drew individuals to the company

- What keeps them there

- What they see as their role and how involved they are in it

- How aligned they are with the company's goals and culture

Engagement seeks to quantify emotional and rational job satisfaction and motivation to think, feel, and act. This combination is extremely important for training, communication, staff management, and individual and group goal-setting.

Though widely accepted by the human resources management community, engagement actually represents a mélange of loosely related concepts. In 2006, the Conference Board published *Employee Engagement: A Review of Current Research and Its Implications*, by John Gibbons. According to this report, 12 major studies on employee engagement had been published over the prior four years by top research firms. Each of the studies used different definitions and, collectively, came up with 26 key drivers of engagement. For example, some studies emphasized the underlying cognitive issues, and others emphasized the underlying emotional issues.

The Conference Board looked across this compilation of data and constructed both a blended definition and key themes that crossed all the studies. They identify employee engagement as "a heightened emotional connection that an employee feels for his or her organization, that influences him or her to exert greater discretionary effort to his or her work." Many of the studies agreed on eight key drivers:

- Trust and integrity—How well do managers communicate and "walk the talk"?

- Nature of the job—Is it mentally stimulating day to day?

- Line of sight between employee performance and company performance—Do employees understand how their work contributes to the company's performance?

- Career growth opportunities—Are there future opportunities for growth?

- Pride about the company—How much self-esteem do the employees feel by being associated with their company?

- Coworkers/team members—How much do they significantly influence one's level of engagement?

- Employee development—Is the company making an effort to develop the employee's skills?

- Relationship with one's manager—Does the employee value his or her relationship(s) with manager(s)?

Brand engagement is an extension of employee engagement. Much of brand engagement is managed through the marketing structure, and it involves the communication of company values and product and service benefits to current and potential customers and to other stakeholders. Some companies have recognized that to deliver the brand promise externally, employees represent the biggest opportunity to arrive at that destination. Involving employees more directly in brand building has definite advantages for HR, such as attracting and retaining good employees and creating a stronger understanding of the company's mission and vision, which then combine to build a more cohesive and aligned workforce.

One quick example of this is Boots the Chemist, the United Kingdom's largest drugstore chain. When the company initially introduced its very successful customer loyalty program, employees were the first participants. Seeing its benefits firsthand, Boots' employees enthusiastically helped promote the program to customers while on the job and with friends and relatives outside their daily employment.

Employees, whether they are customer facing or not, need to "live" the brand and company value promise as company representatives. Concepts and programs such as employee engagement and brand engagement (through employees), though considerably more progressive than satisfaction, may not be sufficient to help companies optimize the customer experience or sustain top-level customer value delivery. Employees may believe they are doing valuable things for their company and they may have positive feelings about their jobs, their employers, and the brands they represent, but where is the specificity around building the best customer experience and relationships?

In its basic thesis, engagement loosely parallels the Service Profit Chain, a model developed by Heskett, Sasser, and Schlesinger (1997) in the 1990s. The model is generally summarized as *happy employees = happy customers = happy shareholders*. In other words, at the core of engagement is the tacit belief that there is a direct relationship or linkage between higher employee satisfaction and customer experience. And, as found by noted customer experience expert Frank Capek (2007),

> just because employee satisfaction and engagement are *correlated* with customer satisfaction doesn't mean that making employees happier will lead to better customer experience. This is one of those classic traps your college professors warned you about: confusing correla-

tion with causation. I've observed that this flaw in logic has led many organizations to invest in trying to make their employees happier in the hope that those happier employees will turn around and deliver a better experience for customers. We've just seen too many companies where, at best, more highly engaged employees simply deliver a sub-par experience more enthusiastically.

One of the shortfalls that can be observed in engagement, particularly as this type of research applies to optimizing customer experience, is that even if employees are trained in brand image, this does not necessarily mean they will deliver on the product or service value promise to customers or other stakeholders. Image needs to be integrated with building a culture of true customer focus. In other words, customers have to experience the external brand promise every time they interact with the company.

. . . and culminates in advocacy, or ambassadorship, where employees "live" the brand promise for themselves and for the benefit and loyalty behavior of customers

Can companies, through employee research, learn how to prioritize initiatives that will generate optimum staff commitment to the company, to the brand value promise, and to the customers?

If employee satisfaction and employee engagement aren't specifically designed to meet this critical objective, and only tangentially correlate with customer behavior, can a single technique provide the means to do that? The answer to both questions is yes, through employee advocacy research. Employee advocacy, like customer advocacy, has been specifically designed to both build on employee satisfaction and engagement and bring the customer into the equation, linking employee attitudes and actions to customer loyalty behavior.

Employee advocacy, or employee brand ambassadorship, has direct connections to—yet is distinct from—both employee satisfaction and employee engagement. As a research frame-work, its overarching objective is to identify the most active and positive (and inactive and negative) level of employee commitment to the company's product and service value promise, to the company itself, and to optimizing the customer experience.

The employee advocacy thesis, with its component elements, can be displayed as shown in Figure 11.1.

- *Commitment to company*—Commitment to, and being positive about, the company (through personal satisfaction, fulfillment, and an expression of pride) and to being a contributing, loyal, and fully aligned member of the culture

- *Commitment to value proposition*—Commitment to, and alignment with, the mission and goals of the company, as expressed through perceived excellence (benefits and solutions) provided by products and/or services

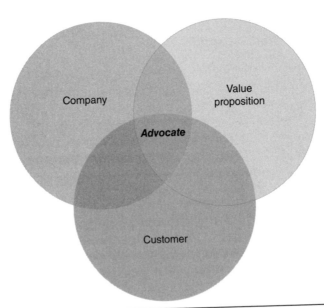

Figure 11.1 Employees who score high on the commitment to the company, the value proposition, and the customer are considered advocates.

- *Commitment to customer*—Commitment to understanding customer needs and to performing in a manner that provides customers with optimal experiences and relationships, as well as delivering the highest level of product and/or service value

Employee advocacy is very definitely linked to the productivity and empowerment elements of employee satisfaction, engagement, and alignment research; however, it more closely parallels achievement of business results and value building because its emphasis is on strengthening customer bonds through direct and indirect employee interaction.

I developed original research utilizing a framework designed specifically to identify drivers of employee advocacy and alienation. It was initially tested with a national panel in 2006, and then it was updated in 2008 with a national sample of 4300 adults who are employed full time. The sample size was sufficient to provide baseline results in close to 20 major business and industry areas.

The three elements of the advocacy research model—company, value proposition, customer—were measured by nine agree/disagree scale attitude statements (three in each of the elements). In addition, a number of loyalty and word-of-mouth (positive and negative communication) metrics were used to help validate the new framework.

Overall Employee Advocacy Baseline Study Results

About 15.5% of adults employed full time and working for a company were identified through the framework as advocates. At the opposite end of the commitment spectrum were employees identified as alienated (about 29.5%). Whereas advocates are beneficial, alienated employees and sabotage levels are of particular concern to organizations because of their "bad apple" potential impact on the productivity and morale of other employees, and on the behavior of customers.

These typical results for advocacy and alienation levels were found in several industries:

- Education
- Healthcare and social assistance
- Technology services
- Banking and finance
- Engineering services
- Insurance

Some industry groups had very high advocacy levels coupled with low alienation levels:

- Religious and nonprofit organizations
- Construction
- Legal services

Conversely, there were industry groups with very low advocacy levels and high alienation levels:

- Telecommunications
- Retail trade, manufacturing
- Transportation and warehousing
- Accommodation and food services

It's interesting and instructive to note that some of the industries so often featured in business studies and in trade stories and articles—especially telecom, retailing, and lodging and food services—represent the poorest reported customer experiences and the highest levels of service complaint.

Advocacy Research Key Findings

In addition to employee motivation, cohesion, productivity, and alignment with corporate values and culture, human resources is perhaps most interested in learning how to increase staff loyalty. Our research identified employee loyalty levels through three specific metrics: rating of the organization as a place to work, likelihood to recommend the organization to friends or family members as a place to work, and level of felt loyalty to the organization. Overall, 18% of our respondents exhibited high loyalty to their organizations, and 20% exhibited low loyalty; importantly, there were strong, almost polar-opposite differences in organizational loyalty depending on whether an employee was categorized as an ambassador or a saboteur, validating ambassadorship framework results shown in Table 11.2.

These are definite "pay attention" findings for human resources. It's a concern, of course, that almost 20% of employees have low organizational loyalty, but it's an even greater challenge that there is three times the level of potential staff turnover among alienated employees, who, before they depart, will undermine the performance and loyalty of other employees. Our research provided very specific insights into why this is occurring. At the same time, the organization will be very well served to emulate the behaviors and attitudes of advocates through the rest of the culture.

Commitment to the company in the form of loyalty and related attitudes and behaviors is a fairly basic requirement for

Table 11.2 Employee loyalty by advocacy group.

	Total	**Advocate**	**Alienated**
Low	19.8%	0.0%	61.0%
Medium	61.9%	27.3%	38.5%
High	18.3%	72.7%	0.5%
Total	100.0%	100.0%	100.0%

Note: Employee loyalty was measured by rating of the organization as a place to work, likelihood to recommend organization as a place to work, and level of loyalty felt to the organization.

employee advocacy. Just as important is feeling that the company is a good place to work and that its products and services are good, and communicating this belief to others, including colleagues, friends, and customers.

Similar to overall employee loyalty findings, advocates were found to be both positive and vocal promoters and representatives of the company as a place to work, while most alienated employees never, or at least less frequently, said anything good about the company as an employer. In terms of the highest frequency of saying positive things about the company as a place to be employed, ambassadors were over 40 times more likely to do this than saboteurs (85.7% compared to 2.1%; see Table 11.3).

When asked if they ever say anything bad about the company as a place to work, almost none of the advocates (1.9%) were frequent or occasional negative communicators in this regard. However, alienated employees were 26 times more likely to communicate to others in negative ways, either frequently or occasionally (49.4%). It's clear that this kind of attitude and behavior can have a significant impact on attracting the best employees, keeping them, and having them be focused on customers.

The third principal component of advocacy is representing the company's products and services, that is, its brand promise, to others both inside and outside the organization. The disparity in saying good things about the company's products and

Table 11.3 Frequency of saying company is a good place to be employed.

	Total	**Advocate**	**Alienated**
Rarely/Never	20.4%	0.9%	55.5%
Sometimes/Often	49.6%	13.4%	42.4%
Almost always/Always	30.0%	85.7%	2.1%
Total	100.0%	100.0%	100.0%

services between advocates and alienated employees was dramatic. Similar to their responses regarding the company as a place of employment, over 20 times more advocates always or almost always said positive things compared to alienated employees (78.3% vs. 3.7%; see Table 11.4).

Saying negative things about the company's products or services was also significantly more prevalent among alienated employees. Over 45% of alienated employees said negative things about products or services at least some of the time, compared to only 2.6% of advocates. Again, companies need to focus on the multilayered consequences of such results.

What actions should companies take with insights such as these? Here are several:

- Employees at all levels and in all functions need to have a thorough understanding of what's important to customers so that their actions match customer expectations and requirements

- Employees' behavior needs to be aligned around customer experiences

- Management must build processes, technology, training, and organizational/cultural practices that support employees being able to optimize customer experience

Table 11.4 Frequency of saying company's products/services are good.

	Total	Advocate	Alienated
Rarely/Never	18.1%	1.6%	45.0%
Sometimes/ Often	54.1%	20.1%	50.3%
Almost always/ Always	27.8%	78.3%	4.7%
Total	100.0%	100.0%	100.0%

Perhaps most of all, companies should evaluate the effectiveness of rules and metrics associated with delivering customer value. For instance, how effective are the company and the employees at unearthing and resolving unexpressed complaints that may be undermining customer loyalty? How are nonfinancial metrics viewed relative to financial ones? What types of automated support processes exist, and how well are employees trained in them to make serving customers easier? How does the company balance taking care of existing customers, particularly those who may be at risk of defection, with acquiring new ones? How much cross-functional collaboration exists in support of the customer?

In order for companies to create and sustain higher levels of employee advocacy, it's necessary to have customer and employee intelligence specifically designed to close gaps among customer experience, outmoded internal beliefs, and rudimentary support and training. It's also essential that the *employee experience* be given as much emphasis as the customer experience. If advocacy is to flourish, there must be value and a sense of shared purpose for the employee as well as the company and customer—in the form of recognition, reward (financial and training), and career opportunities.

Examples of Employee Advocacy at Work

As cited at the outset of the chapter, companies like Virgin, Eastman Kodak, Honeywell, NCR, ING, and Hewlett-Packard are actively creating and sustaining cultures of employee ambassadorship.

Hewlett-Packard, for example, has a program called Demo Days, in which both current and retired employees, irrespective of function or level within the organization, volunteer and are trained to spend days at local electronics retail stores as brand ambassadors for the company, interacting with potential customers. Hewlett-Packard does this several times a year, and it helps the organization build greater customer centricity into the culture.

At Zappos, there's a strong belief that "your culture is your brand." During the hiring process, prospective employees, however talented and experienced, must fit into the culture. Following hiring, all employees—regardless of function or title—are trained in customer loyalty, service, and company values and vision over a four-week period. Two of those weeks are spent on the phone taking calls from customers.

Zappos defines its company culture in terms of 10 core values, the first of which is "Deliver WOW through service." As explained by CEO Tony Hsieh (2009),

> Every employee can affect your company's brand, not just the front line employees that are paid to talk to your customers. It can be a positive influence, or a negative influence. We decided a long time ago that we didn't want our brand to be just about shoes, or clothing, or even online retailing. We decided that we wanted to build our brand to be about the very best customer service and the very best customer experience. We believe that customer service shouldn't be just a department, it should be the entire company. Our belief is that if you get the culture right, most of the other stuff—like great customer service, or building a great long-term brand, or passionate employees and customers—will happen naturally on its own.

Eastman Kodak, in its employee ambassador initiative, has implemented a program called FAST, which stands for focus, accountability, simplicity, and trust. The objective is to drive sustainable, profitable growth by requiring employees to treat everyone—internal and external—as a customer.

High-tech company NCR has created an ambassadorship program that is open to all employees. Its objectives are to drive customer loyalty and advocacy, and to create an enhanced, more customer-centric company culture for both customer-facing and non-customer-facing employees. Employees are recruited to be trained in customer interaction soft skills and NCR overall company and brand information. Ambassadors have enhanced access to company information, participate in a special reward and recognition program for "above and beyond" contributions, and engage in public relations, marketing, and community events. Importantly, they also help build credibility for the company's commitment to employees by reporting back on their experiences as ambassadors.

Summing Up: What's the Value of Advocacy for the Company, the Customer, and the Employee?

In August 2004, the chairman and CEO of Honeywell International, David Cole, sent a message to the company's 120,000+ employees in which he described their role in the company's program to build and protect its brands:

> Every Honeywell employee is a brand ambassador. With every customer contact and whenever we represent Honeywell, we have the opportunity either to strengthen the Honeywell name or to cause it to lose some of its luster and prestige. Generations of Honeywell employees have built our powerful brands with their hard work, spirit of innovation, passion for quality, and commitment to customers. I am counting on every Honeywell employee to continue that legacy. (Lowenstein 2010)

Whether an organization is a major international corporation or a small, embryonic start-up, these words represent the spirit of what employee ambassadorship can accomplish for a company. Simply stated, advocacy is employees living the promise of "wow" customer value delivery, irrespective of whether they interface with purchasers of the company's products or services, other colleagues, or friends and family members. It is also the partnership and the shared destiny between employees and their employer. When this is done well, all stakeholders win.

12

Are We There Yet? Focus on Relationships, Online/Off-Line Social Media Influence, and Clouds

The open society, the unrestricted access to knowledge,
the unplanned and uninhibited association of men for its
furtherance—these are what may make a vast, complex, ever
growing, ever changing, ever more specialized and expert tech-
nological world, nevertheless a world of human community.

— J. ROBERT OPPENHEIMER,
SCIENCE AND THE COMMON UNDERSTANDING, 1953

There are many emerging trends that will influence the continuing growth and impact of social word-of-mouth, including mobile technology evolution; stronger focus on the emotional (as well as the rational) elements of value; brand equity and customer relationships (even in B2B); more active inclusion of customers in branding, marketing, and development decisions (advisory boards, online customer communities, etc.); and further movement away from heavy, almost exclusive use of traditional forms of advertising and promotion to those where consumers live and communicate (microblogging/Twitter, search engines, text messaging, and social networking such as Facebook, LinkedIn, Plaxo, and Digg).

The amount of coverage online social media receives is tremendous. There is a strong and disproportionate amount of attention both as a medium for companies to influence consumers and as a medium for consumers to communicate with one another. There is so much material on how organizations can leverage social media to manage brand perception, dialogue with customers, and increase share of wallet and share of market that it could easily be taken as conventional wisdom that "online social media" is simply a surrogate term for all social media. It must be remembered, however, that off-line word-of-mouth is still the most significant driver of B2B and B2C customer decision making, even among young people for whom mobile communication appears to be a way of life. The results of multiple studies will be presented to reinforce this continued key finding. So, I will endeavor to present a balanced approach in understanding where online social media stands, and where it is going, as an influence on consumer behavior.

One topic that will get particular attention in this chapter is cloud computing, and related technologies for getting closer to the customer. This reflects a significant evolutionary change in how companies manage customer service and customer experiences. Companies want to be where their customers are, and customers have been sending increasingly strong signals that they will be using social applications such as Twitter and YouTube to communicate about vendor experiences. Customers want to be able to access whatever information they want, whenever they want, and wherever they want; and companies will need to harvest and analyze data for patterns and themes using computer-aided qualitative analysis software, such as text mining and cloud techniques.

Service cloud is the convergence, or bridge, of customer conversations through various social media, such as an online community, with more traditional forms of customer service and support. A number of studies have demonstrated the power of service cloud for rapid deployment, responsiveness to change, quicker learning, and improved productivity. One of these, a focused service cloud customer study conducted by Market-Tools and Strativity, showed significant ROI results: higher satisfaction and customer retention, higher service productivity, and reduced costs (Schuster and Arussy 2010). We will cover the emerging importance of service cloud, also known as cloud computing, in the neural communication world.

EVERYBODY SEEMS SMITTEN WITH ONLINE SOCIAL MEDIA, BUT DECISION-MAKING INFLUENCE COMES FROM OFF-LINE WORD-OF-MOUTH

In this time of Xbox, Wii, HD (high definition), PDAs (personal digital assistants), iPads, and sophisticated cell phones, the internet is the acknowledged great, central enabler of social media. Nothing during our lifetime has so influenced the way people live their lives as the internet.

Brand marketers, especially those representing food and drink products and consumer packaged goods, have dramatically increased their word-of-mouth marketing spending, especially online. They are actively creating new communities of product and service users whose principal purpose is to spread the word and, hopefully, influence consumer behavior. Even so, word-of-mouth, through online social media, remains a fraction of the overall advertising and marketing budget.

A phalanx of consulting organizations has evaluated the role of the internet in our day-to-day existence and, at the same time, how it is creating major sea changes in traditional medial channels. One such study was recently completed by McRoberts et al. (2010) of Fleishman-Hillard, a major public relations firm. This study is particularly important in that it represents 48% of the global online population, with respondents in France, Germany, the United Kingdom, the United States, Canada, China, and Japan. Fleishman-Hillard evaluated influence; however, its definition of influence was not impact on purchase behavior but the amount of time consumers spend on each communications medium and the degree of importance each medium has in their daily lives, particularly in their perceptions and attitudes.

The study revealed nine key insights, of which three are discussed here:

- Though digital communications dominate in terms of their use as a medium of conveying information (roughly twice that of television, and 10 times that of print media), relatively little is spent in real marketing dollars. As consumers continue to shift their methods of communication, companies will need to rebalance their media mix so that it is more aligned with what customers are doing.

- Asia is on the march as a digital power. Internet use in China has seen a significant increase over the past few years. At 330 million individuals, China's web-using population now represents an entity larger than the population of the United States. Combined with India, the internet-using population is over 500 million (and is expected to grow to over 700 million by 2015, according to a McKinsey study [Bughin, Doogan, and Vetvik 2010; Atsmon et al. 2010]). In addition to their numbers, internet users in China are different as well, with much heavier researching and expression of personal views through online social media.

- Malaysia, however, wins top prize for internet use, especially where social media are concerned: Though the country has only 15 million internet users, this represents almost 60% of the population (and McKinsey forecasts that this will rise to 25 million, or 80% of the population, by 2015). Malaysians are active users of social media sites and instant messaging, consuming 35% more digital media than internet users in China and 150% more than those in India. India, with only 7% of the population having internet access, is anticipated to grow to 28% penetration by 2015; and they are heavy users of e-mail and downloaded videos and music.

Digital communications influence decision making, especially their facility as a resource to compare options and to identify expert and peer advice, which creates greater confidence. Especially important here is the role of search engines, which often serve as launching points for information research.

As more and more people use online social media and generate content, online information sharing is coming to be seen as somewhat dangerous. Half the respondents in Fleishman-Hillard's study felt that people share too much personal information online, and over one-fifth felt that expressing personal opinions online could have a negative effect on their reputation, career, or financial well-being.

Trust is a critical social media issue. It's one of the key reasons why mass advertising and promotional communication is something of the past. Consumers no longer trust information shoveled at them through a few large channels; they are far more interested in retrieving content from sources they select and cross-checking for accuracy. Though there is increased usage of online postings to glean information on the experiences of others, there is also increasing skepticism. The Fleishman-Hillard study found that 39% believed it was safe to communicate with others online, but 19% felt it was unsafe to do so. We can conclude that as far as online dialogue is concerned, consumers are "cautiously trusting."

Several years ago, when companies began to focus on recommendation as a core metric, or key performance indicator, to understand customer behavior, a new industry started forming. It had to do with paying consumers to make recommendations and paying them to blog. As a method to "job the system," this has largely backfired. The Fleishman-Hillard study found that three-quarters of consumers were less likely to trust content by a blogger who received a free sample or was otherwise compensated by a company or a product he or she was blogging about. This is very much a trust-related element of communication effectiveness.

Microblog sites such as Twitter are growing in both awareness and usage. Of the respondents aware of these sites (about three-quarters), fully one-third have active accounts, and they use microblogging for communication—much more with one another than with organizations. There is a high level of trust in microblogs, and consumers appear to appreciate companies that monitor sites like Twitter, especially when they respond to posted issues in real time.

Mobility in countries like India and Malaysia is a fact of life, and there is active use of mobile applications on PDAs and smartphones. In the United States, Canada, Germany, France, and the United Kingdom, however, actual adoption of these applications remains fairly low, with almost one-quarter of respondents admitting that they don't use the full range of features available on their phones and mobile devices. Among the biggest gaps are the use of e-mail for communication and access to the internet.

Fleishman-Hillard has concluded that in most countries, the internet is just beginning to be an influential tool for peer-to-peer communication. Many consumers felt that the internet would continue to increase in importance and influence, with internet users in China giving the strongest endorsement of this perception.

Much of what transpires on online social media, the interchange between individuals, is what sociologists call "phatic" dialogue, that is, content like "Where should we meet for lunch?," "How are you feeling today?," "Did you see the Phillies game last night?," "I'm going to the zoo next week with my grandkids," and the like. As reported by David Tice (2009) in a

Knowledge Networks study among a nationally representative panel of 500 internet users aged 13–54, though 47% participate in online social media on a weekly basis, less than 5% use these sites for guidance and purchase decisions (and only 16% of social media users said they would have increased likelihood to buy from a company that advertises on social media sites).

Where there is online brand-related communication, it mostly revolves around customer experience and customer service. A study of consumer use of social media by a team led by Nora Ganim Barnes (2008), a senior fellow of the Society for New Communications Research, showed that about one-third of customers considering purchasing a product or service went to social media sites to learn about the customer care offered, and about half of them took customer care learned about online into consideration. Online social media were among the less frequently used online sources, well behind search engines and online rating systems. YouTube, microblogging sites like Twitter and Oownce, and social networking sites like Facebook were seen to have almost no value as trusted sources of information.

The use of social media for at least contributing to consumer decision making, though, does seem to be increasing. In the Knowledge Networks study, one-third of social media site users report increased usage and checking for value components like customer service compared to a year ago, while less than one-fifth uses them less. As stated by Tice (2009), a vice president at Knowledge Networks,

> Our findings show that marketers need to be prudent and people-centric in how they approach social media. Social media users do not have a strong association between these sites and purchase decisions; they see them more about personal connection—so finding ways to embrace that powerful function is key. The fact that they are using social media more now than a year ago is a strong indicator that the influence of these sites is here to stay.

Social media is, if nothing else, becoming a marketer's tool for using two-way dialogue to deepen customer relationships. Though social media is often defined as a set of tools and technologies—blogs, wikis, podcasts, and social networking sites—for people to have conversations with one another, advanced companies are using, or beginning to use, social media to engage customers and build enthusiasm for their products and services.

A recent study by the University of Massachusetts Dartmouth Center for Marketing Research ("Center for Marketing Research" 2011) showed that all forms of online social media, especially sites, blogging, and online video, are experiencing increased adoption as enablers of relationships. The challenge for organizations is to effectively use social media as a tool for inside-out consumer influence. Many consultants believe that online social media has the power to manage customer relationships, but companies have to reckon with the visibility and the "long tail" impact involved in the dialogue.

Several years ago, Dell was badly beaten up for the quality of its customer service, and this situation—known as "Dell Hell"—was broadly reported in the business media. Though the company has made massive, and interactive, strides to improve service quality, a Google search of "Dell Customer Service" still shows negative blogs on the first page of results. In another well-publicized example, and as noted in Chapter 7, a Comcast customer posted a video on YouTube showing a technician who had come to the customer's home to repair a faulty modem and had fallen asleep while waiting to hear back from a CSR. Apparently, he had been on hold for over an hour. This video has been seen by almost 2 million people, and Comcast has been rated low on the American Customer Satisfaction Index and other national service rating studies ever since.

Many companies are also challenged to join customer conversations where these interactions are taking place, and to do so in a manner that appears natural and uncontrived. Twitter is one such emerging conversation marketplace. Because it is a medium principally for conversing with friends and colleagues (professional use of Twitter is greatly outweighed by personal use), companies have to avoid looking too self-serving, Big Brotherish, and commercially obvious if they communicate with customers or consumers.

Quite a few companies have gotten into blogging, micro-blogging, and podcasting as methods of engaging with their customers. Such companies as Accenture, Dell, Cisco, and the Home Depot all have multiple blog sites. In studies like that of the Society for New Communications Research (Barnes et al. 2008), however, the vast majority of consumers using online social media feel that companies are not paying as much attention as they should and are not taking customers' opinions seriously. So, there's clearly some trust to be earned.

At this juncture, it's probably useful to mention that although social media involvement by corporations is principally in the B2C space, there is also much activity in the B2B world. Perhaps the biggest difference is that while B2C social media usage and activity tend to be more passive, conversational, and focused on everyday activities, B2B companies and individuals use it more for professional purposes. These "communities of practice" can be found, for example, in LinkedIn and Plaxo groups, and much content and communication are directed toward specific areas of interest and function. In my case, for instance, this is market research, customer experience management, word-of-mouth marketing, and the like.

As with consumers, much of B2B word-of-mouth influence is off-line, through colleagues and friends, sales representatives, meetings and conferences, and trade shows. In a 2007 multi-country study among business executives by Keller Fay/Jack Morton Worldwide, it was found that 75% of word-of-mouth communications are face to face, with very little taking place through any other medium. Almost all the brand-related conversations were a direct result of executives' personal brand usage. Over half of the 700 executives surveyed said that word-of-mouth was credible and likely to influence their purchase decisions.

A white paper by Peppers & Rogers Group (2008) identified the principal reasons that social media strategies can fail:

- Perhaps most important, much of corporate involvement in social media is haphazard rather than planned. A LinkedIn account here, a Twitter account there, is not a social media strategy.

- Communication continues to be one-way, through advertising, sales activity, promotions, and press releases, rather than having true conversations and dialogues with consumers.

- Honesty and transparency, core components of trust, are often missing, as companies use blogging and tweeting to "grind their own axes" and "polish their own apples," that is, communicate within tight parameters, largely to build their image.

- Additionally, many times companies use "corporate speak," the kind of language and argot they use when communicating on an official basis. Consumers desire interaction in everyday language.

Key findings from the Barnes et al. (2008) study for the Society for New Communications Research, which studied 25- to 55-year-old college graduates to identify the effect of social media on aspects of customer behavior, include:

- Almost 60% use online social media to vent about transactional experiences

- Almost 75% say that their choice of companies or brands is based at least somewhat on the experiences of others that have been shared online

- Over 80% believe that blogs, online rating sites, and discussion forums can give consumers a greater voice regarding desired customer experiences; however, less than one-third believe that businesses actively take customer opinion into consideration

This last study result is especially eye-opening and says a lot about why the internet is seen as a communication enabler more than a decision-making influence. Even if consumers use the internet to do a fair amount of interacting with others and to research products, services, and anticipated experiences, their questioning of others' intentions, as well as how seriously companies take these postings, is a limiting factor.

Still, social media continue to build as an information resource for consumers. OTX (now part of IPSOS Research) conducted research in 2008 among a national sample of males and females over the age of 13. It found that 70% use social media websites (and 68% use company websites) to get information about companies, brands, and products; about half use social media websites to pass along information generated online. Also, most of these consumers find such information valuable, relevant, credible, and honest, with at least modest impact on product perceptions and purchase decision making.

As indicated at the outset of the chapter, although the internet has become a pervasive means of communication, much of the influence on customer brand and product decision making comes through off-line interaction among consumers. OTX conducted a study in 2009 among young people (8000 technology-using 12- to 24-year-olds) in the United Kingdom, United States, Germany, India, and Japan to determine the myths and realities of the role digital technology plays in their lives. What it found was that digital communication was used principally for personal enjoyment. While young people have tremendous access to technology, they don't have as much of an obsession with devices and communicating as how they act as enablers to help them connect and have fun. Most of their favorite things to do—being with friends, listening to music, etc.—are off-line.

Young people are not much interested in using the internet as a means of generating content for its own sake but rather communicating in a social context. For instance, the OTX (2009) study found that only about one-fifth of young people have ever written a blog or filmed and uploaded a clip to a site like YouTube. In purchases of high-tech devices, over two-thirds claim to have learned about the devices from off-line sources, such as word-of-mouth, and not from electronic social media. The same holds true for nontechnical products such as clothing.

Adults demonstrate similar patterns. Informal communication monitoring organization Keller Fay reckons that there are 3.5 billion word-of-mouth conversations each day in the United States, and two-thirds of these involve product and service brands. Its studies, like those of consulting organizations such as McKinsey, show that word-of-mouth has the dominant influence on customer decision making. Data collected through online surveys of consumer panelists aged 13–69 (700 per week, 36,000 per year) and covering word-of mouth in all categories show that:

- Word-of-mouth is mostly positive—63% of brand references are positive, compared to only 9% that are negative

- Word-of-mouth has impact—About half see high credibility, are likely to pass information along to others, and are likely to purchase

In addition, its studies repeatedly show that most of the brand-related informal word-of-mouth takes place off-line. This may change in the future, but it's a present reality.

A 2010 online/off-line word-of-mouth "landscape" study by Wharton Interactive Media Institute and the Marketing Science Institute (MSI) gathered material from NM Incite (a joint venture between Nielsen and McKinsey) and Keller Fay Group.

They evaluated word-of-mouth information sources for 700 US brands, spanning the 2007–2010 time period. Their findings confirmed earlier results, namely, that word-of-mouth is not channel-neutral and that online information doesn't correlate well with off-line behavior (Keller 2010). At the same time, new trends were emerging.

In their research, some brand categories, such as automobiles, sports and hobbies, technology and stores, and media and entertainment, showed high evidence of online conversations compared to off-line. These four categories accounted for almost three-quarters of all brand-related online conversations; media and entertainment alone represented one-third of the online conversations.

Conversely, brands in many other categories—beverages, food and dining, clothing, beauty, and telecommunications—had dominant evidence of off-line communication compared to online. Even technology products and stores, which had extremely high online brand communication in the Wharton/MSI study (17%), had almost as frequent off-line communication (13%).

To increase online inside-out advocacy leverage and to move from fad to strategic marketing tool, organizations will need to more actively engage in conversations with consumers. They will need to identify places online—such as Twitter, LinkedIn, and Facebook, where their customers currently congregate—create interactive blogs, identify brand loyalists and advocates to help them create conversations, engage in 360° communication, and develop social communities of interest for both conversation and insight development purposes. This will make it easier for them to monitor customer dialogues and feedback, use algorithms to find patterns in what consumers are saying to one another, and apply the feedback across the organization for improved customer experiences. Applying these measures will increase bottom-line value for both customers and businesses.

DETERMINATION OF ONLINE AND OFF-LINE WORD-OF MOUTH CUSTOMER DECISION-MAKING IMPACT ("WORD-OF-MOUTH POWER")

There is a definite intersection among customer experience with a product or service (which is where the company should be optimizing the impact of relationship building), informal peer-to-peer communication about that experience, and downstream customer decision making. We make an important distinction between company initiatives through touch points and experiences to create advocacy behavior (inside-out) and outside-in activities that are created by customers and largely free from company control (such as service, promotion, or loyalty and reward programs).

We designed consumer research to help evaluate the incidence and effect of both Web 2.0 social interaction media and off-line communication (which remains, as stated, where the strong majority of information sharing takes place).

The core objective of this research has been to develop well-validated customer perspectives and trends relating to loyalty behavior influenced by experience and downstream word-of-mouth in selected industries.

Study Objectives

This research was intended to identify the impact that word-of-mouth, driven by use and support experience, has on key elements of consumer behavior, as follows.

Initiator (Creator/Sender)

- Product or service experience (category and type of experience) that caused action to be initiated

- Action initiated—*Note*: If back to company, we identify degree of resolution

- Communication mode (formal/informal, online or off-line—phone, face-to-face at business or casual, etc.)

- Tone of communication

- What specific experience message, ranging from passive and benign to positive recommendation, was communicated (one area of particular interest is whether negative messages leading to sabotage get communicated more or less frequently than positive ones)

Recipient (Receiver)

- If information about someone else's purchase, use, or service experience was received, whether it was active (i.e., solicited) or passive (i.e., received without solicitation)

- How communication was received (i.e., mode)

- Content of/reason for communication per respondent recall

- Believability of information received

- Action(s) taken, or intended (purchase/nonpurchase, consideration/nonconsideration, continuity communication, etc.), by respondent as a result of communication

Customer Word-of-Mouth Power Study Design and Field Specifics

We drew a nationally representative sample of 2355 adult respondents. The field period was from March 9 through March 16, 2009. Supported by marketing science colleagues, I prepared nine questions, reflective of the stated objectives, for the respondents to complete. Our qualification criterion was whether the respondent had a product/service purchase experience or a service experience over the past two months that stood out in his or her mind. As noted in Chapter 6, of the study respondents, 1404, or approximately 60%, could recall such an experience.

Key Findings

Methods of Gathering Information for Choices of Product or Service for Purchase

Online social media, known by many names (Web 2.0, social networking, consumer-generated media, etc.), rightly gets a lot of attention. It's certainly compelling and omnipresent. But does it leverage behavior or largely act as a communication enabler? This is a controversial subject.

Those who focus on social media see it as a dominant influence. But we believe that some perspective is useful here. There is ample evidence showing that, irrespective of age group, most word-of-mouth influence comes from off-line sources. For example, Andy Sernovitz (2009a) has made an observation that is similar to the Wharton/MSI study conclusions presented earlier in this chapter: "Only about 20 percent of word of mouth happens online. When it does play a role, it usually sparks the 80% of word of mouth conversations that actually happens face-to-face. Real word of mouth dips in and out of different spaces."

Other research companies examining the sources of information that consumers use in their decision making have, likewise, determined that the majority of information comes from off-line communication methods. In this research, respondents were given the opportunity to select those methods they typically use as information sources, among the following:

- *Traditional media* (advertising or stories from print or broadcast media)

- *Online media* (message boards, chat rooms, blogs, and wikis; company websites; independent websites that have reviews; public social networking sites such as Facebook and MySpace; and private social networking sites such as communities)

- *Direct with company* (phone call or e-mail; face-to-face with a salesperson, such as at a retail store or dealership)

- *Direct informal* (phone call with person not associated with the company, or face-to-face with person not associated with the company)

- *No information gathered* for purchase or service

Methods used were a mixture of "old media" and "new media," and those that would constitute *push* (advertising and websites) and *pull* (information from neural, informal communication). The most frequently identified methods of gathering information were using a company website (36%), face-to-face with a salesperson or other company representative (22%), and face-to-face with a person not associated with the company (21%). Other frequently identified methods or sources were advertising in print media (19%), independent websites that have reviews (19%), and phone call to the company (16%). The rest were cited by 15% or less of the respondents. It was noteworthy that only 4% cited either public or private social networking sites.

There were, as well, some important method differences noted by product or service experience category:

- Traditional advertising as an information source was significantly higher among entertainment experience respondents (58% vs. 29%) but much lower for automotive, healthcare services, and travel category experience respondents (all between 13% and 16%)

- Online message boards/chat rooms/blogs/wikis as a source was significantly higher for tech products (24% vs. 11%), and all online media were higher for this category; travel and entertainment products category respondents were significantly more frequent users of company websites and also independent websites

- Automotive, tech products, and entertainment products experience category respondents were far more likely to receive information through face-to-face communication with a company representative (retailer or auto dealership salesperson), while travel and financial services category respondents were significantly less likely to use this information source

- Restaurant dining, tech products, and entertainment products category respondents were more likely to receive information through informal, face-to-face communication with a person not associated with the company, while automotive and financial services respondents were less likely to do so

Active and Passive Product/Service Information Receipt; Tone and Believability of Information Received

Pundits who monitor how, and what, product and service information is received by consumers often do not distinguish between *active* and *passive* solicitation and receipt of that information. Active information gathering is purposeful seeking by consumers, such as asking someone, looking at a website, or making targeted inquiries via an online community. Passive information receipt occurs when someone tells a consumer about a product or service without him or her having asked, or when it is heard or read about on an incidental, serendipitous basis.

In this study, it was found that 61% actively sought information, 5% obtained it both actively and passively, and the remainder received it only passively. Rates of active seeking were highest among financial services, entertainment products, and travel respondents (between 76% and 79%); restaurant dining was the lowest category in this regard, with 42%.

The only notable demographic differences in terms of where and how information was obtained were the following: (1) less activity online among lower-income (under $50K) respondents and (2) lower use of traditional off-line advertising through print and electronic media, and also off-line print and broadcast stories among white respondents, while it was higher among black and Hispanic respondents. There was more informal face-to-face information gathering among respondents with higher incomes ($50K and above) and also among echo boomers (18- to 32-year-olds). In addition, there was significantly more passive information receipt among respondents with lower education (some college or less).

Respondents were also asked about the tone of informal communication, that is, whether it was seen as predominantly positive or negative. Overall, about 84% of respondents felt that the tone of communication was somewhat positive to highly positive. It should be noted that for telecom products and telecom services, two categories with fewer respondents (but with well-documented negativism in the marketplace), communication tone was significantly less positive.

There was also a question regarding level of believability of information obtained. About two-thirds thought the information was very believable, and almost all of the remainder thought it was somewhat believable. The highest level of information believability was for restaurant dining (74% said "very believable"), followed by automotive; the lowest level of information believability was for financial services. Those who found information "very believable" were more likely to have been among the respondents who actively sought the information out.

Methods of Communication to Others

As noted earlier, about 79% of respondents had communicated to others after their purchase or service experience; of that group, 86% communicated to someone not directly associated with the company (such as contacting customer service or technical support). We asked which methods were used, and received the following responses:

- 63% face-to-face with a family member, business colleague, or friend

- 30% e-mail

- 15% face-to-face with a retail or dealership salesperson

- 12% company website

- 11% text messaging

- 9% public online social networking site, such as Facebook

- 8% online message board, discussion forum, chat room, blog, or wiki

- 7% independent websites that have reviews, such as Amazon

- 5% private online social networking sites, such as communities

Online communication to others seemed to be concentrated among entertainment respondents, and travel and tech product respondents appeared to communicate more frequently through independent websites.

There were several demographic differences by methods of downstream communication. Respondents earning less than $50K tended to use e-mail, text, or independent websites less. Respondents with children in the household texted significantly more, as did echo boomers. Echo boomers, though, were significantly less likely to communicate through a company website or e-mail, and more likely to communicate through public online social networking sites (twice as likely as overall respondents). Males were also significantly more likely to text and to use independent websites.

There was also some correlation between method of communication used and propensity to purchase in the future. Of those who communicated with others face-to-face, 83% said they were definitely or somewhat likely to purchase in the future. This compared to:

- 65% e-mail

- 70% face-to-face with a retail or dealership salesperson

- 68% company website

- 67% text messaging

- 78% public online social networking site, such as Facebook

- 56% online message board, discussion forum, chat room, blog, or wiki

- 77% independent websites that have reviews, such as Amazon

- 80% private online social networking sites, such as communities

Although not conclusive, the data suggested that the action of off-line and online methods of communicating to others about experiences—except for message boards, blogs, and wikis— equally affects, or at least correlates with, customers' own future purchase behavior.

Downstream Behavior Likelihood Based on Customers' Own Communication Behavior, and Overall

There was an interesting and very revealing (for marketers and others) set of correlations to future purchase behavior based on the respondents' own downstream communication behavior:

- Of those who had communicated about their positive product/service experience to others, 76% said they were definitely or somewhat more likely to repurchase, and only 4% said they were definitely or somewhat less likely to repurchase

- Among those who had made a positive recommendation, 78% said they were definitely or somewhat more likely to repurchase in the future, compared to only 6% who said they were definitely or somewhat less likely to repurchase

- Only about one-quarter (23%) of those who had communicated about their negative experience said they were positively inclined to repurchase, compared to 46% who said they were definitely or somewhat less likely to repurchase

- Similarly, about 24% of those who had recommended against purchasing the product or service based on their own experience said they were definitely or somewhat more likely to repurchase, compared to 63% who said they were less likely to repurchase

These findings suggest that the act of communicating to others, positively or negatively, has the same impact on customers' own behavior as the act of actually recommending.

Note that, overall, about 13% of respondents said it was too soon after their experience to determine whether they would purchase the product or service again. This was significantly higher among financial services respondents.

Overall, about 40% of all respondents said they would definitely be more likely to purchase again based on their own experience (see Table 12.1). By category, future purchase likelihood was strongest for tech products (60%) and restaurant dining (55%), and weakest for travel (35%).

Implications of These Findings for Marketers

Customer behaviors are complex and take into account experiences and perceived value, messages received, and messages communicated. The importance of experience on a personal basis must also be taken into account. While the promise of word-of-mouth in the marketing mix has been well reported (almost to the point of saturation), and while many companies see this as a more targeted and efficient use of their budget dollars, the accountability and proof from actual return on investment are still in the process of being proved. Our research findings show very positive potential post-experience, downstream behavioral impact of customer communications.

Organizations will be well served if they can learn to consistently and effectively optimize customer experiences and then find ways to build dialogue around them and keep it going.

Table 12.1 Likelihood to purchase again.

Suppose that you were shopping for that same category of product or service. Based on your recent experience, would you say you would be . . . ?

	Total (%)	Communicated about experience		Recommend	
		Positive (%)	Negative (%)	Yes (%)	No (%)
More likely to purchase (net)	**60**	**76**	**24**	**79**	**24**
Definitely more likely to purchase same product/service again	40	57	9	56	15
Somewhat more likely to purchase same product/service again	20	20	14	22	9
Neither more nor less likely to purchase same product/service again	14	11	20	9	10
Less likely to purchase (net)	**13**	**5**	**46**	**6**	**63**
Somewhat less likely to purchase same product/service again	6	2	22	2	22
Definitely less likely to purchase same product/service again	7	3	24	4	40
It is too soon after the purchase for me to know whether I would purchase that product/service again	13	8	10	6	2

Note: Base is all adults. Percentages may not add up to 100% due to rounding.

The pattern of results from our research suggests the following theses for marketers:

- New technologies complement, rather than replace, traditional forms of communication—example: company websites are simply an updated form of information gathering, more corporate-based media than consumer-generated media

- Even with younger consumers, who have larger social networks and engage in more communication through them, the tendency is still to revert to more traditional communication

- It is far more actionable and productive to seek positive consumer social word-of-mouth as a demonstration of loyalty behavior than to base decisions or judgment *solely* on either intended recommendation or actual recommendation

Companies will need to more actively and more effectively pursue initiatives that (1) drive both online and off-line positive informal communication by customers and others, including optimizing employees' behavior as ambassadors, (2) meld word-of-mouth with the power of traditional advertising, (3) engage customers as enterprise partners and advisors, and (4) learn how to tap into and convert negative word-of-mouth—the complaints and criticisms that customers have (but don't express directly to the company)—into positive outcomes. One of the principal lessons from customer word-of-mouth research is greater clarity on the marketing advantages it portends. This is a strategic, real-world opportunity that will require further investment and learning. What we've done is a good first step.

The increased use of social media also means that contact centers, and related organizational functions that provide service and support to customers, need to have ready access to these conversations so that they can provide rapid response when issues arise. These centers, especially frontline staff, also need to understand when they should be monitoring and "listening" and when they should be directly communicating. Unlike other channels, such as e-mail and telephone, it's easy for conversations between a service rep and a customer to become viral on the internet, which can be a positive or a negative.

These interactions, it's fair to say, can have significant impact on brand reputation. Consulting organizations offer many ideas and practices that contact centers can use for participating in and following social media feedback; however, for our purposes, we'll be looking at how service issues, identified and addressed through social media, are affected by cloud computing.

SERVICE EXPERIENCE INSIGHTS IN THE CLOUDS

Perhaps the simplest way to explain cloud computing from the consumer perspective (not from the standpoint of the complex architecture and engineering of the hardware and software involved) is that it's a massive game of electronic connection of data and communication dots. It's now possible for people to have much easier access to their suppliers than ever before—to be connected anytime and anywhere, through PCs, smartphones, tablets, and mini-laptops.

When they are connected, they are talking about experiences with products and services. Companies—especially in organizational areas of performance having to do with customer *service* and *experience*—need to know what is being said in as real-time a manner as possible, not only to protect their reputation but also to be actively engaged with, and trusted by, their customers. After all, the end goal is to deliver proactive, consistent positive experiences in every customer interaction. This is where the opportunity for treating customers right, and the desired business result of cross-selling and upselling, often resides (such as making these sales through a call or service center), so forward-thinking organizations are paying attention to any methods that will offer a competitive advantage.

For organizations, there are definite cost, platform reliability, scalability, deployment, security, privacy, compliance, legal, and maintenance issues to be considered when beginning the use of cloud-based support. Some companies are big enough and have enough need for frequent relationship-building and service interaction that they have their own hosting operation and software. More frequently, this is outsourced to a vendor that handles maintenance and hosting.

Cloud computing is seeing its most active and most valuable applications in "customer journey" situations such as the following:

- Consumers who have a problem may be able to instantly report the issue, such as by access to a live chat session with a representative trained to provide targeted assistance.

- In addition to chat sessions, the consumer can communicate through knowledge bases, user-driven forums, social networking sites, and other reporting applications (such as e-mail). Consumers should be able to track progress of issue resolution.

- Cloud computing means that data from these problems or complaints, irrespective of online source, can be gathered, collated, and analyzed. When consumers track resolution progress of their problem or complaint, the company or cloud support vendor can "mine" details of the customer's tracking activity so that problem areas can be identified and fixed. Instant action could involve having the issue sent directly from the rep to a technician for resolution, or offering the customer a premium resolution approach.

- The consumer with the complaint or problem can be identified through his or her customer profile. Downstream, this will facilitate more focused follow-up and troubleshooting—or marketing and communications campaigns and sales activity.

Finally, all this information—almost irrespective of online source—can be updated in real time and made available across the enterprise to all authorized users, eliminating financial duplication, confusion, and waste.

If an organization's emphasis were solely on making incremental sales through the customer service center, this would be enough to justify investment in cloud computing. It is well known and well accepted that representative performance (taking ownership of an issue, making the customer feel valued, providing accurate information and timely resolution, etc.) is critical in optimizing the customer experience. In order for customers to be receptive to cross-sell and upsell offers, reps must create trust by first listening to and understanding the customer issue and then resolving the issue as quickly as possible. As reported in a major financial services call center study, once an issue has been successfully resolved, 73% of customers will listen to an offer, and of those, 15% will buy (or, 11% of overall customers who have contacted the service center). These are major dollars.

An impressive cadre of companies across multiple business sectors are actively using cloud computing for improved customer service: Jaguar, Seagate, 3M, Wendy's, Eli Lilly, Outback Steakhouse, Macy's, the *New York Times*, Subway Restaurants, Netflix, Starbucks, ESPN, Dell, Kaiser Permanente, and Sony.

What everything in this chapter—indeed, the entire book—leads to is that customer experience has become less about one-dimensional, passive, reactive, and tactical execution than about customer–supplier collaboration at each touch point. Success in this new relationship will be defined by making complete and unrestricted pictures of customer needs, history and profile, and preferred products and services available to all stakeholders. This results in the proaction, co-creation, personalization, transparency, and honesty that customers not only want but demand, and it is essential to build customer advocacy.

Afterword

Leslie Gaines-Ross, PhD
Chief Reputation Strategist
Weber Shandwick
March 2011

All the changes witnessed over the past several decades in customer decision making and influences on corporate and brand perception have brought companies operating in B2B and B2C marketplaces to a dynamic new frontier. There is an increasingly critical connection among brand and service promise, corporate and brand reputation trustworthiness, the transactional experience (as delivered by people, processes, communications, and culture), and downstream customer behavior.

Any small ripple in reputation change (such as through a product-related issue, online rumor, or executive miscue), brand performance, or customer service can have a tsunami-like effect on business outcomes that may last indefinitely. This is especially true now because of the permanency provided by social media. As one example, Lehman Brothers, which was the fourth-largest investment bank before it declared bankruptcy and collapsed in 2008, has nearly 6 million hits online despite the fact that it technically no longer exists.

Of all the factors that can influence consumer behavior and brand success, employees have a particularly important ambassadorial role in building trust and reputation. Studies have found that employees are often less than enthusiastic about their employers and the goods they produce, particularly in the recent antibusiness shift in public opinion during the economic downturn.

As noted in the chapter addressing the influence of employees, small lapses in their advocacy behavior, identified as "badvocacy" by Weber Shandwick, can cause cataclysmic damage to reputation and financial business outcomes. Poor employee morale and responsiveness, coupled with inflexible processes, often drive customer complaints, a prime cause of customer churn as well as customer defection itself. Some complaints are expressed to the company, but most are suppressed, mentioned in casual online or off-line conversation, or posted on social media sites.

Employees are only one element in an array of scenarios that can affect reputation, consumer perception, and customer behavior. At the end of 2010, a number of my reputation predictions appeared as a blog on the *Huffington Post*:

1. *Hijacked reputations*—In virtually every business, there is the potential for information to get leaked or corrupted via the internet and elsewhere. The long-tail effect and the effort required to repair reputational damage are both substantial. The best approaches, as always, are preparation and quick, open, and decisive action.

2. *Reputation Recoverers Anonymous*—CEOs and companies, increasingly, will find themselves in reputation repair and recovery mode so that they are once again stable. Search engines identified 455,000 mentions of reputation recovery in 2005, and this increased to nearly 2,500,000 mentions in 2010. So, this is a major issue as well as a major opportunity.

3. *Reputation warfare*—The enabling impact of the internet and social media is seen virtually everywhere. There

is little or no restriction for individuals or small groups to sling mud, however valid, at corporations and other entities. This has been seen, for example, in the furor caused by WikiLeaks and the toppling of governments in Egypt and Tunisia. Companies will need to develop countering strategies lest they become further victimized and destabilized.

4. *Online reputation revisionism*—Though very much in the embryonic discussion stage, the (potentially negative) impact on the long-term reputations of individuals represented by social media entries will one day be addressed. Some agreeable form or system of "do over" for suppressing or eliminating these entries is likely to receive increased discussion.

5. *Ascendancy of social CEOs*—Through blogs and other electronic and digital forums, CEOs and senior executives will increasingly represent their companies in more visible ways than ever before. They will not be mere figureheads, but will actively narrate their company's story and build reputations using an array of communication channels.

6. *Reputation blacklisting*—It seems there are lists for everything in the corporate world: best companies to work for, highest satisfaction, best reputation, and so on. Though these rankings can help companies enhance their reputations through third-party endorsement, the reverse is also true. There is likely to be an increase of "worst" company listings.

7. *Reputation risk insurance*—Since there is insurance for virtually everything else, including reputational damage insurance as part of directors' and officers' liability coverage, it is likely that there will be an

increased focus on corporate reputation risk insurance. Broader reputation insurance products would compensate companies whose reputations and sales have suffered through negative off-line or online statements.

8. *The corporate brand rises*—Companies with multiple brands must focus not only on each individual brand's reputation but also on the reputation of the parent organization. The availability of information accessible by consumers means that companies can no longer hope or expect that issues (such as employee treatment, product quality, or leadership capability) affecting a brand won't also have rub-off implications on how they are perceived or how consumers act as a result of that perception.

Going forward, to generate lasting trust, a positive reputation, and continued consumer confidence for brands, products, and services, companies will need to focus on customer-centric leadership as well as become more transparent and authentic. They will have to ramp up inclusion of employees and customers, and more actively engage in off-line and online dialogue with all stakeholders, particularly their advocates. As discussed in the book, successful companies will, at the end of the day, stress inside-out and outside-in advocacy in all of their actions and processes to both drive positive business outcomes and be accountable to all of their constituents—even the virtual ones.

Epilogue

Executing Advocacy Creation: The Branded Customer Experience

Many B2B and B2C companies offer antiseptic, commoditized, and vanilla experiences to customers. These are almost guaranteed not to be memorable, not to be talked about (unless neutrally or negatively), and not to create outside-in advocacy. Through culture, discipline, and purpose, some have succeeded in creating consistent, positive experiences that customers consider appealing and worthy of being passed along through informal conversation and recommendation.

Most brands and corporations get by on transactional approaches to customer relationships. These might include customer service speed, occasional price promotions, merchandising gimmicks, new product offerings, and the like. In most instances, the customers see no brand "personality" or brand-to-brand differentiation, and their experience of the brand is one-dimensional, easily capable of replacement. Moreover, the customer has no personal investment in choosing, and staying with, one brand or supplier over another.

Beyond simply selling a product or service, "experiential brands" connect with their customers. They understand that delivering on the tangible and functional elements of value is just table stakes, and that connecting and having an emotionally based relationship with customers is the key to leveraging loyalty and advocacy behavior.

These companies are also invariably quite disciplined. Every aspect of a company's offering—customer service, advertising, packaging, billing, products, and so forth—is thought out for consistency. They market and create experiences within the branded vision. IKEA might get away with selling super-expensive furniture, but it doesn't. Starbucks might make more money selling Pepsi, but it doesn't. Southwest Airlines could offer first-class seating, but it doesn't. Every function-delivering experience is "closed-loop," maintaining balance between customer expectations and what is actually executed.

Exemplars of branded customer experience also understand that there is a journey for customers in relationships with preferred companies. It begins with awareness, how the brand is introduced—that is, the promise. Then, promise and created expectations must at least equal real-world touchpoint results (such as through service), initially and over time, with a minimum of disappointment. Finally, it requires that the brand's image—its personality, if you will—be sustained and reinforced. Advanced companies map and plan this out, recognizing that experiences are actually a form of branding architecture brought to life through excellent engineering.

Some branded customer experience-centric companies, like Zappos, IKEA, Disney, Target, REI, Nike, American Girl, Starbucks, Southwest Airlines, Baptist Health Care, Whole Foods Markets, the Container Store, and Harley-Davidson, are well known, and several have been discussed in this book. Others deserve mention because they are original and distinctive, and because they represent excellent examples of bringing employees, process, and culture together in highly effective ways.

In her interestingly titled book *I Love You More Than My Dog* (actually a metaphor for how closely consumers bond with companies that create trust and authenticity), author and loyalty consultant Jeanne Bliss identifies several of these companies, as well as what makes them exceptional. In the book, she states: "When customers love you, they'll turn to you first, regardless of the competition. They will tell your story, forming an army of cheerleaders and publicists urging friends, neighbors, colleagues, even strangers to experience your company." This is an almost perfect definition of the inside-out advocacy that creates outside-in advocacy.

As Bliss describes, these companies exhibit five decision traits that separate them from the pack:

- They decide to BELIEVE: They believe their employees, and they believe their customers, that is, they trust them

- They decide with CLARITY OF PURPOSE: They are clear and straightforward about their value proposition

- They decide to BE REAL: They are transparent and "real," making relationships between people, not between company and customer

- They decide to BE THERE: They are "in the moment" with customers, when and as needed

- They decide to SAY SORRY: They have humility and grace, and are willing to apologize when there are experience-delivery shortfalls

In her book, Bliss includes a number of interesting and unique examples of inside-out advocacy creation through branded customer experiences. Companies she identifies include those discussed in the following section.

EXAMPLES

W. L. Gore

When Bill Gore, a research scientist from du Pont, founded the company (known for Gore-Tex fabrics used in outerwear), one of his goals was to give employees more freedom to innovate.

Long a "lattice" organization, with an informal and interconnected structure rather than a conventional hierarchy, the company switched to team-based project initiatives. Team leaders emerge based on both their initiative and ideas, plus their ability to take customer input and put these concepts into action. W. L. Gore & Associates has been listed in *Fortune* magazine's "100 Best Companies to Work For" every year in the 25+ years that the list has been compiled.

Zane's Cycles

Zane's Cycles, based in Connecticut, is one of the largest bike shops in the United States. The lifetime value of each of its customers has been calculated in excess of $12,000. Because the company trusts its staff and customers, a person can take an expensive bicycle out on a test ride without providing any identification or form of collateral. Of the 4,000 bikes sold each year, only about 5 are stolen. Zane's figures this is a small price to pay in exchange for relying on the honesty of both employees and customers. Annual sales growth has been in excess of 20% since the company was founded in 1981. At Zane's Cycles, customers are seen as an asset, not as a cost.

Trader Joe's

Shopping at Trader Joe's is truly a branded customer experience. Each store has a lighthearted South Seas island theme, and the staff dons Hawaiian shirts. Employees at the Monrovia, California, headquarters often serve as a tasting panel, helping determine which new products will be stocked in the stores. At the tasting locations in each store, customers give the final stamp of approval, or rejection, by "voting with their taste buds." This is also a device for bonding with customers at the store level. Even though Trader Joe's stocks about

3000 items, compared to the average supermarket's 30,000 items, sales per square foot are typically two to three times that of chain supermarkets.

What has made Trader Joe's so successful—apart from staff wages, benefits packages, and opportunities for advancement that are well above most companies in the supermarket industry—is the sense that employees *are* the brand, its communication style and fun, upbeat culture. Employees are selected and trained to multitask, and they seem to enjoy what they do. They deliver a great branded customer experience, and they stay (voluntary turnover is only 4%) because they enjoy working there and because the organization is thriving.

Umpqua Bank

Every customer wants a bank that can deliver personalized, customized, and enjoyable experiences. Umpqua is one of the few banks that actually organizes, at a branch level, to make that happen. Employees are rigorously cross-trained so that service reps can make change and tellers can open loans. Like IKEA and Starbucks, Umpqua sees itself as a retail store–type destination; branches function as both bank and community center, with shadings of Internet coffee shop. As a senior bank executive has stated: "The retail model gives people a reason to come to the bank. Many come for entertainment or just to read the paper and enjoy a cup of coffee. When people come to the stores, they experience our culture and are more likely to do business with us or make an 'impulse buy.'"

If Umpqua doesn't sound like a typical bank, then it has achieved its objective. This model is not only good for the customer but good for the employee. Umpqua's voluntary turnover rate is half that of the retail banking industry. Umpqua has regularly been near the top of *Fortune* magazine's "100 Best Companies to Work For" for the past several years.

Wegmans

Though Wegmans is a supermarket, shopping there feels more akin to being in a European outdoor food and beverage emporium. Wegmans's success has been widely publicized. It is built on employee passion, customer-focused training (over 40 hours per employee per year), and empowerment, with a liberal sprinkling of proactive, charismatic customer service throughout the store. It is not at all uncommon, for example, for employees to offer hands-on shopping help if customers are confused or in a hurry.

One of Jeanne Bliss's precepts for creating a company that customers love is the proactive ability to apologize and make amends when and if anything goes amiss with the experience. Recently, Wegmans had to pull and replace a reusable plastic Chinese-made tote bag with a pea design after a consumer group found that the bags had high levels of toxic lead content. Wegmans turned this into a positive event by communicating its recognition of responsibility to protect customers from potential contamination.

Apple Stores

Unlike typical office products and specialty electronics stores, Apple elected to create a sense of community and a supportive, user-friendly environment for customers. One very tangible and visible result of this thinking is the "Genius Bar," where expert employees dispense advice and guidance to customers like bartenders make drinks and engage patrons in dialogue. Customers respond very well to this type of experience, making Apple Stores one of the fastest-growing retailers in the United States.

USAA

USAA is an innovative financial services company for members of the military, including their direct relatives, and children and grandchildren of people who served in the armed forces. It has about 8 million members. One of the differentiators of USAA lies in its training program for new employees. New hires, whether they have military background or not, are required to wear military garb, eat what soldiers and sailors are served in the field, and read letters received from members of the armed services and their families. Through this immersion, employees have stronger affinity for the needs of the members.

USAA is always seeking to provide differentiated, value-added service in an otherwise antiseptic industry. One of its recent innovations is a car-buying service for members that provides detailed pricing information and even helps shop around for the car. The service, which is also available as an iPhone app, promises members the lowest price in the area. After members select their cars, a request for a quote is sent to three USAA-approved dealers in the area. USAA even offers to pay the difference if a member/buyer finds a lower price within three days of purchase. USAA believes that this service will save members an average of $4,500 from new vehicles' sticker prices.

A FINAL OBSERVATION

Today, we are witnessing customer-driven marketing through empowerment, self-management, and consumer-generated media. Many companies have found themselves in the backseat of the new-age vehicles used in customer-supplier relationships. They are forced to modify existing communication techniques or create new ones. They must also rethink interactions between employees and customers, how they hire and train employees, and the experience processes they utilize so that they can be positioned to generate advocates among their customer bases. How they use, or misuse, these techniques, and how they assess the return-on-customer effectiveness and level of monetization of their initiatives will change how word-of-mouth is pursued by both small and large enterprises.

http://customerinnovations.wordpress.com/2007/11/16/a-break-in-the-service-profit-chain-why-improvements-in-employee-engagement-dont-improve-the-customer-experience.

Carnick, Jill, Saji Kumar, and Michael Lowenstein. 2010. *Does Customer Advocacy Exist in B2B?* White paper. Milwaukee, WI: Market Probe. http://www.marketprobe.com.

"Center for Marketing Research Finds that Inc. 500 Continue to Embrace Social Media in 4th Annual Benchmarking Study." *Campanil-E* (blog), University of Massachusetts, January 25, 2011. http://campanile.blogs.umassd.edu/2011/01/25/center-for-marketing-research-find-that-inc-500-continue-to-embrace-social-media-in-4th-annual-benchmarking-study.

Centers for Disease Control. 1994. "Changes in the Cigarette Brand Preferences of Adolescent Smokers—United States, 1989–1993." *MMWR Weekly*, August 19.

Chiarelli, Nick, and Belinda Parker. 2008. *The Influentials.* Presentation, GfK Roper Consulting/World Media Group, July 9.

Chura, Hillary. 2007. "Dealing with the Damage from Online Critics." *New York Times*, October 4.

ClickFox. 2009. *Customer Experience Survey Best Practice Results.* Atlanta, GA: ClickFox.

CMO Council. 2010. *The Leaders in Loyalty: Feeling the Love from the Loyalty Clubs.* Palo Alto, CA: CMO Council.

comScore World Metrix. 2009. *Top 20 Highest Engagement Social Networking Country Audiences.* Reston, VA: comScore World Metrix.

Deming, W. Edwards. 1986. *Out of the Crisis.* Cambridge, MA: MIT.

Dhalla, Nairman. 1980. "Advertising as an Anti-Recession Tool." *Harvard Business Review*, January–February.

Dourado, Phil. 2005. "Tattoo You." *Stakeholder*, July, 26–29.

Drucker, Peter. 2001. *The Essential Drucker: Selections from the Management Works of Peter F. Drucker.* New York: HarperBusiness.

du Toit, Gerard, Beth Johnson, Maureen Burns, and Christy de Gooyer. 2010. *Customer Loyalty in Retail Banking: North America, 2010.* Boston: Bain & Company.

Fay, Brad, Idil Cakim, Scott Carpenter, Steve Hershberger, Sean O'Driscoll, Erik Rabasca, Filiberto Selvas, and Warren Sukernek. 2008. *WOMMA Influencer Handbook: The Who, What, When, Where, How, and Why of Influencer Marketing.* Chicago: Word of Mouth Marketing Association.

Fay, Christopher. 1995. "Can't Get No Satisfaction? Perhaps You Should Stop Trying." *Juran News*, Winter, 1.

Feinberg, Richard, Mike Trotter, and Jon Anton. 2000. *At Any Time . . . from Anywhere . . . in Any Form.* White paper. West Lafayette, IN: Purdue Center for Customer Driven Quality.

Ferguson, Rick, and Kelly Hlavinka. 2009. "The New Champion Customers." Colloquytalk, January. http://www.colloquy.com.

Fischer, Paul, Meyer Schwartz, John Richards, Jr., Adam Goldstein, and Tina Rojas. 1991. "Brand Logo Recognition by Children Aged 3 to 6 Years: Mickey Mouse and Old Joe the Camel." *Journal of the American Medical Association* 266 (22): 3145–3148.

Fornell, C., S. Mithas, F. V. Morgeson, and M. S. Krishnan. 2006. "Customer Satisfaction and Stock Prices: High Returns, Low Risk." *Journal of Marketing* 70 (January): 1–14.

Fou, Augustine. 2009. "What's Wrong with the Net Promoter Score." ClickZ, November 19. http://www.clickz.com/clickz/column/1707482/whats-wrong-with-net-promoter-score.

Freiberg, Jackie, and Kevin Freiberg. 2010. "An Impending Corporate Epidemic." Keynote Resources. http://www.keynoteresource.com/article9jfrieberg.html.

Gaines-Ross, Leslie. 2010. "Reputation Warfare." *Harvard Business Review*, December (reprint).

Gallup Organization. 2006. "Gallup Study: Feeling Good Matters in the Workplace." *Gallup Management Journal,* January 12.

Garvin, David. 1991. "How the Baldrige Award Really Works." *Harvard Business Review*, November–December.

Genesys/Capgemini. 2008. *The Executive Disconnect: The Strategic Alignment of Customer Service.* White paper. Daly City, CA: Genesys/Capgemini.

Georgiadis, Margo, Marc Singer, Katrina Lane, and David Harding. 2000. *"Online Customer Management." McKinsey Quarterly.*

Gibbons, John. 2006. *Employee Engagement: A Review of Current Research and Its Implications.* New York: The Conference Board.

Gladwell, Malcolm. 2000. *The Tipping Point.* Boston: Little, Brown.

Goldenberg, Jacob, Sangman Han, Donald Lehmann, and Jae Weon Hong. 2009. "The Role of Hubs in the Adoption Process." *Journal of Marketing* 73 (2): 1–13.

Goldstein, Adam, Rachel Sobel, and Glen Newman. 1999. "Tobacco and Alcohol Use in G-Rated Children's Animated Films." *Journal of the American Medical Association* 281 (12): 1131–1136.

Goodman, John. 1999. "Basic Facts on Customer Complaint Behavior and the Impact of Service on the Bottom Line." *Competitive Advantage*, June, 1–5.

Griffin, Jill, and Michael W. Lowenstein. 2001. *Customer WinBack: How to Recapture Lost Customers—and Keep Them Loyal.* San Francisco: Jossey-Bass.

Grisaffe, Doug. 2004. "Guru Misses Mark with One Number Fallacy." http://www.creatingloyalty.com.

Gross, T. Scott. 2004. *Positively Outrageous Service.* New York: Kaplan.

Harley-Davidson USA. "Harley Owners Group." http://www.harley-davidson.com/en_US/Content/Pages/HOG/HOG.html.

Hartman Group. 2010. "Loyalty Programs: What Works, What Doesn't." HartBeat. April 7. http://www.hartman-group.com/hartbeat/loyalty-programs-what-works-what-doesn-t.

Hayes, Bob. 2008. *Measuring Customer Satisfaction.* Milwaukee, WI: ASQ Quality Press.

Heffernan, Robert, and Steve LaValle. 2006. *Advocacy in the Customer-Focused Enterprise.* Armonk, NY: IBM Global Business Services.

Henning, Jeffrey. 2009. "Net Promoter Score (NPS) Criticisms and Best Practices." *Voice of Vovici* (blog). April 28. http://blog.vovici.com/blog/bid/18204/Net-Promoter-Score-NPS-Criticisms-and-Best-Practices.

Hepworth + Company. 1999. "Profiting from Customer Dissatisfaction." *Customer Pulse Database*, March 31.

Heskett, James L., W. Earl Sasser, and Leonard A. Schlesinger. 1997. *The Service Profit Chain*. New York: Free Press/Simon & Schuster.

Hlavinka, Kelly. 2010. "What Price Loyalty?" *Retail Talk*. Cincinnati, OH: Colloquy.

Hollins, Christopher, and Carolyn Setlow. 2007. "Who Are Your Active Advocates? What Are They Saying About You?" American Express/GfK, Retail Advocacy Report Presentation, National Retail Federation Convention, New York.

Hsieh, Tony. 2009. "Your Culture Is Your Brand." *Zappos Blogs: CEO and COO Blogs*. January 3. http://blogs.zappos.com/blogs/ceo-and-coo-blog/2009/01/03/your-culture-is-your-brand.

"Internet Users Turn to Social Media to Seek One Another, Not Brands or Products." 2009. Knowledge Networks Press Release, May 20.

Jackson, Peter. 2001. *CRM: Using the Appropriate Mix of Marketing Tools to Create and Manage Relationships with Customers*. Maidenhead, Berkshire, UK: Chartered Institute of Marketing, http://www.connectedinmarketing.com.

Johnson, Bruce. 2011. "Interested in Doubling Your Revenue?" *Because Growth Matters* (blog). http://becausegrowthmatters.com/?s=doubling+your+revenue.

Joseph, Jim. 2010. "Eataly." *The Experience Effect* (blog). September 10. http://jimjosephexp.blogspot.com/2010/09/eataly.html.

Kano, Noriaki, Nobushiro Seroku, Fumio Takahashi, and Shinichi Asuji. 1984. "Attractive Quality and Must-Be Quality." *Quality* 14 (2): 39–48.

Katz, Elihu, and Paul Lazarsfeld. 2005. *Personal Influence*. Piscataway, NJ: Transaction Publishers.

Keiningham, Timothy, Lerzan Aksoy, Bruce Cooil, and Tor Wallin Andreassen. 2008. "The Galileo Effect." *Marketing Management*, January/February, 48–51.

Keiningham, Timothy, Bruce Cooil, Tor Wallin Andreassen, and Lerzan Aksoy. 2007. "A Longitudinal Examination of Net Promoter and Firm Revenue Growth." *Journal of Marketing* 71 (July): 39–51.

Keller, Ed. 2008. "Unleashing the Power of Influencers." Presentation to Bazaarvoice Social Commerce Summit, Keller Fay Group, May 29.

———. 2010. "Wharton Study Shines New Light on Online vs. Offline Word of Mouth." *MediaBizBloggers* (blog). December 16. http://www.mediabizbloggers.com.

Keller, Ed, and Jon Berry. 2003. *The Influentials.* New York: Free Press.

Keller, Ed, and Brad Fay. 2008. "The Future of Advertising in a Word of Mouth Era." Presentation to Empirical Generalizations in Advertising, Keller Fay Group, Philadelphia, December 4.

———. 2009. "Influencers Are Essential in Driving WOM and Affinity with the Brand." *Admap*, April, 20–22.

Keller Fay Group/Jack Morton Worldwide. 2007. *Driving Word-of-Mouth Advocacy among Business Executives: The Experiential Marketing Connection.* White paper 9. New Brunswick, NJ, and New York: Keller Fay Group/Jack Morton Worldwide.

Kirkby, J., J. Wecksell, W. Janowski, and T. Berg. 2003. *The Value of Customer Experience Management.* Gartner Strategic Analysis Report. Egham, Surrey, UK: Gartner.

Leumer, Bill. 2007. "Lessons of the 1997 Teamster Strike at UPS." Parts 1 and 2. *Workers Action*, January 7.

Libai, Barak. 2010. "Assessing the Value of Customers' Word of Mouth." Presentation to WOM UK Conference, London, April.

Lieberman, Scott, and Robert Heffernan. 2006. *Unlocking Customer Advocacy in Retail Banking*. White paper. Armonk, NY: IBM Global Business Services.

Lowenstein, M. 2006. *Linking Employee Loyalty and Ambassadorial Behavior with Customer Commitment and Advocacy*. White paper. Princeton, NJ: Harris Interactive.

————. 2008. *Nurse Retention Wars: Who Wins, Who Loses, and Why.* White paper. Princeton, NJ: Harris Interactive.

————. 2009. "Prospect Value Management: Maximize Profits, Not New Accounts." CustomerThink, July 2. http://www.customerthink.com.

————. 2010. *Linking Employee Behavior to Customer Loyalty and Business Outcomes: Profitably Driving Customer Advocacy through Employee Attitudes and Actions.* White paper. Milwaukee, WI: Market Probe. http://www.marketprobe.com.

MarketingSherpa. 2009. *2009 Social Media Marketing & PR Benchmark Guide.* Warren, RI: MarketingSherpa.

MarketingSherpa and CNET. 2006. *B2B Business Technology Buyers Study.* Warren, RI: MarketingSherpa/CNET.

Marklein, Tim. 2009. "Advocacy, Badvocacy & Upsetting Apple Carts." Inbound Marketing Summit, Weber Shandwick, Boston, October 8.

McDonald, Mark, and Dave Aron. 2011. *Reimagining IT: The 2011 CIO Agenda.* Stamford, CT: Gartner.

McRoberts, Brian, George Terhanian, Ken Alldredge, and Carla Keppler. 2010. *Understanding the Role of the Internet in the Lives of Consumers: Decision Influence Index.* St. Louis, MO, and New York: Fleishman—Hillard/Harris Interactive.

Morgan, Neil, and Lopo Leotte Rego. 2006. "The Value of Different Customer Satisfaction and Loyalty Metrics in Predicting Business Performance." *Marketing Science* 25 (5): 426–439.

Nail, Jim. 2004. *The Consumer Advertising Backlash.* Cambridge, MA: Forrester.

Neolane. 2010. *Social Media & Marketing: Transitioning from Listening to Customer Engagement.* Newton, MA: Neolane.

Nielsen Consumer Research. 2009. *Nielsen Global Online Consumer Survey.* New York: Nielsen Consumer Research.

O'Brien, Kevin. 2010. "Best Buy Transcends the Retail Experience." *CustomerThink* (blog). November 17. http://www.customerthink.com.

OTX. 2009. "Keeping It Real: 'Offline' Communications Still Key to Connecting with Digital Generation." Press release for *A Beta Life—Youth*, March 31.

OTX/Dei Worldwide. 2008. *Engaging Consumers Online: The Impact of Social Media on Purchasing Behavior.* White paper. Los Angeles and Studio City, CA: OTX/Dei Worldwide.

Payne, Adrian. 2005. *The Handbook of CRM.* Boston: Elsevier.

Peppers & Rogers Group. 2008. *The Value of Having Conversations: Using Social Media to Deepen Your Customer Relationships.* White paper. Stamford, CT: Infor/Peppers & Rogers Group.

Peters, Tom. 1992. *Liberation Management: Necessary Disorganization for the Nanosecond Nineties.* New York: Alfred A. Knopf.

Petouhoff, Natalie. 2006. *Customer Advocacy: Creating the Business Case for Customer-Centric Companies with Customer Advocates.* White paper. Dallas, TX: Hitachi Consulting.

Porter, Michael. 1998. *Competitive Strategy.* New York: Free Press.

———. 2008. *On Competition.* Boston: Harvard Business School Publishing.

Preventing Tobacco Use among Young People: A Report of the Surgeon General. 1994. Washington, DC: Government Printing Office.

PricewaterhouseCoopers. 2003. *Recession Study.* New York: PricewaterhouseCoopers.

Putnam, Robert. 2000. *Bowling Alone: The Collapse and Revival of American Community.* New York: Simon & Schuster.

Rainie, Lee, Kristen Purcell, and Aaron Smith. 2011. *The Social Side of the Internet.* Washington, DC: Pew Research Center. http://pewinternet.org.

Ramsdell, E. 1998. "IBM's Grassroots Revival." *Fast Company,* June, 182.

Reichheld, Frederick. 1993. "Loyalty-Based Management." *Harvard Business Review,* March–April, 71.

———. 2003. "The One Number You Need to Grow." *Harvard Business Review,* December 1, 46–54.

RightNow Technologies/Harris Interactive. 2008. *Third Annual Customer Experience Report.* Bozeman, MT: RightNow Technologies/Harris Interactive.

————. 2010. *Fifth Annual Customer Experience Report.* Bozeman, MT: RightNow Technologies/Harris Interactive.

Rosenbluth, Hal. 2002. *The Customer Comes Second: Put Your People First and Watch 'Em Kick Butt.* New York: HarperBusiness.

Scheider, B., J. Parkington, and V. Buston. 1980. "Employee and Customer Perceptions of Service in Banks." Administrative Science Quarterly 25 (2): 423–433.

Schneider, Daniel, Matt Berent, Randall Thomas, and Jon Krosnick. 2008. *Measuring Customer Satisfaction and Loyalty: Improving the 'Net Promoter' Score.* Presentation at the American Association for Public Research Annual Meeting, New Orleans.

Schuster, Justin, and Lior Arussy. 2010. "The Economics of Customer Experience: New Study Reveals the Secrets." MarketTools and Strativity Webinar, IIR Web Seminars.

Sernovitz, Andy. 2009a. "Word of Mouth Is More than Social Media." *Damn, I Wish I'd Thought of That* (blog), May 9. http://www.damniwish.com.

————. 2009b. *Word of Mouth Marketing: How Smart Companies Get People Talking.* New York: Kaplan.

Sisodia, Rajendra, David B. Wolfe, and Jagdish N. Sheth. 2007. *Firms of Endearment.* Upper Saddle River, NJ: Wharton School Publishing.

Stauss, Bernd, and Christian Friege. 1999. "Regaining Service Customers: Costs and Benefits of Regain Management." *Journal of Service Research* 1 (4): 347–361.

Stauss, Bernd, and Wolfgang Seidel. 2004. *Complaint Management: The Heart of CRM.* Cincinnati, OH: Thompson/South-Western.

————. 2008. "Discover the Customer Annoyance Iceberg." Hot Topic of the Month, July. http://www.attentivefm.com.

Stern, Stefan. 2010. "The Marketing Team Must Aim Higher." *Financial Times,* March 1. http://www.ft.com.

Stewart, Thomas. 1996. "Company Values That Add Value." *Fortune,* July 8.

Stubblefield, Al. 2005. *The Baptist Health Care Journey to Excellence: Creating a Culture That WOWs!* Hoboken, NJ: John Wiley & Sons.

Thompson, Bob. 2008. *Accelerate Your Customer-Centric Journey.* White paper. Burlingame, CA, and Bozeman, MT: CustomerThink/RightNow.

Tice, David. 2009. "How People Use Social Media/The Home Technology Monitor." Knowledge Networks Press Release, May 20. http://www.knowledgenetworks.com.

"Toyota Resale Value, Reputation Fall from Heights." 2010. Associated Press, February 6. http://www.msnbc.msn.com/id/35300033/ns/business-autos.

Urban, Glen. 2005. *Don't Just Relate—Advocate! A Blueprint for Power in the Era of Customer Power.* Upper Saddle River, NJ: Wharton School Publishing.

Watts, Duncan. 2003. *Small Worlds: The Dynamics of Networks Between Order and Randomness.* Princeton, NJ: Princeton University Press.

Weber Shandwick. 2007. *The Return on Advocacy.* New York: Weber Shandwick.

———. 2009a. *Do Fortune 100 Companies Need a Twittervention?* New York: Weber Shandwick.

———. 2009b. *The Good Book of Badvocacy.* New York: Weber Shandwick.

———. 2009c. *Risky Business* (Reputations Online study conducted with the Economist Intelligence Unit). New York: Weber Shandwick.

———. 2010. *Socializing Your CEO: From (Un)social to Social.* New York: Weber Shandwick.

Weber Shandwick/KRC Research. 2007. *The New Wave of Advocacy.* New York: Weber Shandwick/KRC Research.

Wynn, Steve. 2009. Interview by Charlie Rose. *60 Minutes*, CBS, July 26.

Index

Note: Page numbers followed by f *or* t *refer to figures or tables, respectively.*

About the Author

Michael Lowenstein, PhD, CMC, is executive vice president of Market Probe, a leading worldwide market research and consulting organization. He is broadly experienced in many B2B and B2C product and service industries. His particular areas of interest are the impact of word-of-mouth communication on downstream customer behavior, employee commitment and ambassadorship, and how organizations build trust and authenticity and use customer insight in reaching their strategic goals.

Drawing on over 30 years' management and consulting experience in customer and employee loyalty research, customer relationship and experience management (CRM), loyalty program and product/service development, customer win-back, service and channel quality, customer-driven corporate culture, human resources management, and strategic marketing and planning, Lowenstein is an active international conference keynote presenter and speaker, workshop facilitator, and trainer. He is a regular featured contributor to two customer loyalty newsletters. He also provides expert customer and stakeholder loyalty resource commentary to several professional CRM, marketing, customer service, and HRD sites on the internet and is an active blogger on these subjects.

He is the author of several widely regarded stakeholder and enterprise management books: *Customer Retention: Keeping Your Best Customers* (1995), *The Customer Loyalty Pyramid*

(1997), and *One Customer, Divisible* (2005). He is also coauthor of *Customer WinBack: How to Recapture At-Risk and Lost Customers—and Keep Them Loyal* (2001), a Soundview Executive Book Summaries Best Book of 2002. Additionally, he is a principal contributing author to *Redefining Consumer Affairs* (Society of Consumer Affairs Professionals, 1995) and *The Answer Book for Customer Service Managers* (Bureau of Business Practice/International Customer Service Association, 2000), and he has written several sections and the afterword for *Customer.Community: Unleashing the Power of Your Customer Base* (2002). He has written over 150 customer-related white papers, journal articles, and columns, with material appearing in online and off-line publications in Europe, North America, Asia Pacific, Africa, Australia, and South America.

Lowenstein is a customer life-cycle workshop developer/ facilitator for the Direct Marketing Association and has been a customer loyalty/stakeholder behavior instructor for Pennsylvania State University, the American Marketing Association, the American Society for Quality, the Conference Board, ESOMAR, the Bank Administration Institute, Frost & Sullivan, the Institute for International Research, SOCAP, Marcus Evans, UNI, eCustomer Service World, and the American Management Association. He has presented at industry and professional conferences across the United States and in over 25 foreign countries, and for corporations such as Toyota, Aetna, Nestle, MetLife, National City, General Motors, Earth-Link, Sprint, Wachovia, Daimler-Chrysler, Bell South, and Charles Schwab. Additionally, he has lectured in the MBA and EMBA programs of the University of Pennsylvania, New York University, and Columbia University.

He holds an MBA degree in marketing and management from the University of Pittsburgh and a BS degree in economics and marketing from Villanova University. His PhD is in strategy, program development, and program management from

ISGI Groupe Ecole Superieure de Commerce de Lille (ESC Lille), Euralille/Paris, France (now SKEMA Business School). He also holds a certified management consultant (CMC) professional designation, awarded by the Institute of Management Consultants, USA.

Lowenstein is a member of both the Advisory Council and the Executive Roundtable of the Villanova University Center for Business Analytics, whose mission is to forward thought leadership for the critical business skill of developing and applying performance metrics in the marketplace. He is listed in several regional, national, international, and professional *Who's Who* editions. He has been an expert panel or advisory board member for several online stakeholder behavior, customer loyalty, HRD, CRM, and customer experience management information sources, including CustomerThink, the leading CRM/customer loyalty portal.

Belong to the Quality Community!

Established in 1946, ASQ is a global community of quality experts in all fields and industries. ASQ is dedicated to the promotion and advancement of quality tools, principles, and practices in the workplace and in the community.

The Society also serves as an advocate for quality. Its members have informed and advised the U.S. Congress, government agencies, state legislatures, and other groups and individuals worldwide on quality-related topics.

Vision

By making quality a global priority, an organizational imperative, and a personal ethic, ASQ becomes the community of choice for everyone who seeks quality technology, concepts, or tools to improve themselves and their world.

ASQ is...

- More than 90,000 individuals and 700 companies in more than 100 countries
- The world's largest organization dedicated to promoting quality
- A community of professionals striving to bring quality to their work and their lives
- The administrator of the Malcolm Baldrige National Quality Award
- A supporter of quality in all sectors including manufacturing, service, healthcare, government, and education
- YOU

Visit www.asq.org for more information.

ASQ Membership

Research shows that people who join associations experience increased job satisfaction, earn more, and are generally happier*. ASQ membership can help you achieve this while providing the tools you need to be successful in your industry and to distinguish yourself from your competition. So why wouldn't you want to be a part of ASQ?

Networking

Have the opportunity to meet, communicate, and collaborate with your peers within the quality community through conferences and local ASQ section meetings, ASQ forums or divisions, ASQ Communities of Quality discussion boards, and more.

Professional Development

Access a wide variety of professional development tools such as books, training, and certifications at a discounted price. Also, ASQ certifications and the ASQ Career Center help enhance your quality knowledge and take your career to the next level.

Solutions

Find answers to all your quality problems, big and small, with ASQ's Knowledge Center, mentoring program, various e-newsletters, *Quality Progress* magazine, and industry-specific products.

Access to Information

Learn classic and current quality principles and theories in ASQ's Quality Information Center (QIC), *ASQ Weekly* e-newsletter, and product offerings.

Advocacy Programs

ASQ helps create a better community, government, and world through initiatives that include social responsibility, Washington advocacy, and Community Good Works.

Visit www.asq.org/membership for more information on ASQ membership.

*2008, The William E. Smith Institute for Association Research

ASQ Certification

ASQ certification is formal recognition by ASQ that an individual has demonstrated a proficiency within, and comprehension of, a specified body of knowledge at a point in time. Nearly 150,000 certifications have been issued. ASQ has members in more than 100 countries, in all industries, and in all cultures. ASQ certification is internationally accepted and recognized.

Benefits to the Individual

- New skills gained and proficiency upgraded
- Investment in your career
- Mark of technical excellence
- Assurance that you are current with emerging technologies
- Discriminator in the marketplace
- Certified professionals earn more than their uncertified counterparts
- Certification is endorsed by more than 125 companies

Benefits to the Organization

- Investment in the company's future
- Certified individuals can perfect and share new techniques in the workplace
- Certified staff are knowledgeable and able to assure product and service quality

Quality is a global concept. It spans borders, cultures, and languages. No matter what country your customers live in or what language they speak, they demand quality products and services. You and your organization also benefit from quality tools and practices. Acquire the knowledge to position yourself and your organization ahead of your competition.

Certifications Include

- Biomedical Auditor – CBA
- Calibration Technician – CCT
- HACCP Auditor – CHA
- Pharmaceutical GMP Professional – CPGP
- Quality Inspector – CQI
- Quality Auditor – CQA
- Quality Engineer – CQE
- Quality Improvement Associate – CQIA
- Quality Technician – CQT
- Quality Process Analyst – CQPA
- Reliability Engineer – CRE
- Six Sigma Black Belt – CSSBB
- Six Sigma Green Belt – CSSGB
- Software Quality Engineer – CSQE
- Manager of Quality/Organizational Excellence – CMQ/OE

Visit www.asq.org/certification to apply today!

ASQ Membership

Research shows that people who join associations experience increased job satisfaction, earn more, and are generally happier*. ASQ membership can help you achieve this while providing the tools you need to be successful in your industry and to distinguish yourself from your competition. So why wouldn't you want to be a part of ASQ?

Networking

Have the opportunity to meet, communicate, and collaborate with your peers within the quality community through conferences and local ASQ section meetings, ASQ forums or divisions, ASQ Communities of Quality discussion boards, and more.

Professional Development

Access a wide variety of professional development tools such as books, training, and certifications at a discounted price. Also, ASQ certifications and the ASQ Career Center help enhance your quality knowledge and take your career to the next level.

Solutions

Find answers to all your quality problems, big and small, with ASQ's Knowledge Center, mentoring program, various e-newsletters, *Quality Progress* magazine, and industry-specific products.

Access to Information

Learn classic and current quality principles and theories in ASQ's Quality Information Center (QIC), *ASQ Weekly* e-newsletter, and product offerings.

Advocacy Programs

ASQ helps create a better community, government, and world through initiatives that include social responsibility, Washington advocacy, and Community Good Works.

Visit www.asq.org/membership for more information on ASQ membership.

*2008, The William E. Smith Institute for Association Research